Home Care
for the
HIGH RISK
Infant

A Holistic Guide
to Using Technology

Contributors

B. Patrick Cox, PhD
Professor and Chair
Department of Audiology
Gallaudet College
Washington, D.C.

Karen D. Dixon, parent

Jeanne O'Connor Egan, RN, MSN
Neurosurgery Clinical Specialist
Children's Hospital National
Medical Center
Washington, D.C.

Janice George, MSW, ACSW
Home Care Program
Children's Hospital National
Medical Center
Washington, D.C.

Rebecca Ichord, MD
Assistant Professor in Child Health
and Development
George Washington University
School of Medicine;
Associate Director, Pediatric
Residency Training Program
Children's Hospital National
Medical Center
Washington, D.C.

Connie Jo Lierman, RN, MSN
Clinical Nurse Specialist
Home Care Program

Children's Hospital National
Medical Center
Washington, D.C.

Sally A. McCarthy, MSN, RN
Discharge Planning Specialist
Children's Hospital National
Medical Center
Washington, D.C.

Teri Peck, BSN, CPNP
Home Care Program
Children's Hospital National
Medical Center
Washington, D.C.

Bonnie M. Simon, MA, CCC-SP
Home Health Care Services:
Pedicare, Quality Care, and
Community Home Health of
Philadelphia
Philadelphia, Pennsylvania

Nancy Weinstock, MSW, ACSW
Home Care Program
Children's Hospital National
Medical Center
Washington, D.C.

Margaret Wilson, MS, OTR
Home Care Program
Children's Hospital National
Medical Center
Washington, D.C.

Home Care
for the
HIGH RISK
Infant

A Holistic Guide
to Using Technology

by
Elizabeth Ahmann, RN, MS, FNP

AN ASPEN PUBLICATION®
Aspen Publishers, Inc.
Rockville, Maryland
Royal Tunbridge Wells
1986

Library of Congress Cataloging in Publication Data
Main entry under title:

Home care for the high risk infant.

Bibliography: p.
Includes index.
1. Infants (Premature)—Home care. 2. Infants (premature)—Diseases. I. Ahmann,
Elizabeth. [DNLM 1. Home Care Services. 2. Infant, Premature, Diseases. WS 410
H638]

RJ250.H54	1986	649'.8	86-1056

ISBN: 0-87189-285-5

Editorial Services: Carolyn Ormes

Library of Congress Catalog Card Number: 86-1056
ISBN: 0-87189-285-5

Printed in the United States of America

1   2   3   4   5

This book is dedicated to the many children and families
who have taught me so much about home care
of the high risk infant.

Table of Contents

Foreword

In the past 20 years there have been major strides in perinatology, resulting in improved survival of high-risk neonates. Though there is a decreased incidence of long term sequelae, a larger number of small infants are discharged with a plethora of ongoing complications. Until the present, most of the emphasis in perinatology has been on hospital care. This book takes on the difficult and important task of describing the often complex nursing and management of the high-risk infant at home.

The authors properly approach both the medical and behavioral needs of the infants and their families. They first explore in detail the problem in the hospital and how to prepare the infant and parents for discharge. As in the hospital care of the small neonate, anticipation is a necessity. Extensive care outlines are then presented for each complication and special care procedure. The authors share their many years of practical experience covering problems ranging from minor illnesses to mechanical ventilator management. For each complication the authors carefully describe the care during the first visit as well as subsequent home visits.

The home care of many complications are complex, tedious, and sometimes exhausting. Fortunately the authors describe the management of each problem in sufficient detail to simplify even complicated procedures. Nurses and parents should be encouraged to read each area carefully since small details of care can have major reverberations. The reader should also explore the extensive appendixes for valuable care plans and useful tables and charts.

The authors are to be especially commended for all their hard work in preparing this most needed book. Since it will serve as a handbook for the home care of the high-risk infant, we hope the author Elizabeth Ahmann and collaborators will accept the challenge to revise this valuable book frequently.

Marshall Klaus, M.D.
Professor and Chairman
Department of Pediatrics/Human Development
Michigan State University

Preface

As medical technology improves, increasing numbers of early premature infants are surviving. Infants who would not have survived ten and even five years ago because of respiratory, neurologic, and other impairments are now not only surviving, but, in fact, going home. Many of these infants have multiple and complex chronic impairments, and even after transition from the hospital to the home environment, many continue to rely on high-technology support systems. As a result, homes may become mini–intensive care units, and parents* must face the challenge of providing complex care for their infants.

Community health nurses must keep pace with the changes in home care. Currently, information pertinent to home care of the high risk premature infant is widely scattered among journals and books of many disciplines, including nursing, medicine, social work, and rehabilitation therapies. This text synthesizes a wide range of material and provides a practical instructional guide and a useful reference. Although written primarily for the community health nurse, the book will also be useful to other professionals, including physicians, discharge planners, social workers, rehabilitation therapists, and other home care professionals, as well as to parents.

The term "high risk infant" has been used in a variety of ways by different authors. In this text, the term refers to the premature infant with multiple problems resulting from both prematurity and the aggressive medical care often necessary to ensure the infant's survival. Although the text emphasizes home care of the high risk infant, its usefulness extends to the child of any age requiring complex, high-technology home care.

Chapter 1 provides readers with an overview or profile of the high risk infant. Chapter 2 discusses the principles and practice important in discharge planning for

---

*Although a wide variety of family configurations and caregiving systems exists, for simplicity and uniformity throughout the text, the term "parent" is used to refer broadly to either a parent or any other primary caregiver of the infant.

the high risk infant (or other child with complex, multiple problems). Readers are provided with guidelines for recognizing both special needs and potential problems in discharge planning. Sample discharge instructions are included, and the chapter appendix includes a sample discharge teaching checklist.

Chapter 3 provides readers with an overview of important principles for interviewing and documentation in home care. The chapter also provides a framework for the nursing intake history and includes, in the chapter appendix, documentation forms that can be used for obtaining a complete history, review of systems, and physical examination. The documentation forms were developed especially for use with the high risk infant. The reader is encouraged to review them carefully as they add significantly to the text of the chapter.

Chapters 4 through 13 each address separate aspects of what might be a total plan of care for the high risk infant at home. Chapter 4 addresses special challenges in meeting the health maintenance needs of the high risk infant, including locating a source of primary pediatric care, responses to minor illnesses, safety issues, parent-infant interaction (assessment and intervention), and coordination of services. A standard nursing care plan for health maintenance of the high risk infant and a home safety checklist are provided in appendixes to the chapter.

Chapter 5 discusses nutrition and feeding of the high risk infant, offering guidelines for assessment and intervention related to common problems. The chapter appendix contains a nutrition assessment form targeted to the high risk infant. Chapter 6 complements Chapter 5 by addressing gastrostomy and nasogastric tube feedings. Indications for tube feedings, guidelines for choice of tube, and practical details about various methods for both gastrostomy and nasogastric feedings are provided, as well as a care plan for home tube feeding.

Each of Chapters 7 through 13 addresses respiratory and neurologic problems pertinent to care of the high risk infant. Each chapter provides a general discussion of the particular subject, followed by practical suggestions related to the transition from hospital to home, routine home visits, the first home visit, subsequent home visits, and ongoing concerns. Suggestions for assessment and teaching are included in each chapter, and many care procedures are described in detail. Each chapter appendix contains a standard home care plan. The appendixes of chapters 8 through 11 also contain home assessment forms. The assessment forms are designed to be used in conjunction with the care plans both as guides to assessment and teaching and as simple documentation forms. The reader is encouraged to review the care plans and assessment forms carefully as they add significantly to the text of each chapter.

Chapters 14 through 17 address developmental concerns related to care of the high risk infant. Overall development, hearing, speech, and vision are discussed. The reader is provided with an overview of potential problems, guidelines for assessment, and suggestions for intervention and referral. The appendixes of Chapters 14 and 16 also include assessment forms that can be used both as guidelines for assessment and as simple documentation forms for hearing and vision screening.

Chapters 18 and 19 address common challenges faced by families and siblings in the adjustment to home care. Common stresses, adjustment difficulties, and coping strategies are discussed. The chapters also suggest approaches to mitigating many commonly encountered problems. These chapters are supplemented by Chapter 20, which identifies and discusses community services and resources that can be useful to the family providing home care. Financial, therapeutic, family support, and informational resources are addressed.

The community health nurse plays a pivotal role in any home care program through assessment, instruction, support, screening, referral, and case management. Because of this pivotal role, maintaining current information and skills is essential. This text offers a comprehensive review of the medical and nursing, developmental, and social and emotional issues relevant to planning and providing home care of the high risk infant and other children requiring high-technology care in the home.

The Ad Hoc Task Force on Home Care of chronically ill infants and children suggests that:

> The goal of a home care program for infants, children, or adolescents with chronic conditions is the provision of comprehensive, cost-effective health care within a nurturing home environment that maximizes the capabilities of the individual and minimizes the effects of the disabilities.[1]

It is my sincere hope that this text will help further that goal for many children.[2]

Elizabeth Ahmann

NOTES

1. Ad Hoc Task Force on Home Care of Chronically Ill Infants and Children: Guidelines for home care of infants, children, and adolescents with chronic disease, *Pediatrics* 74: 434, September 1984.
2. The following resource may be useful to individuals either setting up or currently administering home care programs: *Home Health and Hospice Manual: Regulations and Guidelines.* National Health Publishing (prepared by the editorial staff): 1985 Rynd Communications, 99 Painters Mill Rd, Owings Mill, MD 21117.

Acknowledgments

The preparation of this comprehensive manual could not have been accomplished without the assistance of the following individuals in critiquing the chapter content, offering suggestions for organization of material, and adding important details.

Margaret C. Ahmann, MLS
Marilyn Clare, RN
   Cardiology Ambulatory Service
   Children's Hospital National Medical Center
   Washington, D.C.
Athleen B. Coyner, RN, MS, FAAN
   Nurse consultant
Mary Dickie, MS, RD
Mary E. Donar, RN, BSN
   Head Nurse
   Pediatric Intensive Care–Intermediate
   The Children's Hospital of Philadelphia
   Philadelphia, Pennsylvania
Judy Anne Duncan, MA, MSW
   Coordinator, Apnea Program
   Department of Pediatrics, Mercy Hospital and Medical Center
   San Diego, California
David S. Friendly, MD
   Chairman, Department of Ophthalmology
   Children's Hospital National Medical Center
   Washington, D.C.
Cheryl L. Henson
   Word Processor—Home Care Program

Children's Hospital National Medical Center
Washington, D.C.

Marilyn B. Hartsell, MS, NS, RN
Project Coordinator, Tri-Regional Education and Networking Development
System
University of Delaware College of Nursing
Newark, Delaware

Pat Hennessy, RN
Formerly Tracheostomy Nurse Coordinator
Children's Hospital National Medical Center
Washington, D.C.

G. Scott Lea, BS, RRT
Assistant Director, Respiratory Care Services
The Children's Hospital of Philadelphia
Philadelphia, Pennsylvania

Susan Leibold, RN, MS
Pediatric Clinical Specialist
Apnea Program Coordinator
Children's Hospital National Medical Center
Washington, D.C.

Cheryl Person Margulies, MA, CCC-SP
Coordinator of Speech and Language Pathology
Children's Hospital National Medical Center
Washington, D.C.

Cheryl Naulty, MD
Department of Neonatology
Children's Hospital National Medical Center
Washington, D.C.

Cynthia Poindexter
Office Manager, Home Care Program
Children's Hospital National Medical Center
Washington, D.C.

Elizabeth Riggs, RN, ET
Enterostomal Therapist
Children's Hospital National Medical Center
Washington, D.C.

Melissa Van Wey, RN, MSN
Joan Ward, RN, MA
Clinical Specialist, Parenteral/Enteral Therapy
Children's Hospital National Medical Center
Washington, D.C.

Carolyn Willard, MLS
  Family Library
  Children's Hospital National Medical Center
  Washington, D.C.

I am especially grateful to Wayne Schwandt for his careful typing, to Linda Harteker for her helpful editing, to Teresa Ahmann for her artwork, and to Richard Saviet for both his editing assistance and his constant encouragement.

Chapter 1

Profile of the
High Risk Infant

Rebecca Ichord, MD

Rapid advances in neonatal intensive care have dramatically improved the survival rates of ever smaller premature infants.[1] Improved survival has been effected through the use of aggressive, multisystem therapies requiring prolonged hospital stays. When these infants are "ready" for discharge, parents frequently face complex home care demands for a multitude of medical problems.

This chapter provides a profile of the high risk premature infant. The discussion begins with a description of the infant population at risk for multiple long-term medical problems, and then proceeds to a review, system by system, of the most common chronic medical problems of prematurity. Finally, the implications of these medical problems are considered in broad relationship to the field of home care.

DESCRIPTION OF THE POPULATION

Prematurity is defined as a gestational age of less than 37 weeks. *Low birth weight* (LBW) refers to a weight of less than 2500 grams (gm)—approximately 5½ pounds—at birth. *Very low birth weight* (VLBW) premature infants weigh less than 1500 gm at birth, and *extremely low birth weight* (ELBW) prematures weigh less than 1000 gm at birth. Some infants experience growth retardation during gestation and are called *small for gestational age* (SGA) at birth. Gestational age, rather than birth weight alone, is a better indicator of the medical problems an infant may face since these problems are directly related to the immaturity of various organ systems.

The magnitude of the problem of prematurity can best be appreciated by considering its relative contribution to infant mortality and morbidity. In the United States, 7 percent of all live-born infants are under 2500 gm at birth.[2] Yet LBW infants account for 66.7 percent of neonatal deaths. The mortality risk increases directly as gestational age decreases.[3] A premature infant weighing less than 1500 gm is 200 times more likely to die than a full-term infant. Morbidity is another indicator of the problems associated with this population. As a group, these infants require long periods of hospitalization, particularly if they have significant lung disease.

Nonetheless, advances in neonatal care have led to a steady improvement in the survival of premature infants. In 1960 the lower limit of viability was a birth weight of 1000 gm; now this figure is 500 gm. In one recent study, the survival rate was 50 percent for birth weights between 700 and 800 gm, and more than 75 percent for birth weights of 1000 gm or higher.[5]

The impact of premature birth is unevenly distributed among groups of the United States population. For example, the incidence of LBW is much greater in nonwhites than whites (12.7 versus 5.9 percent).[6] Teenage pregnancy, a low level of maternal education, and an abnormal obstetric history are other factors associated with an increased incidence of LBW. These socioeconomic factors translate into hard, cold reality for those planning and implementing home care services for this population. Plans for home care must take into account the infant's needs in the context of the home environment and the familial or parental resources and motivation to provide complex and demanding care.

MEDICAL DISORDERS OF PREMATURITY

The medical disorders of the premature infant occur because of both the immaturity of a multiplicity of organ systems and the invasive treatment technologies necessary to maintain the infant's viability. Problems may be encountered with every organ system at one time or another. In most cases, the dominant problems relate to respiratory disease and neurologic, gastrointestinal, and nutritional disorders. Table 1–1 summarizes the common medical disorders of the premature. It classifies the problems of each major organ system according to acute and chronic forms. It is by no means an exhaustive list. Rather, like the following discussion, it highlights the most common disorders that have a long-term impact on the infant's health care needs.

Respiratory Disorders

The most common medical disorder related to prematurity is respiratory disease. The immature lung does not have the mechanical or biochemical characteristics necessary to provide for adequate exchange of oxygen and carbon dioxide. Because of this, *respiratory distress syndrome* (RDS) develops shortly after birth, and treatment with supplemental oxygen and frequently mechanical

Table 1–1 Common Medical Disorders of Prematurity

Organ System	*Disorders*	
	Acute	*Chronic*
Respiratory system	Respiratory distress syndrome Apnea of prematurity Pneumonia	Bronchopulmonary dysplasia Apnea of prematurity Tracheostomy Subglottic stenosis Croup syndromes Frequent respiratory infections
Cardiovascular system	Patent ductus arteriosus Cor pulmonale	Cor pulmonale
Central nervous system	Hypoxic brain damage Intraventricular hemorrhage Seizures	Neurodevelopmental disorders Hydrocephalus Seizures
Gastrointestinal system	Necrotizing enterocolitis Jaundice	Malabsorption syndrome Malnutrition Growth retardation
Hematologic system	Anemia	Anemia
Other	—— Sepsis Meningitis Pneumonia	Hernias Retinopathy of prematurity Sepsis Recurrent respiratory and gastrointestinal infections

ventilation becomes necessary. Although these treatment measures are life-saving, their use is associated with tissue injury and altered physiologic responses in the lung.

When RDS is acute (ARDS), the syndrome may evolve into a chronic picture of respiratory insufficiency called *bronchopulmonary dysplasia* (BPD). Infants with BPD have problems with excessive bronchial secretions, narrowed airways, and inefficient oxygen and carbon dioxide exchange. (See also Chapter 7). In its most severe form, BPD necessitates continued mechanical ventilation. In less severe forms, it causes dependence on supplemental oxygen, decreased exercise tolerance, increased work of breathing, and increased susceptibility to infection. The impact of BPD on other organ systems is difficult to measure. However, it certainly alters the energy economy of the infant as a whole, with wide-ranging implications for feeding, nutrition, growth, cardiovascular function, behavior, and neurodevelopmental status.

Most infants with BPD slowly grow out of their worst symptoms of chronic lung disease through a careful balance of several treatment strategies. These strategies aim to maintain adequate nutrition, minimize cardiac decompensation, and prevent respiratory infection. With time, for most infants, the healing of damaged tissue occurs more rapidly than does continued tissue damage, and healthy new lung tissue develops. However, in a small minority of infants, the respiratory insufficiency is so severe, and so compromises cardiac function, that a steady downhill progression occurs, ending in death.

Lung disease in the premature infant affects respiratory function in other ways. Prolonged and repeated endotracheal intubations may injure the upper airway, leading to *subglottic stenosis* (narrowing or constriction). This problem may not be manifested until a viral infection is superimposed, causing a croup-like syndrome that may be life-threatening. Some infants showing a prolonged dependence on mechanical ventilation will require a tracheostomy both to provide for maximal control of the airway and to avoid permanent upper airway damage. The small lower airways, or bronchioles, may also be damaged, giving rise to a disorder that closely resembles asthma. Asthma-like symptoms may be present all the time in more severe cases or only intermittently in less severe cases; symptoms are precipitated by viral infection, exercise, or exposure to irritants such as cigarette smoke in the air.

Respiratory disorders involving the large or small airways may have their onset at variable times, beginning in the nursery or not appearing until months after discharge. These disorders differ from the croup and asthma syndromes in normal children in that they generally occur at a younger age, are more severe and more frequent, and last longer. Although the majority of survivors of prematurity-related lung disease do not develop the most severe forms of these late-onset respiratory complications, they do have a greatly increased vulnerability.

Cardiovascular Disorders

Disorders of the cardiovascular system are closely linked to respiratory disorders in the premature infant. In the transition from intrauterine to extrauterine life, the cardiovascular system rapidly adapts to channel blood flow appropriately to lung and systemic circuits. This channeling requires closure of the ductus arteriosus, a vessel that connects the two circuits in utero. In the premature infant, because of lung immaturity, respiratory physiology is abnormal, and this vessel remains patent—that is, it is a *patent ductus arteriosus* (PDA). PDA increases the workload of the heart and exacerbates respiratory insufficiency already imposed by the immature pulmonary mechanisms. In some infants, treatment can be effected medically. In others, PDA ligation, a very safe and effective surgical procedure, may be required.

A more difficult management problem is posed by the chronic cardiac insufficiency, or *cor pulmonale*, caused by chronic lung disease (see Chapter 7). When cor pulmonale occurs, the heart becomes enlarged, pumps less efficiently, and causes total body fluid build-up. The infant can then tolerate less fluid intake and frequently develops metabolic disturbances owing to fluid imbalances and necessary diuretic drug therapy. The cardiac dysfunction and both fluid and metabolic imbalances in turn further compromise pulmonary function. In these infants, recovery of normal cardiac function parallels recovery of pulmonary function.

Apnea

One of the most common cardiorespiratory disorders in this population is *apnea of prematurity*. This type of apnea (described in Chapter 8) has many causes, all of which relate to immaturity and ineffectiveness of the brain's respiratory control centers. Apnea may occur independently of other heart or lung disease, or it may be the presenting symptom of a correctable condition such as anemia or sepsis. In the absence of a treatable cause, apnea is attributed to brain immaturity.

When apnea occurs, a transient decrease in blood oxygen levels results, frequently accompanied by bradycardia, or slowing of the heart beat. Although episodes of apnea are sometimes self-limited, in many premature infants some intervention is needed. Intervention ranges from light tactile stimulation, to vigorous stimulation, to oxygen administration, to use of bag and mask. In most cases, the infant eventually outgrows apnea. In the meantime, however, continuous monitoring is required, in conjunction with a readiness on the part of the caregivers to provide immediate intervention, including cardiopulmonary resuscitation (CPR), if needed.

Neurologic Disorders

Central nervous system (CNS) disorders are another common problem affecting premature infants.

Acute Disorders

Acute disorders include intraventricular hemorrhage, hypoxic brain damage, and brain infections or meningitis.

Intraventricular hemorrhage (IVH) refers to bleeding in the brain. IVH arises from fragile immature blood vessels whose integrity has been disturbed by some other disorder of prematurity, such as hypoxia, low blood pressure, or infection. The acute manifestations of IVH are highly variable, ranging from clinically "silent" episodes to a sudden life-threatening syndrome of hemorrhagic shock, seizures, and coma. IVH also ranges in severity according to the extent of brain substance involved and is graded as I or II (mild), III (moderate), or IV (severe). Ultrasound diagnostic scanning can be used to pinpoint the exact location and severity of the bleed and to monitor its resolution.

The significance of IVH depends on its severity. Mild bleeds may have few or no symptoms in the acute phase. Moderate or severe bleeds, in the acute phase, may diminish consciousness, cause seizures, or alter neurologic function in such a way as to interfere with other vital processes (e.g., breathing or circulation). The long-term effects of IVH on brain growth and on development, however, remain controversial.

Hypoxic brain damage, also called asphyxial brain damage, can occur as a result of fetal distress during labor or delivery, lung disease, or cardiovascular instability, among other factors. Hypoxic brain injury is much more difficult to quantify than hemorrhage, partly because there are no discrete laboratory or radiologic indicators, and partly because the premature infant's neurologic system responds in nonspecific and global ways to brain injury.

Chronic Disorders

The chronic forms of brain disorders in prematures include *hydrocephalus, microcephaly, seizure disorders,* and *neurodevelopmental handicaps.* Chronic brain disorders in this population have multiple causes but most commonly are directly related to acute brain insults, namely, IVH, hypoxic brain damage, and meningitis. The symptoms of chronic brain disorders may be subtle and diffuse, including poor feeding, irritability or drowsiness, altered muscle tone and movements, and delayed acquisition of developmental skills. Treatment for hydrocephalus may be surgical, through placement of a ventriculoperitoneal shunt, or medical, through the use of drugs that decrease brain fluid production (see Chapter 12). In either case, therapy requires close monitoring for effectiveness and complications. Similarly, therapy for seizure disorders must be closely monitored (see Chapter 13). Treatment for neurodevelopmental handicaps (addressed in Chapter 17) is at best symptomatic; however, it should be realized that neurodevelopmental assessment begins in the nursery and helps to define the starting point for the infant as normal, suspect, or abnormal for gestational age.

Gastrointestinal Disorders

VLBW premature infants are also susceptible to gastrointestinal (GI) diseases. Immaturity of the digestive system, combined with an increased vulnerability to tissue injury imposed by cardiorespiratory instabilities, can lead to *necrotizing enterocolitis* (NEC). NEC is a destructive infection of the small bowel, which can be associated with signs of severe illness such as excessive bleeding, cardiovascular collapse, or respiratory decompensation. In milder forms NEC can be managed with medications and supportive measures; in the severe forms, however, surgery to remove the most damaged portions of bowel is required. Such surgery usually leads to a temporary interruption of the intestinal passage by way of an ileostomy, a surgically created connection through the abdominal wall. After some months of healing and growth, another surgical procedure can usually be performed to restore a normal passageway through the colon and rectum.

Whether or not intestine is removed, the infant with NEC will permanently lose some length of functional intestine; this can have an impact on the infant in several ways. First, during the acute phase, intravenous feeding, also called total parenteral nutrition (TPN), is necessary for a variable period of time. Second, it may take much longer than normal to advance the amount and/or frequency of formula feedings to a point that sustains growth. Third, in the chronic stage, the infant is highly susceptible to symptoms of malabsorption, such as diarrhea and abdominal discomfort, which are triggered more easily by dietary changes or intestinal infections. All of these factors combined may contribute to feeding disorders and delayed physical growth.

As with chronic lung disease, the minor diseases of normal infancy can lead to major setbacks for the infant with chronic GI sequelae of prematurity. An intestinal virus that would cause a few days of vomiting in a normal infant may, in the premature with a history of NEC, lead to a rapid and severe dehydration, rehospitalization, and prolonged recovery time to reach an acceptable feeding regimen and growth rate.

Infections

Infections constitute another group of diseases to which the premature infant is highly susceptible. Every aspect of the infant's immunologic system is immature, including antibody production, cellular immune defenses, and even the integrity of simple barrier defenses such as skin and mucous membranes. Superimposed is the dramatically increased exposure to infectious agents necessitated by the use of invasive treatment devices such as umbilical vessel catheters, endotracheal tubes, and chest tubes. When infections do occur in the unstable neonate, they tend to be serious systemic infections of the blood (sepsis), the brain (meningitis), or the lungs (pneumonia). Thus infections can prolong the neonatal hospital stay by virtue of both the symptoms they produce and the treatment they require.

Hematologic Disorders

Premature infants suffer from a variety of hematologic disorders. These include both inadequate numbers and immature functioning of the cellular components of the blood—red blood cells, white blood cells, and platelets. Among these, deficiencies in red blood cells are most common, giving rise to *anemia*. Anemia may be caused by multiple factors including low iron stores due to premature birth, immature or damaged bone marrow due to other diseases, and blood loss from either hemorrhage or necessary laboratory studies. The symptoms will vary according to the infant's other problems. There may be unexplained lethargy, irritability, an exacerbation of underlying cardiac or lung disease, or even no symptoms. Most premature infants will require some iron supplementation after discharge from the nursery. Chronic disorders involving other components of the blood system are infrequent and are not further discussed here.

Other Disorders

Premature infants have, for unknown reasons, a very high prevalence of *inguinal hernias*. In many cases, these require surgical repair, which usually proceeds without complication. It is important, however, for surgeons and anesthesiologists to be knowledgeable of the increased risk of complications in this population. Ideally, surgery is planned through close cooperation between medical and surgical experts in order to minimize the surgical risks resulting from such chronic sequelae of prematurity as malnutrition and lung disease.

In addition, premature infants suffer from a unique eye disorder called *retinopathy of prematurity* (ROP), also known as retrolental fibroplasia (RLF). This develops because of a toxic effect of oxygen on the immature eye tissues. The severity ranges from mild abnormalities in eye structure, causing nearsightedness, to more severe damage to the retina, causing severe visual impairment or even blindness. Routine medical care should thus include timely screening for ROP in all premature infants exposed to supplemental oxygen (see Chapter 16).

CHRONIC SEQUELAE OF PREMATURITY: UNDERSTANDING THE WHOLE CHILD

Most of the research in neonatal medicine focuses on disease processes occurring within the intensive care nursery setting. Unfortunately, the hazards of prematurity do not end at the time of discharge. This section describes the impact of chronic neonatal disorders in terms of prevalence, contribution to postdischarge morbidity and mortality including rehospitalization, and natural history. As was pointed out in a study by Hack (one of the few studies published on this subject), this "broader spectrum of morbidity" has strong implications for home care services and follow-up care.[7] In Hack's study, a cohort of VLBW infants (birth weight less than 1500 gm) was followed until the age of 3 years. Demographic data in this study illustrate both the biological complications and adverse socioeconomic factors common within this population. Although the data in this study come from infants cared for in only one center, and born between 1975 and 1979, the principles illustrated remain valid.

Acute biological complications in the study population included the following:

- intrauterine growth retardation (20 percent)
- birth asphyxia (21 percent)
- RDS (71 percent)
- apnea of prematurity (42 percent)
- sepsis and meningitis (12.6 percent)
- NEC (5 percent)

The indicators of socioeconomic disadvantage among mothers of the study infants included the following:

- belonging to lower socioeconomic classes (62 percent)
- having less than a high school education (41 percent)
- being unmarried (35 percent)

By the time of hospital discharge, infants in the study were near the equivalent of term age (36 to 40 weeks) and were feeding orally. A minority had chronic physical sequelae at the time of discharge: chronic lung disease (8 percent), chronic GI disease (14 percent), and hydrocephalus (1.7 percent). Growth retardation, on the other hand, was highly prevalent, occurring in 54 percent of the infants at the time of discharge.

Follow-up of chronic medical sequelae in those infants who survived beyond 3 years of age offers reasons for some optimism. The prevalence of chronic lung disease had fallen from 8 percent to 3.8 percent by 8 months, and to 0.5 percent at 3 years. All chronic GI diseases had diminished in severity by 21 months of age. Although 42 percent of the infants had some neuromotor abnormality at 3 years, only 5 percent had a major motor handicap; 4 percent had mental retardation, and 1.8 percent had serious sensory deficits. Likewise, the prevalence of growth retardation decreases from 54 percent at discharge to 23 percent at age 3 years, with most of the catch-up growth occurring during the first year of life. These data suggest that a gradual normalization and recovery occurs in the vast majority of VLBW and premature infants, but that this normalization takes up to 2 to 3 years to occur.

Another indication of the ongoing biological hazards these infants face can be measured in rate of rehospitalization. Fully one third of Hack's cohorts required rehospitalization during the first year of life, and one tenth during the second year of life. Most of these rehospitalizations were for infections, exacerbations of chronic sequelae of prematurity, and inguinal hernia repairs. By contrast, only 8 percent of normal birth weight infants need hospitalization during the first year of life. Furthermore, survivors of prematurity have more frequent visits to physicians and longer hospital stays than are noted for normal birth weight infants.

The statistics Hack presents on prevalence of chronic sequelae represent only a part of the picture. Survivors of prematurity also suffer a disproportionate share of mortality well into the third year of life. In Hack's cohort of VLBW infants, 20 percent of the deaths occurred after 28 days of age, and 6 percent of the deaths occurred after discharge. When these data are viewed from another perspective, it can be seen that VLBW infants account for 25 to 30 percent of deaths between 1 and 12 months of age, even though they account for only 1 percent of all births.[8]

CONCLUSION

The full impact of higher rates of mortality and morbidity in this population has not been measured. It is reasonable to expect that for the infant's family, family functioning in general, and adaptation to the premature infant's special needs in particular, would be severely stressed. The potential certainly exists for timely and competent home-based intervention to reduce the disproportionate burden related to both illness and death among these infants. As home care of the high risk infant is such a promising field, its success will be enhanced by linking service to research. Experienced practitioners should be encouraged to ask critical questions and to document the results of their interventions so that their contribution to the total service network can be appropriately recognized.

One of the greatest current challenges in neonatal medicine is posed by the explosion of knowledge and treatment technology. For example, newer methods of treating lung disease of the premature such as extracorporeal membrane oxygenation (ECMO), are being used; intrauterine surgery for life-threatening birth defects is being attempted; and organ transplantation for malformations such as congenital heart disease or renal failure is being performed in younger infants than ever before.

As increasingly sophisticated technology promotes survival from more severe illness, so too must the long-term care of the survivors be supported. In relation to these technologies, more and more infants will require specialized, long-term, multidisciplinary supportive care and monitoring. Paradoxically, the development of these technologies occurs in an era of shrinking health dollars and a transfer of care from expensive acute care facilities to more cost-effective chronic care or home care settings. The long-term success of new medical technologies will depend in part on the extension of specialized knowledge and skills to nontraditional settings such as the home.

NOTES

1. Hack M: Changing trends in neonatal and postnatal deaths in VLBW infants, *Am J Obstet Gynecol* 137: 797–800, 1980.
2. *United States Health, 1982*, DHHS publication 83–1232. US Department of Health and Human Services, 1983.
3. McCormick M: The contribution of low birth weight to infant mortality and childhood morbidity, *N Engl J Med* 312, no. 2 (1985):82–90.
4. Horn S: Interhospital differences in severity of illness: problems for prospective payment based on DRG's, *N Engl J Med* 313: 20–23, 1985.
5. Saigal S: Outcome in infants 501 to 1000 gm birth weight delivered to residents of the McMaster Health Region, *J Pediatr* 105: 969–976, 1984.
6. McCormick M: The contribution of low birth weight, p. 84.
7. Hack M: The very low birth weight infant: the broader spectrum of morbidity during infancy and early childhood, *J Dev Pediatr* 4: 243–249, 1983.
8. McCormick M: The contribution of low birth weight, p. 3.

REFERENCES

Avery G: *Neonatology: Pathophysiology and Management of the Newborn,* ed 2. Philadelphia, JB Lippincott Co, 1981.

Hack M: Changing trends in neonatal and postnatal deaths in VLBW infants. *Am J Obstet Gynecol* 137: 797–800, 1980.

Horn S: Interhospital differences in severity of illness: problems for prospective payment based on DRG's. *N Engl J Med* 313: 20–23, 1985.

McCormick M: The contribution of low birth weight to infant mortality and childhood morbidity. *N Engl J Med* 312: 82–90, 1985.

Saigal S: Outcome in infants 501 to 1000 gm birth weight delivered to residents of the McMaster Health Region. *J Pediatr* 6: 969–976, 1984.

United States Health, 1982. DHHS publication 83–1232. US Department of Health and Human Services, 1983.

Chapter 2

Discharge Planning for the High Risk Infant

Sally McCarthy, MSN, RN

The American Nurses' Association has defined discharge planning as that "part of the continuity of care process which is designed to prepare the patient or client for the next phase of care, whether it be self-care, care by family members, or care by an organized health care provider."[1] Discharge planning for the high risk infant is a planned process of activities involving the family and professionals from various disciplines. Its goal is to facilitate the transition of health care for the infant from the hospital to another environment. Although home care is generally most desirable for the high risk infant, it may not be feasible because of medical, psychosocial, or financial reasons. Consequently, alternative modes of care may be required, at least for an interim period.[2]

The current emphasis on home care versus institutionalization makes it difficult for many parents to admit that having their infant at home may not be their choice. In addition, lack of financial support from third party payers may rule out home care as an option. In other instances, a family may attempt home care, only to find the burden too overwhelming. For these reasons, it is imperative that health professionals recognize various alternatives and provide parents with the necessary support for informed decision making.

RATIONALE

The rationale for discharge planning is continuity of care and cost effectiveness. Fiscal restraints brought about by federal legislation, as well as cost containment measures imposed by many third party payers, have recently highlighted the need for effective discharge planning. Although children's hospitals are temporarily exempt from the "Diagnostic Related Groups" (DRGs) imposed upon Medicare patients, many states have devised their own similar systems for Medicaid patients. Other health care payment programs, such as health maintenance organizations (HMOs), and private insurance companies are adopting their own systems to curb health care costs.[3] Third party payers are no longer automatically reimbursing hospitals for extensive lengths of stay and multiple diagnostic tests even with clear documentation of medical necessity and evidence of discharge planning throughout the hospitalization.

Thus, hospitals nationwide are reviewing and revising policies related to discharge, developing aggressive discharge planning programs, and taking measures to educate staff members and to streamline the discharge planning process. The challenge is to streamline the process to reduce costs without reducing the quality of care.

PHILOSOPHY

Every infant has the right to discharge planning. Some infants will require relatively simple preparation for discharge, with a focus on well baby care and routine medical follow-up. Others, with more complex needs, will require special planning with a multidisciplinary approach in order to meet their needs for continuity of care. Each member of the health care team providing care for the infant is responsible for integrating discharge planning into delivery of that care and for documenting the process as it evolves.[4]

It is the right of every family to be actively involved in discharge planning and to be assured that all efforts, beginning at the time of admission, have been directed toward planning and providing them with necessary information and support required for continuity of care. Indeed, a successful discharge plan demands that the family be involved in the decision-making process. Professionals in institutions must avoid setting the goals for families and thus depriving parents of their role and responsibility. Goals that are mutually established will be realistic and more readily attained.

DISCHARGE PLANNING PROCESS

The discharge planning process, like any other nursing process, involves assessment, planning, implementation, and evaluation, as indicated in Figure 2–1. Although the components follow a logical progression, two or more may be operational at the same time. The process is cyclic in nature, and between and among the components there is constant movement.[5]

Assessment

In the nursery, the assessment phase of discharge planning begins with the admissions interview. At this time the nurse obtains information for a nursing data

Figure 2–1 Discharge Planning Process

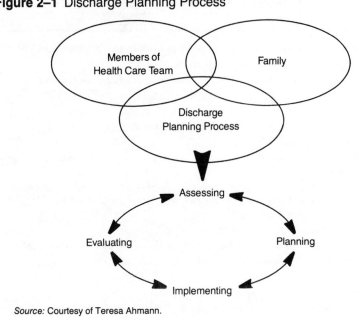

Members of
Health Care Team

Family

Discharge
Planning Process

Assessing

Evaluating

Planning

Implementing

Source: Courtesy of Teresa Ahmann.

base and identifies the primary caregiver and support persons for the infant and family. A comprehensive assessment is essential in order to provide direction for effective discharge planning. Assessment continues throughout the course of hospitalization as the infant's condition changes and new data become available through collaboration with professionals from other disciplines involved in the infant's care.

Assessment may reveal various psychosocial or other factors that indicate a need for special attention in discharge planning. Exhibit 2–1 provides a comprehensive listing of such factors that can be used as a nursing assessment tool.

Since many high risk infants belong to "high risk families," accuracy in family assessments is essential. Primary nurses in the hospital spend considerable time with both infant and caregivers and are thus in a unique position to observe both verbal and nonverbal cues during caregiving and teaching sessions. Areas of caregiver-infant interaction that should be observed and documented are detailed in Exhibit 2–2.

Planning

The planning phase begins with the formulation of the nursing care plan. Through the admissions interview and nursing data base, the nurse has identified

Exhibit 2–1 Factors Indicating Special Needs in Discharge Planning

- Congenital anomalies or conditions that will impair normal growth and development
- Progressive, chronic, or life-threatening disease
- Adolescent or single parents, particularly those with minimal or no available family support systems
- Illegal alien status of family members
- History of drug or alcohol abuse in the immediate family
- Multiple psychosocial problems
- Insufficient family financial resources to pay for hospitalization or for needed home-care equipment or services
- Family residence beyond reasonable commuting distance to hospital, indicating need for initially intensive support from the hospital, with identification of the family's local community resources for continuity of care
- Lack of regular visits by family members
- Inability of family to accept the infant's condition and to cope with the stresses involved
- Unresponsiveness of family members to the infant's needs
- Life-sustaining equipment required for home care
- Extended hours of nursing required for home care
- Need for respite care (e.g., by properly trained neighbors or by professionals)
- Need for supportive follow-up by various community agencies
- Need for transfer of infant to another specialty hospital or institution

the primary caregiver, community agencies that may already be involved, discharge teaching needs, and psychosocial factors important to discharge planning. The discharge plan is never a static plan but is continually evaluated and altered as new data indicate a need for change in the original plan.

Daily physician and nursing rounds also provide a forum for discharge planning, albeit brief. At least weekly, professionals from the various disciplines involved in the infant's care should participate in patient care and discharge planning rounds, where patients' readiness for discharge can be addressed and appropriate plans implemented. In consideration of nurses' limited time and resources, it is generally advisable to incorporate discharge planning into regularly scheduled multidisciplinary meetings or patient care rounds.

Primary caregivers and consultants from various disciplines involved in patient care should attend these meetings or rounds. For example, those attending rounds in the nursery might include physicians; nurses; social workers; physical, occupational or respiratory therapists; dietitians; chaplains; patient care representatives; psychologists; and possibly home care coordinators from appropriate community agencies or the hospital's home care program. Patient care and discharge planning rounds should be held on a consistent basis in order to address the following issues:

Exhibit 2–2 Caregiver-Infant Interaction Assessment Tool

Positive Cues

Eye contact, touching and talking with infant in soothing manner
Favorable comments regarding infant
Responds to diapering needs appropriately
Progressive involvement in infant's care
Interactions during feeding that are supportive of infant
Positive behavioral responses to infant's negative behavior
Realistic goals for infant or self
Statements indicating that infant is seen as an individual, respected human being
Statements associating infant's characteristics with those of other respected family members
Visits or calls nursery regularly
Verbalizes plans for ways to care for infant at home
Responds positively to suggestions and requests by staff in preparing for discharge

Negative Cues

Overstimulation or understimulation of infant
Negative comments regarding infant
Visits or calls nursery irregularly
Fails to keep appointments (i.e., for discharge teaching)
Does not become progressively involved in infant's care
Unrealistic goals for infant or self
Interprets infant's behavior as rejection

- the family's understanding of the diagnosis, prognosis, and discharge teaching
- the parents' attitude toward both the illness and the evolving discharge plan
- the parents' ability to provide adequate care and their coping abilities
- financial resources
- the physical environment of the home
- the need for therapeutic or supportive services.

Readiness for discharge is assessed, and potential community resources for assisting the family in providing continuity of care are identified. It is important that as discharge planning needs are identified, specific disciplines or individuals who will be accountable for making plans that address these needs also be identified. When this information is documented, accountability is established, and implementation of the discharge plan is more certain.

The high risk infant with complex care needs may require several individual predischarge conferences in addition to the regular nursery-wide patient care and discharge planning rounds. The purpose of the individual predischarge conference is to develop and implement discharge plans for a specific patient requiring special planning. The timeliness of such predischarge conferences is another important factor. They must be held early enough in the hospitalization to allow for comfortable planning and implementation rather than crisis intervention.

Although it may be helpful to have only health team members attend the first such conference, it is imperative that the family or primary caregiver be directly involved in all subsequent predischarge conferences. Parents, together with health team members, can identify discharge teaching that has been accomplished and can outline the need for further teaching of parents or other caregivers. Family members should be given an opportunity to discuss their concerns regarding home care and to participate in the problem-solving process. In this way, the family and the health professionals can mutually establish the goals for the discharge plan and assess readiness for discharge. This involvement also enables parents to begin establishing the advocacy role they must later assume for their child. The remaining predischarge steps to be taken by the family and by each health team member should be identified, and accountability clearly established. Families' involvement in the decision-making process assures their commitment to the plan, develops their confidence, and increases the likelihood of a successful discharge plan.

These conferences should include primary care providers and consultants from all appropriate disciplines within the institution, as well as representatives from any community agency to be involved in the infant's care. In this way, discharge planning goals are clearly understood, and continuity of care is more likely.

The community health nurse plays a pivotal role in case management and the monitoring of home care. The community health nurse can provide invaluable input to the discharge plan by identifying resources within the community. A predischarge home visit by the community health nurse will assure both family and hospital staff that the home is ready for the infant. If the community health nurse and family have not met previously, this home visit gives them an opportunity to establish a relationship before discharge. The nurse becomes familiar with the mutually established discharge planning goals and is viewed as an active member of the health care team. The infant, family, community health nurse, and hospital staff benefit from the liaison that is established.

Implementation

Implementation of the discharge plan includes discharge teaching, ordering equipment needed for home care, arranging for follow-up appointments, and making appropriate community referrals.

Discharge Teaching

Home care of a high risk infant may be very complex. Thorough teaching, emphasizing the details of each aspect of routine and potential emergency care, is essential. Teaching methods should include discussion, instructional materials, and demonstration by the nurse, with a return demonstration by the caregivers. The nurse should also observe for evidence of caregivers' confidence and competence, as indicated through routine performance.

An increasingly standard approach to discharge teaching is for nursing staff to contract with parents and other caregivers for a series of specific teaching sessions. These are followed by an 8- to 24-hour period (or more) during which family members and other caregivers take over complete responsibility for the infant's care as a "trial run." Regardless of how skilled and confident caregivers appear, this total-care experience provides an essential step in confidence building for the family and in assuring hospital staff of the family's competence. Countless families have attested to the value of this experience, even when they have spent months providing the infant's care intermittently within the hospital. Some hospitals arrange to provide a room located away from the nursery for this experience; others make arrangements outside but near the hospital.

Documentation of the discharge teaching standards that have been established, what teaching has actually occurred, and what degree of understanding and skill the caregivers are able to verbalize or demonstrate is, of course, an essential component of discharge teaching. Standardized teaching criteria and discharge teaching checklists facilitate both measurement and documentation of the skills and knowledge acquired by the caregivers. A brief overall view of discharge teaching is reflected in a checklist; a more detailed view of the progress is reflected in the nursing progress notes accumulated by all nurses participating in the teaching. An example of a discharge teaching checklist is provided in Appendix 2–A. Ideally the checklist should also be shared with the community health nurse to enable confirmation and enhancement of discharge teaching in the home setting.

Written discharge instructions are an important part of teaching and should be given to parents and caregivers whenever possible. *Going Home: A Handbook for Parents* is an example of the kind of booklet that can be devised to serve as a guide to well baby care.[6] Providing parents with information on well baby care will be an invaluable aid in helping them to focus on the "normal" aspects of their infant's care, which is often difficult after the infant has spent several weeks in a hospital nursery.

Preprinted instruction sheets for certain disease conditions or medications can also be devised to assist the caregiver and to streamline the teaching process. (See Appendix 2–B). These must be individualized, however; written instructions do not substitute for individualized and patient teaching but serve as a source of reference and increase the family's confidence after the infant's discharge. For maximum benefit, instruction sheets should be given to parents and caregivers prior to discharge, allowing them time to read and formulate questions while health team members are available for clarification.

An essential component of the discharge teaching plan is the identification and training of at least one secondary caregiver. These back-up caregivers must comprise a reliable support system that is readily available to the primary caregiver. Even when two parents are trained in the care, one may not be readily available for providing care to the infant; for example, the father may work excessive hours or be employed in two jobs. In such cases, a relative or neighbor can then be trained as a secondary caregiver. Single parents may also need assistance in identifying a secondary support person.

Equipment Ordering

Early identification of equipment needed for home care is important in order to avoid obstacles in obtaining reimbursement and resultant delays in discharge. Individual state Medicaid programs have different limitations regarding exactly what home equipment and supplies they will provide.[7] Some private insurance companies and HMOs contract only with specific durable medical equipment companies, whereas others provide no reimbursement whatsoever for home care equipment. It is important to determine the availability of funding for equipment before preparing families for home care or ordering equipment.

In some instances, it is possible to negotiate with third party payers regarding home care coverage. Although it is a time-consuming process, documenting the cost of hospital care compared with the cost of providing equipment for home care will often provide the data needed to negotiate and obtain reimbursement for the necessary equipment.[8] Successful negotiations are often easier when the prognosis is favorable and the need for the equipment is not viewed as chronic, maintenance care. When reimbursement by the third party payer seems at all unlikely, it is important to pursue alternative funding sources, such as private associations and foundations, church groups, local community organizations, national organizations, or the state Crippled Children's program (see also Chapter 20).

Once questions of reimbursement for home care equipment and supplies are settled, a vendor must be carefully selected. Hartsell and Ward suggest that important criteria to consider in selecting a vendor include the following:[9]

- pediatric experience
- 24-hour availability
- provision of a range of equipment and supplies
- provision of preventive maintenance on equipment

- provision of free "loaner" or replacement equipment when equipment malfunctions
- provision of written instructions for operation and maintenance of equipment
- timely responses to telephone calls regarding problems.

Follow-up Appointments

Arranging for appropriate medical follow-up with specialty clinics (e.g., for pulmonary or neurologic problems) is also an essential component of the discharge plan. Prior to discharge, parents or caregivers should be given follow-up appointments with specific dates and times. The community health nurse, if informed of scheduled appointments, can reinforce their importance and can often provide assistance with transportation arrangements. Locating a physician who will act as primary care physician is of vital importance and is discussed further in Chapter 4.

Community Referrals

Community referrals might be made to a variety of resources, including, for example, the local visiting nurse association or parent-infant education programs. Some referrals may need to be made significantly before the anticipated date of discharge in order to ensure continuity of care. An early referral for community health nursing will allow the nurse both to come to the hospital to meet the infant and family and to make a predischarge home visit, if indicated. When the infant care needs are complex or unfamiliar to the community health nurse, arrangements can be made for the nurse to come to the hospital for a demonstration or review of specific procedures or medical equipment required in the infant's care. A written plan of care should also be provided for the community health nurse. In addition, sharing discharge teaching checklists, as previously indicated, will enable the nurse to be familiar with the infant's care and the caregivers' need for follow-up teaching.

Because home care of the high-risk infant may be very demanding, respite care is often an essential component of the discharge plan (see Chapter 20). For the very fragile infant, extended hours of professional care provided by a home health agency may be necessary.

When extended hours of nursing care are necessary, careful selection of a home health agency is essential. The discharge planner should consider the degree of pediatric or neonatal expertise available, the willingness of practitioners to spend time in the hospital refining skills, and the quality of feedback provided by the agency or nurse to families and physicians.

Chapter 20 provides further discussion of community resources, including financial, therapeutic, and family support resources.

EVALUATION

Evaluation of discharge planning is essential in order to make home care a safe and successful alternative for infants and families. Discharge planners and all health professionals are responsible for evaluating the adequacy of home health agencies, equipment companies, and any community agency providing support at home.

Parents and caregivers can be helpful in providing feedback about such things as the reliability of equipment companies or the readability and usefulness of parent teaching materials. They may also provide valuable information regarding what additional assistance might have helped them in the transition to home care.

One effective mechanism for evaluation is the enclosure of a follow-up form with all referrals, to be mailed back to the hospital within a designated period of time. One copy of the form can then be shared with the primary team members who initiated such referrals. This provides not only personal satisfaction for staff members but gives them the opportunity to evaluate their discharge plan and referral decisions. Another copy of the form should also be shared with physicians and health team members involved in the ongoing care of the infant. Establishing such a communication mechanism keeps all involved professionals aware of the family's needs and progress and thus promotes continuity of care.

NOTES

1. American Nurses' Association Publication. Code NP-49, 3000-3, 1975.

2. McCarthy SA: Discharge planning in a primary nursing system, *Discharge Planning Update* 4: 10–14, Fall 1983.

3. Rutkowski BL: DRG's—now all eyes are on you, *Nursing Life*, March/April 1985, pp 26–29.

4. McKeehan KM (ed): *Continuing Care: A Multidisciplinary Approach to Discharge Planning*, St Louis: CV Mosby Co, 1981, p 8.

5. Yura H, Walsh MB: *The Nursing Process: Assessing, Planning, Implementing, Evaluating*, ed 3, New York, Appleton-Century-Crofts, 1978, p 93.

6. *Going Home* is a booklet offering a guide for well baby care, based on the nursing and medical philosophies of the Department of Neonatology at Children's Hospital National Medical Center (House MB, Kimura PS: *Going Home: A Handbook for Parents*, Washington, DC, Children's Hospital National Medical Center, 1982).

7. Medicaid coverage of the pediatric population, *Caring*, May 1985, p 52; Private health care coverage for children, *Caring*, May 1985, p 53.

8. Examples can be found in Cabin B: Cost effectiveness of pediatric home care, *Caring*, May 1985, pp 48–50.

9. Hartsell MB, Ward JH: Selecting equipment vendors for children on home care, *MCN: The American Journal of Maternal/Child Nursing* 10: 26–28, January/February 1985.

REFERENCES

American Nurses' Association. Publication Code NP-49, 3000-3, 1975.

Cabin B: Cost effectiveness of pediatric home care. *Caring*, May 1985, pp 48–50.

Hartsell MB, Ward JH: Selecting equipment vendors for children on home care. *MCN: The American Journal of Maternal/Child Nursing* 10: 26–28, January/February 1985.

House MB, Kimura PS: *Going Home: A Handbook for Parents*. Washington, DC, Children's Hospital National Medical Center, 1982.

McCarthy SA: Discharge planning in a primary nursing system. *Discharge Planning Update* 4: 10–14, Fall 1983.

McKeehan KM (ed): *Continuing Care: A Multidisciplinary Approach to Discharge Planning*. St Louis, The CV Mosby Co, 1981.

Medicaid coverage of the pediatric population. *Caring*, May 1985, p 52.

Private health care coverage for children. *Caring*, May 1985, p 53.

Rutkowski BL: DRG's—now all eyes are on you. *Nurs Life*, March/April 1985, pp 28–29.

Yuna H, Walsh MB: *The Nursing Process: Assessing, Planning, Implementing, Evaluating*, ed 3. New York, Appleton-Century-Crofts, 1978.

Discharge Checklist—Tracheostomy Home Care

Nurse's Name   Initials   Caretaker _____   Caretaker's level of
                                        (Indiv. checklist for each caretaker)   Performance
_____ _____   V—Verbalized
_____ _____   D—Demonstrated
_____ _____   RP—Routinely Performs
_____ _____

	NURSING ACTIVITIES				CARETAKER ACTIVITIES			COMMENTS
	Disc.	Demon.	Reinf.		V	D	RP	
Disch.	Date/ Intl.	Date/ Intl.	Date/ Intl.		Date/ Intl.	Date/ Intl.	Date/ Intl.	
Std.								
V								

"Home Care of Your Child with a
Tracheostomy" booklet given to
caretaker.

24

Anatomy and physiology of the upper airway system explained and how it is related to a tracheostomy.	V
Purpose of tracheostomy for this child explained.	V
Identified general symptoms of respiratory distress.	V
Identified appropriate steps in handling respiratory difficulty.	V
Identified the difference between moist and dry breath sounds.	D

B-114/Disk11

[Explanation of abbreviations on checklist:

Disch. std. = Discharge Standard (level of performance)
Disc. = Discussed
Demon. = Demonstrated
Reinf. = Reinforced
Intl. = Initial (of nurse)]

	Disch.	NURSING ACTIVITIES			CARETAKER ACTIVITIES			COMMENTS
	Std.	Disc. Date/Intl.	Demon. Date/Intl.	Reinf. Date/Intl.	V Date/Intl.	D Date/Intl.	RP Date/Intl.	
Identified significance of changes in color, nature and amount of secretions.	V							
Demonstrated use of mist collar.	R.P.							
Instilled normal saline into child's tracheostomy tube.	R.P.							
Demonstrated correct technique for suctioning.	R.P.							
Verbalized understanding of purpose and use of resuscitation bag.	V							
Demonstrated use of resuscitation bag.	R.P.							
Demonstrated chest physical therapy.	R.P.							

Provided skin care around the tracheostomy area and explained how to assess for skin breakdowns.	R.P.
Prepared and changed child's tracheostomy ties.	R.P.

Explained and demonstrated correct technique in changing child's tracheostomy tube:
  with assistance
  without assistance
	R.P.

Described correct procedure to follow when tracheostomy tube is difficult to insert.	D
Verbalized and demonstrated on a doll what to do if, child accidentally decannulated himself/herself.	D
Identified appropriate steps in handling plugging of tracheostomy tube.	D

		NURSING ACTIVITIES			CARETAKER ACTIVITIES			COMMENTS
	Disch. Std.	Disc. Date/Intl.	Demon. Date/Intl.	Reinf. Date/Intl.	V Date/Intl.	D Date/Intl.	RP Date/Intl.	
Demonstrated correct CPR procedure for a child of this age with a tracheostomy.	D							
Provided total care for 24 hours or more.	R.P.							
Travel kit assembled and given to caretaker with purpose and contents explained.	D							
Home Care supplies: ordered:	V							
delivered and demonstrated by vendor	V							
Caretaker has demonstrated competence in troubleshooting problems with equipment.	D							

	Completed Date/Initials
Caretaker describes arrangement of supplies/equipment at home.	V
Parents instructed to post emergency phone #'s by telephone.	V
Parents instructed to post CPR guidelines by child's bed.	V
Community Support and Resources	
Nursing referral written and sent	
Name of Agency _____	

	Completed Date/Initial	COMMENTS
Local Hospital Emergency Room:		
Name		
Phone #		
Notified in writing of child's need for services		
Emergency Squad:		
Name		
Phone #		
Notified in writing of child's need for services		
Telephone Company		
Written notification sent re: child's need for priority service.		
Instructions given caretaker re: procedure to follow if service is interrupted		

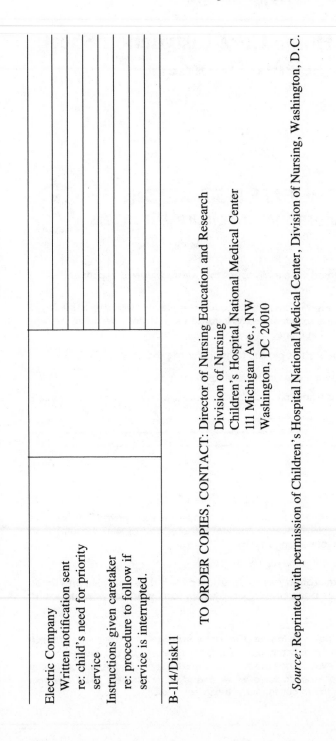

Electric Company

Written notification sent re: child's need for priority service

Instructions given caretaker re: procedure to follow if service is interrupted.

B-114/Disk11

TO ORDER COPIES, CONTACT: Director of Nursing Education and Research
Division of Nursing
Children's Hospital National Medical Center
111 Michigan Ave., NW
Washington, DC 20010

Source: Reprinted with permission of Children's Hospital National Medical Center, Division of Nursing, Washington, D.C.

Discharge Home Care Instruction Sheet: Seizure Disorders

HOME CARE INSTRUCTIONS
for Children with Seizure Disorders

Activity:

Your child should be treated as normally as possible with play activities, sports and school appropriate for age and ability.

There are a few special precautions to follow: avoid activities that would result in injury to your child or others if he lost consciousness, for instance, bicycling in heavy traffic, climbing in high places, or swimming alone.

Avoid excessive fatigue, such as playing to the point of exhaustion.

Do not leave a small child alone on the toilet or in the bath.

Your child may return to school on _____ .

Other restrictions _____
_____
_____ .

General Guidelines:

Diet - no restrictions.

Any **illness** or **fever** may affect your child's seizure pattern. Fevers above 101° should be treated promptly with aspirin or acetaminophen (tylenol or other aspirin substitute) and if necessary, with a lukewarm sponge bath.

Be sure your child has a **regular family doctor**.

Other drugs or alcohol may affect your child's seizure pattern, therefore, **give only those medications that have been prescribed by your family doctor or neurologist.**

Medication:

The medicine that is being given to your child has been selected to control the seizures. It is very important to give the right amount at the right time every day as instructed below. **Never miss a dose.** Never change the amount of medicine or schedule without talking with the doctor. Contact the doctor a week ahead of time when you know your medications are going to run out so that you can get a refill.

Additional Instructions:

_____

_____

_____

When to Call the Doctor:

- Prolonged seizures
- Change in pattern or frequency of seizure
- Significant side effects from anticonvulsant medications:

_____

_____

_____

When Your Child has a Seizure:

- Remain calm. You cannot stop a seizure once it has begun. Do not try to restrain the child.
- Clear the area around the child so he does not injure himself.
- **Do not force anything between his teeth.** If his mouth is open, you may place a soft object like a folded handkerchief between his side teeth so he does not bite his tongue.
- If you can, turn him on his side, so that saliva may flow from his mouth.
- Allow the child to rest if he desires, after the seizure is over.

Additional Instructions:

_____

_____

_____

Return Appointments:

_____

_____

_____

Phone Numbers:

Neurology Office: 745-2198 or 745-2120

Emergency Room: 745-5204

Nights or weekends: 745-3060 (ask for neurology resident on call)

General Information:

Emotional behavior— as a result of hospitalization and surgery, your child may regress in some areas of his emotional development. This behavior is not unusual, but it must be handled carefully. He may for example, develop one or more of the following problems:

1. Nightmares: he may awaken at night crying and upset. Reassure him that he is home, that you are there, he is safe and that he just had a bad dream. Remain with him until he falls asleep again.

2. Appetite: his appetite may be poor when he returns home. This should gradually improve.

3. Demanding: he may be demanding and always want his own way, or he may be more dependent upon his mother than before hospitalization. Give him a great deal of love and affection, including physical contact. Do not let him have his own way all the time.

4. Discipline: treat the child with seizures as any other child, including rewards and punishment appropriate for the age of the child and situation. If parents have difficulty with discipline, it can be helpful to discuss feelings with a member of the health care team.

Available Services:

Arrangements can be made to have a visiting nurse visit you and your child after his discharge from the hospital. She can be helpful in discussing instructions, making observations and answering any questions that you may have concerning your child's care at home. Our social worker is also available to help you with any futher service you desire.

CL/sa
B2/309

Source: Reprinted with permission of Children's Hospital National Medical Center, Division of Nursing, Washington, D.C.

Chapter 3

The Nursing Intake Process, Interviewing, and Documentation

NURSING INTAKE PROCESS

The first home visit is important for several reasons. First, it is the beginning of the relationship between the community health nurse and the family. The tenor of this visit will in all likelihood set the tone of the relationship and thus influence subsequent visits. Second, in most agencies the first home visit requires the most documentation (permission forms, insurance information, intake history, and so forth). As a third and final factor, the first home visit must include an immediate assessment of the infant's status and safety at home.

Because of the necessary assessment and documentation requirements, the first visit may tend to be lengthy. It should generally be limited, however, to 1½ to 2 hours; longer periods may seem overwhelming and invasive to a family. In this regard, parents should be informed before the visit of the expected amount of time the nurse will need. They should also be reassured that not all visits will be as lengthy. The first home visit should be planned at a time when parents will be relatively free from interruptions (e.g., older children at school and baby napping). However, patience is necessary if interruptions do occur; the home environment is quite different from the hospital or clinic.

To ensure an acceptable time period for the first home visit, the nurse may need to assign priorities among necessary intake activities. Of course, certain permission forms will need to be signed, and insurance information obtained. In addition, for an infant with multiple problems who is dependent on medical technology for life support, the infant's condition must be assessed; equipment must be checked for proper functioning; the presence of all needed supplies determined; and a

---

Note: Documentation forms for a nursing intake history focused on the technology-dependent infant, a review of systems tailored to the infant, and an outline for pediatric physical examination are provided in Appendixes 3–A, 3–B, and 3–C, respectively.

preliminary assessment made of the parents' preparation for providing appropriate routine and emergency care.

Although it is often thought that a complete health history is the first step in providing health care services, if time on the first visit prohibits obtaining this information, the health history can be obtained on a subsequent visit. Alternatively, the history can be obtained bit by bit, in an informal manner, over several visits.

The importance of obtaining a thorough and accurate health history cannot be overemphasized, however. The elements of a complete health history are listed in Exhibit 3–1. The history, including a review of body systems, together with a physical examination and an observation of the child and family, provides the data on which both the initial care plan and ongoing nursing interventions are based. The history-taking process not only provides facts but, as Korsch and Aley suggest, allows the nurse to identify family perceptions, concerns, and dynamics: "If we [nurses] are to relate well to parents, it is helpful to explore some of their attitudes, to learn something of their social and emotional reactions, and to familiarize ourselves with the familial interpersonal relationships."[1]

PRINCIPLES OF HEALTH INTERVIEWING

When either the initial history or interim histories are obtained, attentiveness and a nonjudgmental attitude are important both for establishing rapport and for creating an environment in which the parent feels free to discuss any concerns openly. In most cases, health interviewing and history taking will be most

---

Exhibit 3–1 Elements of a Complete Health History for the High Risk Infant*

- Home and family data
- Family health history
- Prenatal history
- Birth history
- Newborn history
- General health history—immunizations, allergies, accidents, illnesses, previous hospitalizations

- Parent-child interaction
- Daily patterns—feeding, sleeping, urinary and bowel habits
- Nutrition†
- Development
- Special care needs—equipment, treatment, diet, medications
- Review of body systems‡

*See also Appendix 3–A.
†See Appendix 5–A for nutritional assessment.
‡See Appendix 3–B.

productive when open-ended questions are used (e.g., "Can you tell me about your pregnancy?") rather than a series of direct questions (e.g., "When did you first know you were pregnant? Did you have any infections or bleeding? take any medications?) When open-ended questioning is used, the parent (or patient, if old enough to be questioned) should rarely be interrupted. If pauses occur, they can be used for the interviewer to indicate interest or to ask for clarification. Open-ended questions usually generate significant health information and reveal parental perceptions and concerns and family dynamics.

If specific details needed for a complete history or assessment are not addressed by the parent in response to open-ended questions, some direct questions may be necessary. The following principles, suggested by Bernstein and colleagues, outline the most appropriate way to use direct questions:[2]

a) The sequence of questions should progress from the general to the specific; b) The questions should progress from the less personal to the more personal; c) The questions should be worded to elicit answers of a sentence or more and to avoid "yes" or "no" responses; d) The questions should be worded to avoid bias.

In any health interview, it is important to use language comprehensible to the persons being interviewed. Although language that is too elementary may be insulting, medical jargon is often not understood, and some parents may be hesitant to ask for an explanation. In addition, some questions that seem important to health care providers may seem unnecessarily prying to parents, who then become reluctant to reply openly. This problem can often be avoided by explaining to the parents what will be asked and why—for example, "Now I am going to ask about the health of the family members. It is important to know if there are any hereditary or contagious diseases."

A child at home is part of the family, and that child's problems and care occur in the family context, both affected by and affecting each family member and the family as a whole. For this reason, the reaction of family members to any problem the child has, whether chronic or acute, is important and should be an aspect of both the initial history and subsequent interviews. Korsch and Aley suggest that it is particularly important to explore the parent's main concern or worry at each visit and the reason for this concern.[3] If these concerns are not addressed, the level of parent frustration will be high, and cooperation with the health care provided may suffer.

DOCUMENTATION AND THE PLAN OF CARE

Thorough and clear documentation is essential in home health and must be based on identification of problem areas in the development of a plan of care.

Exhibit 3–2 The SOAP Format for Documentation

Problem _____

S   *Subjective data:* reports, concerns, observations, and feelings of patient or patients' caregivers

O   *Objective data:* findings on physical examination and screening tests; observations of interactions or environment

A   *Assessment:* an attempt to synthesize the subjective and objective data, discuss the problem, and give rationale for the plan

P   *Plan:* in concretely defined terms, may include further data collection, therapeutic intervention, health education, and follow-up plans

---

Problem areas can include medical, nursing, social, emotional, and environmental concerns. Identification of problem areas is based on information obtained in the initial history, the review of systems, and the physical assessment.[4] Throughout each home visit, the information elicited from parents and other caregivers, together with the nurse's skilled observation and examination, will allow updating of the problem list as necessary.

The plan of care, for each problem identified, may consist of several components. It may include, for example, further data collection, therapeutic interventions, education, and coordination. The care plan should address the identified problems, while building on the strengths of the infant and family. It can, in fact, be developed jointly by the nurse and family. (Sample care plans are provided in the Appendixes of Chapters 4 through 13.)

The care plan should in all cases be documented in writing, and a copy made available to the family. Sharing a copy of the care plan with other professionals involved in the infant's care may also assist in coordination of services. Of course, regular evaluation and refinement of the care plan are essential.

Each home visit should address one or more aspects of the overall plan of care. Thorough and clear documentation of each home visit is also important. A procedure for documentation that has widespread use is the SOAP format.[5] Based on recording *s*ubjective and *o*bjective data, *a*ssessment and *p*lan, the SOAP format provides a well-organized system, assuring that all necessary components of thorough documentation are included. An outline of the SOAP format is provided in Exhibit 3–2.

NOTES

1. Korsch BM, Aley, EF: Pediatric interviewing technics, *Current Problems in Pediatrics* VIII: 5, 1973.

2. Bernstein L, Bernstein RS, Dana RH: *Interviewing: A Guide for Health Professionals,* ed 2, New York, Appleton-Century-Crofts, 1974, p 103.
3. Korsch BM, Aley EF: Pediatric interviewing technics, p 5.
4. Physical assessment is an important part of nursing evaluation. The reader is referred to other sources for details about pediatric physical assessment: Alexander MM, Brown MS: *Pediatric History Taking and Physical Diagnosis for Nurses,* ed 2, New York, McGraw-Hill Book Co, 1979; Bates B: *A Guide to Physical Examination,* ed 2, Philadelphia, JB Lippincott Co, 1979, particularly pp 368-462; Chow MP, Durand BA, Feldman MN, et al: *Handbook of Pediatric Primary Care,* ed 2, New York, John Wiley and Sons, 1984.
5. The SOAP system was developed by Weed LL: *Medical Records, Medical Education, and Patient Care,* Cleveland, Case Western Reserve University Press, 1970; it and similar systems have become widely accepted in both medicine and nursing practice. (See also Bonskowsky ML: Adapting the P.O.M.R. to community child health care, *Nursing Outlook* 20: 515-518, August 1972; Schell PL, Campbell AT: P.O.M.R.—not just another way to chart, *Nursing Outlook* 20: 510-514, August 1972; Woody M, Mallison M: The problem-oriented system for patient-centered care, *Am J Nurs* 73: 1168-1175, July 1973.)

REFERENCES

Alexander MM, Brown MS: *Pediatric History Taking and Physical Diagnosis for Nurses,* ed 2. New York, McGraw-Hill Book Co, 1979.

Bates B (ed): *A Guide to Physical Examination,* ed 2. Philadelphia, JB Lippincott Co, 1979.

Bernstein L, Bernstein RS, Dana RH: *Interviewing: A Guide for Health Professionals,* ed 2. New York, Appleton-Century-Crofts, 1974.

Bonskowsky ML: Adapting the P.O.M.R. to community child health care, *Nursing Outlook* 20: 515-518, August 1972.

Brunner LS, Suddarth DS (eds): *The Lippincott Manual of Nursing Practice,* ed 3. Philadelphia, JB Lippincott Co, 1982, Chapters 1 and 2.

Chow MP, Durand BA, Feldman MN, et al: *Handbook of Pediatric Primary Care,* ed 2. New York, John Wiley and Sons, 1984.

Hoekelman RA: The pediatric physical examination, in Bates B (ed): *A Guide to Physical Examination,* ed 2. Philadelphia, JB Lippincott Co, 1979, p 368.

Holt SJ, Robinson TM: *FAT: The Family Assessment Tool for School Nurses and Other Professionals.* Boulder, Colo., Family Assessment Tools, 1979. (FAT Kit available from Family Assessment Tools, Box 4941, Boulder, Colorado 80306).

Klijanowicz AA: Pediatric history taking, in Brunner LS, Suddarth DS (eds): *The Lippincott Manual of Nursing Practice,* ed 3. Philadelphia, JB Lippincott Co, 1972.

Korsch BM, Aley EF: Pediatric interviewing technics. *Curr Prob Pediatr* VIII: 3-42, 1973.

Schell PL, Campbell AT: P.O.M.R.—not just another way to chart, *Nursing Outlook* 20: 510-514, August 1972.

Weed LL: *Medical Records, Medical Education, and Patient Care,* Cleveland, Case Western Reserve University Press, 1970.

Woody M, Mallison M: The problem-oriented system for patient-centered care, *Am J Nurs* 73: 1168-1175, July 1973.

Appendix 3–A

Nursing Intake History

Name _____ DOB _____
Address _____ Phone _____
_____

Mother's name _____ Work Phone _____
Father's name _____ Work Phone _____

DIAGNOSES _____
_____
_____

Doctors _____ Phone _____
_____ Phone _____
_____ Phone _____
_____ Phone _____
_____ Phone _____
_____ Phone _____

HOME & FAMILY

Description of home and community (Observation for safety, location of equipment, availability of telephone, transportation) _____
_____
_____
_____
_____
_____

Family constellation (List names and ages of family members) _____

_____

_____

_____

_____

_____

Family dynamics (Parental confidence, parental interaction, sibling roles, parent-child interactions) _____

_____

_____

_____

_____

_____

FAMILY HEALTH HISTORY

Source of information _____
(Note if positive for asthma/allergies, diabetes, hypertension, anemia, sickle cell, cancer, alcoholism, drug abuse, hearing/vision loss, mental retardation, deaths)

Mother _____

_____

Father _____

_____

Siblings _____

_____

_____

_____

Maternal grandmother _____

_____

Maternal grandfather _____

_____

Paternal grandmother _____

_____

Paternal grandfather _____

_____

PRENATAL HISTORY

Age of mother _____   # of pregnancies _____   # of births _____
# of miscarriages _____   # of abortions _____
Prenatal care (frequency, source) _____

Complications of pregnancy (infections, bleeding, etc.) _____

Alcohol _____   Smoking _____   X-rays _____   Weight gain _____
Caffeine _____   Medications _____

BIRTH HISTORY

Hospital _____
Gestational age _____   Type of delivery _____
Length of labor _____   Apgars(blue?) _____
Birth weight _____   Length _____ Head circumference _____
Comments _____

NEWBORN PERIOD

Respiratory difficulties (describe) _____

Jaundice _____   Seizures _____   Anemia _____
Feeding problems (describe) _____

Infections (describe) _____

Physical abnormalities (describe) _____

ICU _____ Length of stay _____
Length of initial hospitalization _____
Comments _____

IMMUNIZATIONS

DT or DPT (circle), CPV, (I) _____ (II) _____ (III) _____ MMR _____
reactions _____

ALLERGIES

Foods _____
Medications _____
Other _____

ACCIDENTS

_____
_____
_____

ILLNESSES

measles _____   rubella _____
chickenpox _____   mumps _____
scarlet fever _____   strep throat _____
meningitis _____   hepatitis _____
pneumonia _____   otitis _____
tuberculosis _____   abscesses _____
febrile convulsions _____ other _____

PREVIOUS HOSPITALIZATIONS

_____
_____
_____
_____
_____

Brief history of most recent hospitalization _____
_____
_____
_____
_____
_____

THE CHILD

Source of information _____

Parental description of child _____
_____
_____

How do you know when your child is upset? _____
_____

How do you quiet your child? _____
_____

Do you recognize different cries? _____
_____

DAILY PATTERNS

Caretakers _____
_____

Feeding (see nutritional assessment)
Appetite _____   schedule _____
Problems _____
Sleeping schedule (including naps) _____
Where child sleeps _____
Bedtime routine _____
Problems _____
Urinary habits (freq/amount/odor) _____
Bowel habit (freq/type/color) _____
Problems _____
Bathing (freq/method) _____
Discipline _____

Activity/play/toys _____
_____

Peer relationships _____
_____

School (performance/reactions) _____
_____

Self-care: feeding _____   bathing _____
              dressing _____   toileting _____
_____

Do you have any problems managing your child in the home? _____

_____

_____

_____

DEVELOPMENT

Source of information _____

Development milestones (List age acquired)

hold up head _____ responds to name _____

smile responsively _____ cruise _____

roll prone to supine _____ walk _____

roll supine to prone _____ babble _____

voluntary grasp-release toys _____ first word _____

sit alone _____ finger feed _____

4-point crawl _____ cup drink _____

pull to stand _____ spoon feed _____

Parent summary of child's development (compared to normal child) _____

_____

_____

Summary of developmental screening: (DDST & Milani under 1 yr.*; DDST, 1-3 yrs.) _____

_____

_____

_____

*Denver Developmental Screening Test (DDST)

Milani-Comparetti Motor Development Screening Test

SPECIAL CARE NEEDS

Source of information _____

Parental description of child's medical problems _____

_____

_____

_____

EQUIPMENT (type, location, arrangement, and prescribed settings)

_____

_____

_____

_____

_____

Supplier(s) _____   Phone _____
               _____   Phone _____
               _____   Phone _____

TREATMENTS (frequency, schedule)

_____
_____
_____
_____
_____
_____

DIET PRESCRIPTION

_____
_____
_____
_____
_____

MEDICATIONS

_____
_____
_____
_____
_____
_____

Nursing completing intake _____ Date _____

Source: Reprinted with permission of Home Care Program (Ahmann, Lierman, & Peck), Children's Hospital National Medical Center, Washington, D.C.

Appendix 3–B

Review of Systems

Review of Systems (Circle if Present)

1. SKIN: Itching, dryness, rashes, acne,
    bruises easily, hypersensitivity to tactile
    input, hyperpigmented spots, nodules.

2. EYES: Glasses ＿＿ Last Eye Exam ＿＿
    Itch, water, tire easily, redness, stands
    close to TV, clumsy, sensitive to light,
    cross, rubs eyes, squints, slanted
    downward, upward, epicanthal folds,
    wide spacing. Other ＿＿＿＿＿＿＿＿
    _____

    Risk factors from history

    _____

    _____

3. EARS: Earaches, hearing loss,
    infections, sensitive to noise, drainage,
    ringing, fears strangers, wakens from
    sleep when called, low set, malformed.
    Other ＿＿＿＿＿＿＿＿＿＿＿＿＿＿
    Risk factors from history

    _____

    _____

47

LIST AREAS OF CONCERN
OR AREAS WNL

Review of Systems (Circle if Present)

4. NOSE: Frequent colds, itching,
    discharge, infections, paroxysmal
    sneezing, nose bleeds, broad flat bridge.
    Other _____

5. MOUTH-THROAT: Dental cavities,
    toothache, bleeding gums, sore throat,
    strep, hoarseness, swollen glands, loss of
    color of teeth, pitted teeth, thin upper
    lip.
    Other _____

6. CARDIO-RESPIRATORY: Coughing,
    wheezing, shortness of breath, cyanosis,
    tires easily with running, hyperventilates.
    Other _____

7. GASTRO-INTESTINAL: Diarrhea,
    constipation, bleeding, abdominal pain,
    vomiting. Other _____

8. GENITO-URINARY: Strong stream,
    dribbling, dysuria, burning, frequency,
    odor, color, undescended testicles.
    Other _____

9. MUSCULO-SKELETAL: Pain,
    swelling, leg pains, redness in joints,
    limited range of motion in joints, back
    pains, fractures easily or multifractures,
    lax joints, nails malformed, webbing of
    digits, hyper or hypomuscle tone.

10. NEUROLOGICAL: Headaches,
    dizziness, twitches, blackout spells,
    tremors, fainting spells, reflexes
    appropriate for age.

LIST AREAS OF CONCERN
OR AREAS WNL

11. ENDOCRINE: Deviation in growth
pattern, hyper or hypo activity, excessive
thirst, frequent voiding, coarse hair
texture, hair pattern whorls, excessive
body/facial hair.

12. GENETIC: Family history of delays,
seizures, mental retardation, still births,
diagnosed genetic or congenital defect,
failure to thrive. Other _____

Source: Reprinted from *FAT: The Family Assessment Tool for School Nurses and Other Professionals* by Sandra Holt and Thelma Robinson, revision authors, Thelma Robinson (school-aged) and Melissa Van Wey (infant/preschool) with permission of Family Assessment Tools, © 1979, 1985.

Appendix 3–C

Physical Examination

Name _____ DOB: _____ DATE: _____

SYSTEM

General appearance (size, activity level, etc.) _____
_____
_____
_____
_____

HEAD   head circumference _____
fontanelle (size) ____ flat ____ bulging ____ depressed ____
facial symmetry _____
abnormal facies _____

eyes: ptosis _____   nystagmus _____
sunsetting _____   red reflex _____
PERRLA _____   EOM _____
focus _____   following _____
discharge _____   redness _____

ears: pinna _____
TMs _____
turns to sound _____

nose: _____

mouth: lesions/thrush _____
palate _____

50

NECK   ROM _____
         adenopathy _____
         throat:pharynx/exudate _____

CHEST   symmetry _____ retractions _____
          lungs: RR _____
          adventitious sounds _____
          heart: AP _____ cardiac murmur _____
          peripheral pulses _____

ABDOMEN   bowel sounds _____
            tenderness _____ masses _____
            liver size _____

GENITALIA/ANUS _____

MUSCULOSKELETAL   ROM _____
                    tone/strength _____
                    abnormal extremities _____

NEUROLOGICAL   reflexes _____
                 _____

SKIN   cleanliness _____
          color _____ turgor _____
          rashes/lesions _____

OTHER _____
_____
_____
_____

Examiner _____ Date _____

Source: Reprinted with permission of The Home Care Program (Ahmann, Lierman, & Peck), Children's Hospital National Medical Center, Washington, D.C.

Chapter 4

Health Maintenance for the High Risk Infant

Health maintenance for the infant with multiple handicapping conditions or chronic illness poses special challenges for the family and for health care providers. For example, some families may have difficulty finding a source of pediatric care; immunizations may be significantly off schedule; parent-infant interactions may be strained; managing minor illnesses can be complicated. These and other health maintenance issues discussed in this chapter are important for the nurse to address when working with the family of a high risk infant.

PRIMARY PEDIATRIC CARE

If a family has previously worked with a certain pediatrician, this physician may be the best source of primary pediatric care for the high risk infant. Since many pediatricians have had little or no training in managing the multiple problems of this population, reluctance to accept these children as patients is not unusual. If offered the opportunity for regular phone consultations with the hospital neonatologist or other specialist, preferably one who has followed the child's early course, a pediatrician may be more willing to provide the high risk infant's primary care. In addition, some pediatricians may be more inclined to accept a patient with multiple problems if they know that the developmental assessment and intervention are being provided elsewhere, and that a nurse will be making regular home visits.

If a willing pediatrician cannot be located, perhaps a staff pediatrician, neonatologist, or other specialist at a conveniently located hospital can be encouraged to provide pediatric care for the high risk infant. Whatever source of care is

---

Note: A sample home care plan for health maintenance can be found in Appendix 4–A.

planned, families should be assisted in arranging for pediatric primary care either prior to or shortly after the infant's arrival home from the hospital.

A second issue related to primary care is the immunization schedule. Immunizations may be significantly off schedule owing to prolonged hospitalization or repeated minor illnesses. Parents may be relieved to know that immunizations can be given on an altered schedule. They should be informed that if the infant has any history of seizures or other central nervous system (CNS) disorders, the pertussis vaccine will not be given.

DENTAL CARE

Although a dentist is not needed in the first 2 years of life, there are several important dental issues that warrant discussion with families. First, many parents wait expectantly for the baby's first tooth. It will normally erupt between 4 and 10 months of age. The high risk infant's schedule should not be any slower, if correction for prematurity is taken into account in determining age.

Second, as with any baby, the concern about "bottle mouth" should be addressed as a preventive measure before teeth erupt. Bottle mouth is a form of decay of the primary teeth that is associated with frequent and prolonged sucking on a bottle containing carbohydrate liquids, such as milk or juices. Bottle mouth occurs most commonly when the infant is often given a bottle at nap or bed time. Optimally, a bottle should be given only while the infant is being held; however, if parents feel a bottle is necessary at nap or bed time, only water should be used.

NUTRITION

Nutrition, of course, is an important aspect of health maintenance. Assessment of both nutrition and feeding status, as well as interventions for the infant with problems of nutrition or feeding, are discussed in Chapter 5.

DEVELOPMENTAL STIMULATION

Developmental stimulation is another important aspect of health maintenance. Appropriate stimulation is based on the developmental age and takes into account any sensory impairments the infant may have. For example, for a visually impaired infant, stimulation experiences should emphasize touch, sound, and proprioception (use of balance and movement to increase the infant's internal awareness of position). The infant who tires easily because of severe lung disease provides another example. In such infants, stimulation should be minimized during particularly stressful periods, and bursts of high activity and overstimulation should be avoided. Visual stimulation, however, should be encouraged and can be supplemented by gentle sounds and activity for short periods of time.

Appropriate activities should, of course, be based on the infant's developmental age and can be planned in conjunction with an occupational, physical, or speech therapist if the child needs such services. Chapter 17 provides more detailed information about developmental issues and infant stimulation. The reader may find the Home Observation for Measurement of the Environment scales useful for assessing the home environment in relation to infant stimulation.[1]

MINOR ILLNESSES

Fever, vomiting, diarrhea, and constipation are minor illnesses discussed in this section. Respiratory disorders are discussed in Chapter 7. The reader is referred to other resources for a further discussion of minor illnesses, for example, Chow et al., *Handbook of Pediatric Primary Care.*[2]

Fever

Temperature taking is an important skill for any parent. The nurse can stimulate a discussion on this subject by requesting to use the family's thermometer on the first visit. Asking caregivers whether they have ever been taught to take temperatures correctly and then observing them using the thermometer during home visits is a nonthreatening way to explore their knowledge. If temperature taking is to be taught, demonstration, parents' return demonstration, and written instructions left in the home can be helpful.

Guidelines for treatment of fevers should be worked out with the child's pediatric care provider. Generally, if the infant has a rectal temperature of 101° F (39.5° C) or more, the pediatrician or nurse practitioner should be notified. The family should be encouraged to keep acetaminophen drops (e.g., Tylenol or Tempra) available at home for use if needed. Aspirin is generally not recommended, particularly not for varicella infections or respiratory febrile illnesses, because of the association with an increased incidence of Reye's syndrome.[3]

Vomiting

Management of vomiting in the high risk infant can be complicated, and parents should be encouraged to contact the infant's primary care provider when vomiting occurs. Although some spitting up may be normal, prompt identification and treatment of certain vomiting problems are important.

Reflux vomiting, for example, may be a problem. The term *reflux* refers to the return flow of stomach contents into the esophagus, caused by relaxation at the distal esophagus. Mild reflux can be noted clinically in up to 40 percent of newborn infants, presenting as regurgitation or vomiting after meals, usually when the infant is laid down after feeding.[4] Reflux is more prevalent in premature infants and children with mental retardation and cerebral palsy. It can contribute to the risk of aspiration[5] and aspiration pneumonia and may also be related to the development of recurrent apnea and cyanosis in some infants.[6] In children with frequent and copious vomiting, reflux can lead to failure to thrive.[7] (Interventions for reflux vomiting are discussed in Chapter 5.)

Vomiting may also be related to any of the following problems. Some infants with copious secretions may cough and vomit. Other infants receiving theophylline and medicated aerosol treatments may vomit if fed shortly after treatments; vomiting can also signal toxic theophylline levels. If an infant has a history of intraventricular hemorrhage or hydrocephalus, vomiting may be a sign of increased intracranial pressure (see Chapter 12). Gastroenteritis is another possible cause. Vomiting may upset a tenuous fluid or electrolyte balance in the infant. In addition, feeding problems may contribute to vomiting, and vomiting can, conversely, contribute to failure to thrive.

Because of the many possible causes of vomiting and the associated risks, episodes in the high risk infant should be assessed thoroughly. A thorough assessment of vomiting episodes includes amount, frequency, timing, and related activities such as positioning; use of aerosol medications; coughing; and general activity. Overestimation of the volume of emesis is a common problem: 15 milliliters (ml)—about a teaspoon—makes a spot 4 inches in diameter on clothing or sheet; 60 ml—2 ounces—makes a spot 8 inches in diameter.

Diarrhea

Diarrhea is also a signal for parents to contact the infant's health care provider, since dehydration can occur rapidly in infants. Nursing assessment of diarrhea addresses the following: amount, frequency, color, odor, texture, and relationship to feedings. If diarrhea is a recurrent problem for the infant, parents may wish to keep a supply of oral electrolyte solution available in the home for use in accordance with recommendations by the primary care provider.

Constipation

Constipation (difficulty in passing stools, which typically are hard and rock-like) can become a problem for a variety of reasons, including inadequate dietary fluids, hyper- or hypotonus, limited mobility, and medication side effects. Both nutritional and nonnutritional interventions for constipation can be considered. As a *nutritional intervention*, unless fluid restriction is necessary for management of cardiac or pulmonary problems, fluids should be offered frequently. Prune juice, an ounce at a time, can also be given as needed. Karo syrup, 1 teaspoon in 2 to 3 ounces of formula, as needed, can help loosen stools and is often used in infants requiring fluid restriction; however, there may be an associated risk of botulism (see Chapter 5). If solids have been introduced very early or increased quickly, they can be discontinued until the constipation is relieved. Subsequently, solids should be reintroduced slowly and in small amounts to prevent a recurrence of constipation.

Nonnutritional interventions include rectal stimulation with a thermometer and the use of glycerine suppositories in an acute episode. Only in extreme cases of impaction should an enema be used.

SAFETY

Accidents are the leading cause of death of children in the United States; most accidents, however, are preventable. The community health nurse visiting the home is in an ideal position to address safety issues. The nurse can identify safety hazards in the home or neighborhood and educate family members about such hazards. Anticipatory guidance and preventive teaching about age- and development-specific safety issues can also be provided. Appendix 4–B lists important general safety precautions for the home, as well as specific considerations for infants and toddlers.

PARENT–INFANT ATTACHMENT AND INTERACTION

Every parent–infant relationship is unique; each relationship develops in the combined context of infant and parental characteristics and environmental influences. *Attachment* is defined by Ainsworth as ''an affectional tie that one person . . . forms between himself and another specific one—a tie that binds them together . . . and endures over time.''[8] Attachment is the basis for positive and nurturing parent–infant relationships.

Positive and nurturing parent–infant relationships foster optimal growth and development. Poor parent–infant relationships, on the other hand, can adversely affect the infant's development, feeding, and growth, and the quality of home care. In some instances, poor parent–infant interactions can contribute to neglect or abuse (see Chapter 18). The community health nurse should be aware of parental, infant, and environmental factors influencing attachment and interactions; should observe parent–infant interactions for either attachment or attachment problems; and should be prepared to offer therapeutic interventions and referrals for appropriate assistance if problems are noted.

Parental factors influencing the parent–infant relationship are multiple. Parents bring to the relationship their past histories and their current energies. Although

Exhibit 4–1 Parental Factors Leading to Poor Parent–Infant Attachment

Previous experiences of the mother (caregiver)
   Early parental life deprivations
   Loss of parent figures early in life of parent
   Illness during childhood
   Death or illness in prior children
Pregnancy
   Emotional or physical illness
   Death or major illness of key family figures
   Other loss of significant relationships
Perinatal events
   Complications of delivery causing prolonged separation of mother and child
   Acute illness in mother or infant
   Prematurity
   Congenital defects
   Other diseases and disturbances
Current life events
   Marital stress
   Mental or medical illness causing caregiver to be unavailable
   Drugs and alcohol
   Financial crisis

Source: Reprinted from *Failure to Thrive in Infancy and Early Childhood: A Multidisciplinary Team Approach,* by P.J. Accardo (Ed.), p. 101, with permission of University Park Press, © 1982.

most research has focused on maternal–infant attachments, the importance of assessing the contribution of the father, or other caregiver, to the infant's interpersonal relationships should not be underestimated. Past events in the life of the parent and events during the pregnancy that may influence parental ability to attain and maintain a nurturing attachment with the infant are listed in Exhibit 4–1.

Infant factors that affect the parent–infant relationship include numerous infant behaviors and characteristics. Behavior problems and other disorders commonly found in disturbed parent–infant interactions are indicated in Exhibit 4–2. Many of these disorders are fairly common among premature infants, particularly those with multiple medical and developmental problems, and may place these infants at high risk for poor attachment.

In addition to parent and infant factors, a number of *environmental factors* also place the premature infant at risk for problems of poor parent–infant attachment. Klaus and Kennell identify *prematurity* itself as a significant factor, as follows:[9]

Parents of a premature infant are deprived of about six weeks of psychological preparation. The changes that occur in the last six weeks

Exhibit 4–2 Infant Behavior Problems and Other Disorders Found in Disturbed Parent–Infant Interactions

Feeding disorders	Developmental delay
Failure to gain weight	Listlessness or lethargy
Food refusal	Sleep disturbances
Recurrent vomiting	Minimal vocalization
Recurrent diarrhea	Decreased "cuddliness"

Source: Green M: A developmental approach to symptoms based on age groups, *Pediatr Clin North Am*, 22:571–583, 1975.

are very important. Parents prepare for the birth of the baby both physically and psychologically, and the parents of a normal full-term infant experience a labor that is not associated with concern for the welfare of the baby. In contrast, the entire experience of labor, birth, and attachment for the mother of a premature infant takes place under a cloud of fear.

Associated with prematurity, *handicapping anomalies or birth injuries* may lead to parental feelings of inadequacy, which can affect attachment. Similarly, acute illness in the infant can cause parental fear about the baby's survival, also affecting attachment. The prolonged parent–infant separation that can occur in association with the infant's long-term hospitalization is another factor.

Assessment of interaction between parent or caregiver and infant is of great importance for the community health nurse caring for the high risk infant and the family. Assessment begins with obtaining a thorough prenatal and perinatal history from each parent, as well as a history concerning the parent's recollections of his or her own childhood and parenting. History taking should also explore each parent's current health status and both personal and professional support systems. Parental perception of the infant and its abilities should be explored: "How would you describe your baby?" is a useful open–ended lead question. The questions listed both in the Neonatal Perception Inventory and in the Degree of Bother Inventory can also be helpful for assessing specific problem areas for both parent and infant.[10]

Assessment of the parent–infant interaction relies not only on a thorough history but also on the nurse's observations. The nurse should observe for the overall energy level of parents, for the infant's characteristic behaviors, and for both adaptive and maladaptive behaviors in the parent and in the infant (see Exhibits 4–1 and 4–2). Impressions may be most accurate if observations are gathered over time.

Exhibit 4–3 Nursing Interventions to Promote Healthy Parent–Child Interactions

---

Point out strengths and appropriate interactions.
Avoid blame or criticisms of parent.
Offer parent acceptance and support.
Mother the parent: "And how are *you* doing?"
Encourage parent to attend to own needs.
Promote family communication.
Assist parent to identify and use personal support systems.
Encourage use of respite care.
Invite telephone calls from parent.
Provide parent with hot line number for crisis.
Assist parent in close observation of infant's traits and skills (Brazelton's Neonatal Behavioral Assessment Scale may be useful).
Assist parent to see infant's needs.
Instruct in age- and development-appropriate behaviors.
Offer encouragement and instruction to provide nurturing and stimulating environment for infant.
Role-model appropriate parenting behaviors.
Instruct in appropriate discipline by demonstration and parent's return demonstration.
Praise and reinforce parent for positive response to child.
Teach parent to use praise.

Source: Brazelton TB, *Neonatal Behavioral Assessment Scale*, Clinics in Developmental Medicine Series 50, Philadelphia, JB Lippincott Co, 1973; Clark AL, Alfonso DD: Infant behavior and maternal attachment: two sides to the coin, *MCN: The American Journal of Maternal/Child Nursing*, March/April 1976, pp 94–99; Clark AL: Recognizing discord between mother and child and changing it to harmony, *MCN: The American Journal of Maternal/Child Nursing*, March/April 1976, pp 100–106; Webster–Stratton C, Kogan K: Helping parents parent, *Am J Nurs*, February 1980, pp 240–244.

Disturbances in parent–infant interactions can in some cases be prevented if screening for risk factors is undertaken in conjunction with preventive intervention.[11] Suggestions for nursing interventions that may be helpful in promoting healthy parent–infant interactions, in preventing disturbances, or in correcting early problems can be found in Exhibit 4–3. If serious disturbances are noted, or if nursing interventions fail to improve the parent–infant relationship, psychologic intervention for the parent or parent–infant dyad may be indicated. If at any time the quality of the parent–infant interaction is such that abuse or neglect is suspected (see signs and symptoms in Chapter 18), a referral to state child protective services should be made in order to protect the infant.

FAMILY ADJUSTMENT AND USE OF COMMUNITY RESOURCES

Care of the child with multiple disabilities or chronic illness can have a profound impact on the entire family. Family patterns and routines must change; and normal social support mechanisms may be unavailable due to economic or time restraints (and sometimes due to fear on the part of friends and relatives). Care of the child can stretch family resources in a wide range of areas:

- financial
- environmental
- emotional
- interpersonal
- social.

Assessment and promotion of the family's adjustment to the infant's care and of their awareness and use of available community resources are important aspects of nursing care for the high risk infant. Further discussion of assessment and intervention in these areas is found in Chapters 18 through 20. A bibliography of materials that may be of special interest to parents is available in Appendix C at the end of this book.

COORDINATION OF SERVICES

A premature infant with multiple problems will often receive health care services from a variety of professionals. Often a pediatrician, neonatologist, pulmonologist, neurologist, and psychiatrist may each provide ongoing evaluation and interventions. In addition, the infant may receive developmental intervention from an occupational therapist, physical therapist, speech therapist, or even all three. A dietitian and social worker, as well as clinic nurses and the community health nurses, may also be involved. Because of the many care providers involved, coordination is essential.

A designated case manager, often most appropriately the nurse, can provide a focus for communication and coordination. A case manager can help parents to ensure consistency in treatment plans and comprehensive, coordinated care. The nurse as case manager will take responsibility for informing each involved professional, as appropriate, of both the others' intervention plans, the infant's overall status, and the general plan of care. In addition, the case manager will advocate for the child and family as necessary. In both these regards, the nurse may plan occasional or even regular meetings of all involved professionals to discuss with the family both the overall plan of care for the high risk infant and the family's ideas about and reactions to the plan of care. Coordination of services through case management is an essential part of the care of infants or children with multiple problems and should be a part of every care plan developed.[12]

NOTES

1. Caldwell B, Snyder C: *Home Observation for Measurement of the Environment* (prepared as part of the Nursing Child Assessment Satellite Training Project), 1978 (unpublished). Copies may be ordered from NCAST, WJ–10, University of Washington, Seattle, Washington 98195.

2. Chow MP, Durand BA, Feldman MN, et al: *Handbook of Pediatric Primary Care,* ed 2. New York, John Wiley and Sons, 1984.

3. Waldeman R, et al: Aspirin as a risk factor in Reye's Syndrome. JAMA 247: 3089–3094. June 11, 1982.

4. Palmer FB: Gastroenterology, in Accardo PJ (ed): *Failure to Thrive and Infancy and Early Childhood: A Multidisciplinary Team Approach,* Baltimore, University Park Press, 1982, p 152.

5. Darling DB, McCauley RGK, Leonidas JC, et al: Gastroesophageal reflux in infants and children: correlation of radiologic severity and pulmonary pathology, *Radiology* 27: 735–740, 1978.

6. Leape LL, Holder TM, Franklin JD, et al: Respiratory arrest in infants secondary to gastroesophageal reflux, *Pediatrics* 60: 924, 1977.

7. Kibel MA: Gastroesophageal reflux and failure to thrive in infancy, in Gellis SS (ed): *Gastroesophageal Reflux: Report of the Seventy-Sixth Congress on Pediatric Research,* Columbus, Ohio, Ross Laboratories, 1979, pp 39–47.

8. Ainsworth M, Bell S: Attachment, exploration and separation: illustrated by the behavior of one-year-olds in a strange situation, *Child Dev* 41: 50, March 1970.

9. Klaus MH, Kennell JH: *Bonding: The Beginnings of Parent-Infant Attachment,* New York, CV Mosby Co, 1983, p 133.

10. Broussard EB, Hartner MSS: Further considerations regarding maternal perception of the newborn, in Hellmuth J (ed): *Exceptional Infants: Studies in Abnormalities 2,* New York, Brunner/Mazel Inc, 1971, p 440. The Inventories are also reprinted in Chow MP, Durand BA, Feldman MN, et al: *Handbook of Pediatric Primary Care,* ed 2, New York, John Wiley and Sons, 1984, pp 198–201.

11. The Harrison tools were developed for use as an assessment and intervention tool related to mother and infant behaviors (Harrison LL: Nursing intervention with the failure to thrive family, *MCN: The American Journal of Maternal/Child Nursing,* March/April 1976, pp 111–116).

12. Case management of chronically ill children is the subject of the Rural Efforts to Assist Children at Home (REACH) project, a demonstration program funded jointly by the Robert Wood Johnson Foundation and Florida Medicaid. The case managers, nurses, provide coordination and family support. Thus far, both improved care for the children and a 17 percent reduction in cost of care have been observed, as reported in Perrin JM: Chronically ill children in America, *Caring,* May 1985, pp 21–22.

REFERENCES

Ainsworth M, Bell S: Attachment, exploration and separation: illustrated by the behavior of one-year-olds in a strange situation. *Child Dev* 41: 49–65, March 1970.

Bishop B: A guide to assessing parenting capabilities. *Am J Nurs*, November 1976, pp 1784–1787.

Bradley RH, Caldwell BM: Home observation for measurement of the environment: a validation study of screening efficiency. *Am J Ment Defic* 81: 417–420, 1977.

Brazelton TB: *Neonatal Behavior Assessment Scale.* Clinics in Developmental Medicine Series 50. Philadelphia, JB Lippincott Co, 1973.

Broussard EB, Hartner MSS: Further considerations regarding maternal perception of the newborn, in Hellmuth J (ed): *Exceptional Infant: Studies in Abnormalities 2*. New York, Brunner/Mazel Inc, 1971, pp 442–447.

Caldwell B, Snyder C: *Home Observation for Measurement of the Environment* (Nursing Child Assessment Satellite Training Project). 1978 (unpublished). Copies may be ordered from NCAST WJ–10, University of Washington, Seattle, Washington 98195.

Chow MP, Durand BA, Feldman MN, et al: *Handbook of Pediatric Primary Care*, ed 2. New York, John Wiley and Sons, 1984.

Clark AL: Recognizing discord between mother and child and changing it to harmony. *MCN: The American Journal of Maternal/Child Nursing*, March/April 1976, pp 100–106.

Clark AL, Alfonso DD: Infant behavior and maternal attachment: two sides to the coin. *MCN: The American Journal of Maternal/Child Nursing*, March/April 1976, pp 94–99.

Darling DB, McCauley RGK, Leonidas JC, et al: Gastroesophageal reflux in infants and children: correlating radiologic severity and pulmonary pathology. *Radiology* 27: 735–740, 1978.

Elmer E, Gregg GS: Developmental characteristics of abused children. *Pediatrics* 40: 596–602, 1967.

Green M: A developmental approach to symptoms based on age groups. *Pediatr Clin North Am* 22: 571–583, 1975.

Harrison LL: Nursing intervention with the failure to thrive family. *MCN: The American Journal of Maternal/Child Nursing*, March/April 1976, pp 111–116.

Hunter RS, Kilstrom N, Kraybill EN, et al: Antecedents of child abuse and neglect in premature infants: a prospective study in a newborn intensive care unit. *Pediatrics* 61: 629–635, 1978.

Kennedy JC: The high-risk maternal-infant acquaintance process. *Nurs Clin North Am* 8: 549–556, 1973.

Kibel MA: Gastroesophageal reflux and failure to thrive in infancy, in Gellis SS (ed): *Gastroesophageal Reflux: Report of the Seventy-Sixth Ross Congress on Pediatric Research*. Columbus, Ohio, Ross Laboratories, 1979, p 39.

Klaus MH, Kennell JH: *Bonding: The Beginnings of Parent-Infant Attachment*. New York, CV Mosby Co, 1983.

Klein M, Stern L: Low birth weight and the battered child syndrome. *Am J Dis Child* 122: 15–18, 1971.

Klijanowicz AS: Pediatric health maintenance, in Brunner LS, Suddarth DS (eds): *The Lippincott Manual of Nursing Practice*, ed 3. Philadelphia, JB Lippincott Co, 1982.

Leape LL, Holder TM, Franklin JD, et al: Respiratory arrest in infants secondary to gastroesophageal reflux. *Pediatrics* 60: 924–928, 1977.

Lynch MA, Roberts J: Predicting child abuse: signs of bonding failure in the maternity hospital. *Br Med J* 1: 624–626, 1977.

Palmer FB: Gastroenterology, in Accardo PJ (ed): *Failure to Thrive in Infancy and Early Childhood: A Multidisciplinary Team Approach*. Baltimore, University Park Press, 1982, p 153.

Perrin JM: Chronically ill children in America. *Caring*, May 1985, pp 16–22.

Webster-Stratton C, Kogan K: Helping parents parent. *Am J Nurs*, February 1980, pp 240–244.

Appendix 4–A

Children's Hospital National Medical Center Home Care Team
Plan of Treatment

Date _____

Name _____

Page _____

Case manager _____

Hosp # _____

DOB _____

PROBLEM: **HEALTH MAINTENANCE**

GOALS/OBJECTIVES	METHODS	STAFF/REVIEW
Family will have a source of primary pediatric care and will appropriately utilize same.	Assist family in obtaining and teach appropriate use of pediatric primary care.	
Child will be up-to-date on immunizations if medically indicated.	Discuss alterations in immunization schedule with family, prn; facilitate obtaining appropriate immunizations.	

Family will demonstrate appropriate well child care re: nutrition, growth and development, stimulation, responses to minor illness, dental and safety needs.	Assess/teach provision of well child care as needed in each aspect. Coordinate with primary care provider prn.
Parent-infant interaction will facilitate child's growth and development.	Assess relationship for positive interactions and alert to risk factors for poor interactions in infant, parent, and dyad. Provide intervention and/or referrals as necessary.
Family will demonstrate a workable adjustment to care of the child and will utilize available community resources as needed.	Assess family dynamics, strengths and weaknesses. Provide counseling and support to facilitate adjustment prn. Educate family and assist in accessing appropriate community resources prn.
Child will receive coordinated, integrated care.	Assist in coordination of care and facilitate communication between care providers.

Source: Reprinted with permission of Home Care Program (Ahmann, Lierman, and Peck), Children's Hospital National Medical Center, Washington, D.C.

Appendix 4–B

Home Safety Precautions for Families of High Risk Infants

General Precautions

Use only Underwriter's Laboratories (UL)-approved electrical equipment.

Avoid overloading electrical systems.

Store medicines and poisons in child-proof containers and out of reach of children.

When giving medications, measure doses carefully; know side effects and toxic effects.

Do not give any medications without prescription.

Post emergency telephone numbers near the home telephone.

Learn first aid and CPR.

Immunize pets.

If child is on apnea monitor, make sure alarm can be heard from all parts of house; observe other safety precautions (see Chapter 8).

If child has tracheostomy or is on oxygen or a ventilator, observe all safety recommendations (see Chapters 9 through 11).

Preventing Falls

Keep crib sides up.

Strap child carefully in infant seat or feeding chair; crotch strap is important.

When child uses infant seat, place on floor or in playpen.

Do not leave infant unattended on bed, couch, or changing table.

Place gates at head and foot of stairways.

Put guards on windows; secure screens.

Keep chairs or stools away from windows.

Keep stairs free of clutter.

Preventing Choking or Strangulation

Do not use cribs with slats more than 2⅜ inches apart.
Use bumper pads in crib.
Do not tie anything around infant's neck.
Thread apnea monitor wires through lower end of clothing.
Remove loose or small parts from toys.
Avoid small hard foods (e.g., candy, nuts, raisins).
Avoid bottle propping.
Burp infant well before putting into crib; place infant on stomach or propped on side.
Keep drapery cords tied up high or cut short.
Tie plastic bags in a knot and discard.
Avoid play with balloons.

Preventing Burns

Label flammable liquids, and store away from heat or sparks.
Develop and practice a fire escape plan.
Install smoke detectors.
Keep a small fire extinguisher available.
Check temperature of bath water carefully.
Use flame-resistant clothing, sheets, and blankets.
Avoid holding infant while cooking or handling hot liquids.
Keep pot handles turned in toward stove.
Keep hot drinks and foods away from counter or table edges.
Do not warm formula in microwave—bottle and formula will be different temperatures.
Avoid use of tablecloths with hanging edges.
Place guards around fireplaces, radiators, and heaters.
Keep crib or bed away from radiators or heaters.
Avoid use of heating pad.
Place safety caps on unused electrical outlets.
Keep kitchen door closed or gated.
Keep vaporizers out of child's reach.

Preventing Drowning

Do not leave child unattended in bath or pool.
Place fences around pools.
Empty tub or sink when not in use.

Preventing Injuries

Keep sharp items out of child's reach.
Pad sharp corners of furniture.
Secure small rugs.
Keep fans out of reach.
Avoid toys with sharp or breakable parts.
Teach safe play.

Car Safety

Always use an approved car seat:

- anchors to vehicle seat
- restrains child with protective shield harness
- provides head support.

Never leave children alone in car.
Keep car doors locked.
Avoid litter and loose objects inside car.
Provide fenced-in play area.
Do not allow play in driveways or street.

Source: Handbook of Pediatric Primary Care, 2d ed., by M.P. Chow et al., Tables 5–22 and 6–9, John Wiley and Sons, Inc., © 1984; *Lippincott Manual of Nursing Practice*, 3d ed., by L.S. Brunner and D.S. Suddarth (Eds.), Chapter 35, J.B. Lippincott Company, © 1982.

Chapter 5

Nutrition and Feeding of the High Risk Infant

Providing adequate nutrition for the high risk infant poses a challenge to parents and health care providers. The first two years of life, however, are a period of rapid growth; and malnutrition during this time may have long-range effects.

The community health nurse plays an important role in promoting adequate nutrition and feeding of the high risk infant. This role has several aspects. First, the nurse will need a sound knowlege of normal feeding behaviors and progressions (see Appendix 5–B). Second, the nurse must be able to offer a comprehensive assessment if feeding or nutritional problems are suspected. Third, the nurse must have a knowledge of interventions appropriate to the more common nutrition and feeding problems. These points are addressed in this chapter and augmented by a discussion of the problem of failure to thrive. In addition, since nutritional and feeding problems are often multifaceted, a multidisciplinary approach to assessment and intervention may be indicated in many cases. As a result, the nurse must be prepared to obtain consultation as needed. Occupational, physical, or speech therapists may be important team members. Consultation with a nutritionist or a physician may also be necessary if nutritional problems are not responsive to the more common interventions.

FACTORS CONTRIBUTING TO NUTRITIONAL AND FEEDING PROBLEMS

The factors affecting nutritional and feeding patterns in the high risk infant can be multiple and interrelated. The following problems may contribute to low weight and poor growth:

Note: Appendix 5–A contains a sample nutrition history form.

- disturbed parent-infant interaction
- oral motor disturbances
- inadequate amount of food offered
- easy fatigability (tires before feeding completed)
- high energy requirements (e.g., related to work of breathing)
- reflux vomiting
- diarrhea or malabsorption
- behavioral food refusal
- central nervous system (CNS) damage affecting appetite
- genetic factors
- food allergies
- other chronic illnesses.

Delays in achieving normal developmental milestones are common among high risk infants. Such delays can contribute to oral motor disturbances affecting both oral feeding and eventual self-feeding and may be associated with very individualized calorie requirements owing to widely variable activity levels. The high risk infant with cardiac or respiratory compromise may have high metabolic calorie requirements but may at the same time have difficulty enduring the work of feeding necessary to take in the needed calories by mouth. Fluid restrictions may also complicate meeting the nutritional needs of infants with respiratory compromise.

In addition, long-term intubation of the high risk infant may contribute to the need for prolonged tube feedings, and to the development of oral hypersensitivity, lack of homeostasis, and persistent food refusal. Reflux vomiting, particularly if frequent or copious, can cause loss of valuable nutrients and calories. Anticonvulsants can affect nutritional requirements, and other medications may cause nausea or anorexia. Long-term hospitalization of the infant can affect parental bonding and may thus contribute to poor parent-infant interaction during feedings. For these multiple and interrelated reasons, the high risk infant may be at risk for nutritional and feeding disorders and even failure to thrive.

ASSESSMENT OF FEEDING AND NUTRITIONAL PROBLEMS

Appropriate plans for feeding and nutrition of the high risk infant will be based on a thorough individualized assessment, including the following areas: the serial measurement of growth parameters, a thorough history including a diet record, and observations of both oral motor skills and parent-infant interactions during feeding.

Growth Parameters

Weight should be obtained on a balance beam scale.[1] Spring scales will lose accuracy over time, particularly if they are often carried in a car. For purposes of accurate assessment, the scale should be set to zero before each use, and the infant weighed nude. Serial weights, including birth weight, should be plotted on an NCHS (National Center for Health Statistics) growth chart, at regular intervals, to assess the pattern of weight gain.[2] Table 5–1 details normal daily weight gain at different stages during infancy.

Length should also be measured. Length is the supine measurement; height is the standing measurement. Since the child while "standing" will appear shorter than while lying down, length is generally used as the measurement for the first 3 years.[3] Numerous studies have shown that children with mental or physical handicaps are shorter than nonhandicapped children of the same age.[4] Length, rather than age, is thus important in determining the appropriate weight and calorie needs for a handicapped child. For this reason, length should be measured carefully and plotted regularly on the growth chart.

To measure length at home, the infant can be placed supine on an even surface such as the floor or a table. One person holds the measuring tape even with the top of the infant's head. Another person stretches the tape alongside the infant and straightens the infant's hips and knees to get an accurate measurement. The distance from the base of the heel to the top of the head is the length.

Weight can be plotted as a function of length, serially, on the growth chart. A smooth, upward-sloping curve (a "positive" curve) suggests that the infant is growing optimally. If this is not seen, nutritional intervention may be warranted. *Weight for length* is obtained by plotting weight against length on the appropriate portion of the NCHS growth chart. A weight for length of less than 5 percent will necessitate close nutritional follow-up. The "ideal" weight for length is the

Table 5–1 Normal Daily Weight Gain in Infancy

Age (months)	Daily Gain	
	Grams	Ounces
0–3	30	1
3–6	20	2/3
6–9	16	1/2
9–12	10	1/3
12–24	7	2/10

Source: Adapted from *Supplemental Nutrition Support of Babies with Respiratory Distress* (unpublished), Children's Hospital National Medical Center, Washington, D.C., 1984, with permission of M. Dickie.

Table 5–2 Guide to Calorie Requirements in Children with Growth Problems

Age (months)	cal/kg Ideal Weight
0–6	115
6–12	105
12–36	100

Source: Reprinted from *Supplemental Nutrition Support of Babies with Respiratory Distress* (unpublished), Children's Hospital National Medical Center, 1984, with permission of M. Dickie.

weight in kilograms (kg) at the 50th percentile, on the NCHS charts, for the infant's length. Calorie (cal) requirements for the child with growth problems should be based on this ideal weight, as indicated in Table 5–2.

Head circumference is an index of brain growth. (It is also assessed as an indicator of hydrocephalus.) Head circumference is measured around the widest part of the head, over the forehead and occiput. It should be plotted serially on the growth chart.

Nutritional History

Feeding problems can be very tension-producing for caregivers. To facilitate the goal of obtaining as much information as possible about the child's nutrition and feeding, therefore, a nonjudgmental approach to interviewing is important. Only if thorough information is obtained can nutrition and feeding problems be accurately assessed and appropriate plans for intervention be developed. The nutrition and feeding history should include the following elements:

- overall health status
- underlying medical problems
- feeding history, including the use of total parenteral nutrition (TPN), a nasogastric (NG) tube, or a gastrostomy (G) tube, and age at introduction of oral feedings
- history of reflux vomiting
- current medications
- nutritional supplements
- source of iron
- method of preparing feeding (caregiver description)
- duration of a typical feeding
- self-feeding skills

- feeding-related problems noted by caregivers
- a diet record.

A *diet record* is more accurate than mere recall. Depending on the child's nutritional status and the patience of the caregiver, a record of from 1 to 7 days is recommended for assessment of intake and feeding patterns. A thorough diet record will yield valuable information about total intake (both calories and nutrients), frequency and amounts of feedings, and appropriateness of preparation techniques. The record should include the following information: time, the food or liquid given, type of preparation, and exact amount in ounces (oz) or tablespoons (tbsp). If the child frequently vomits, caregivers should be instructed to include the time and amount of vomiting on the same record. To assist calculation of calorie intake based on the diet record, the guide in Table 5–3 can be used.

Feeding Observation

It is often the nurse who, through careful observation, first becomes aware of feeding problems in the high risk infant. Observation of one or more feedings can provide a wealth of information that will contribute to the overall assessment of an infant's feeding or nutrition problems. Observation should include an assessment of feeding skills and behaviors, assessment of the parental ability to use appropriate positions and techniques in order to feed the infant in a reasonable length of time, and an assessment of the psychosocial context of the feeding.

Feeding Skills and Behaviors

Adequate nutritional intake by the infant can be hindered by delayed or abnormal acquisition of feeding skills and by behavior disorders. Normal development of feeding skills is reviewed briefly in Appendix 5–B. A knowledge of the

---

Table 5–3 Guide to Calculation of Caloric Intake

Food	Caloric Content
Standard commercial formula	20 cal/oz
Baby cereal	10 cal/tbsp
Baby fruits and vegetables	5–10 cal/tbsp
Baby meat	15–18 cal/tbsp

Note: 4 tbsp = ¼ cup = ½ small jar baby food.

Source: Adapted from *Supplemental Nutritional Support of Babies with Respiratory Distress* (unpublished), Children's National Medical Center, 1984, with permission of M. Dickie.

Table 5–4 Common Feeding Disorders in the High Risk Infant

Disorder	Effects on Feeding
Suck-swallow uncoordination	Choking possible Decreased efficiency and increased energy output Prolonged feeding time Frustration
Poor lip seal	Loss of liquid Prolonged feeding time
Abnormal oral development Tongue thrust Tongue retraction Poor tongue control Lip immobility Lip retraction Limited movement of oral musculature	Interference with progression of feeding skills Prolonged feeding time Frustration Disturbed infant-parent attachment Need for tube feeding
Vomiting or reflux	Frustration Need for tube feeding Need for increased frequency of feedings Need for special positions during feeding
Food refusal	Disturbed infant-parent attachment Weight loss Need for tube feeding
Respiratory compromise	Interference with rhythm of suck-swallow-breathe Tiring during feeding Need for prolonged intubation or TPN Tube feeding
Lethargy	Prolonged feeding time Parental frustration Need for tube feeding
Lack of oral experience	Interference with progression of feeding skills Food refusal Need for tube feeding

Source: Table developed with the assistance of M. Wilson, OTR, and C. Berg, OTR, Children's Hospital National Medical Center, Washington, D.C.

---

normal patterns, coupled with an awareness of potential disorders (see Table 5–4) provides the basis for a thorough nursing assessment.

The most common feeding problems seen in the high risk premature infant include the following:

- ineffective sucking
- poor coordination of breathing with suck-swallow
- neck hyperextension
- tactile defensiveness
- lethargy
- food refusal.

(For details about infants with neurologic impairments, the reader is referred to other sources.[5])

The nurse should observe the infant for *sucking skills:* the ability to initiate and maintain an effective seal on the nipple with minimal leakage of formula; to initiate and maintain a rhythmic suck; and to coordinate a smooth and rhythmic suck-swallow pattern. In addition, the nurse should observe for *coordination of breathing with suck-swallow* in a rhythmic pattern; it is not normal for an infant to gasp for breaths or to become cyanotic during feedings.

A related problem, *hyperextension of the neck,* is frequently noted in infants with respiratory compromise, a tracheostomy, or certain types of cerebral palsy. Hyperextension during feeding will interfere with both suck and swallow. In addition, it may interfere with the timely development of hand-to-mouth motor skills and oral experiences.

Oral tactile defensiveness, seen as an adverse reaction to touch, can develop in the infant who has been without oral intake (maintained with TPN or tube-fed) for long periods. Use of a pacifier and other means of oral stimulation can prevent the problem. Once tactile defensiveness develops, the infant may resist any texture in or around the mouth; oral motor development and oral feeding are hindered.

Lethargy is a feeding behavior that is observed among many high risk infants. It may result from poor bonding and attachment, causing lack of interest, or from exhaustion related to the work required to coordinate breathing with eating. The nurse will observe that the infant seems to tire easily during a feeding and shows little interest in maintaining a suck. Prolonged feeding times may also be noted.

Food refusal, perhaps the most frustrating feeding disorder, may evolve because of early oral deprivation, resulting from lengthy illness and hospitalization.[6] Forced oral feeding can also contribute to the development of food refusal. Food refusal may be manifested similarly to tactile defensiveness: the infant may turn or back away from food stimuli or, in some cases, vomit.

Positions and Techniques

In infants who have problems with general or oral muscle tone, tactile defensiveness, reflux vomiting, lethargy, and food refusal, special positions and techniques may be required to facilitate optimal feeding. Once parents have been taught an optimal feeding program, the nurse should assess both the parental ability to use and the consistency of use of positions and techniques appropriate for the particular infant. The assistance of an occupational, physical, or speech therapist may be necessary to thoroughly evaluate this aspect of feeding.

Psychosocial Context of Feeding

A feeding observation should also include an assessment of the psychosocial context of feeding. The high risk infant is particularly vulnerable to poor parental attachment, owing to several factors including prolonged separation of parent and child, prematurity, and the presence of chronic diseases.[7] Attachment is essential to feeding an infant because feeding is an interactional process. Clarity of the infant's cues (regarding hunger, satiation, and so on), the caregiver's responsiveness to both the infant and these cues, and the infant's responsiveness to the caregiver are factors related to attachment and are essential in the feeding process. The Nursing Child Assessment Satellite Training (NCAST) Project feeding assessment tool provides a model for a thorough feeding observation.[8] General guidelines for a feeding observation are included in Appendix 5–A.

NURSING INTERVENTIONS FOR COMMON PROBLEMS

Nutrition and feeding problems are often multifaceted, and appropriate interventions will be based on a thorough assessment addressing the multiple related factors, listed earlier in the chapter, contributing to the problem. Although a multidisciplinary team approach can be helpful in many cases, the interventions discussed in this section can be implemented by nurses whether or not a team approach is possible.

Increasing Calories

The simplest method of increasing the infant's caloric intake is to increase the volume or frequency (or both) of feedings. For infants requiring fluid restriction or with frequent vomiting or those who are difficult to feed because of oral motor problems or food refusal, this solution may not be practical.

If an infant is taking the maximum volume of formula per day that is appropriate or practical but still needs additional calories, the caloric concentration of the formula can be increased. Most infant formulas (excepting "premie" varieties) contain 20 cal/oz. A 24 cal/oz formula can easily be made by mixing a 13-oz can of concentrated formula with only 9 oz of water. If the formula needs to be even more dense in calories, commercial supplements such as Polycose, Moducal, or vegetable oil can be added to achieve a caloric concentration of 26 to 30 cal/oz. A concentration of more than 30 cal/oz may be required in very exceptional cases.

Table 5–5 describes various calorie supplements and will assist the nurse in making an appropriate choice.

Corn syrup is a frequently recommended calorie supplement. However, recent research suggests that both honey and corn syrup may contain Clostridium botulinum spores.[9,10] While the spores pose no apparent risk of contracting botulism in older children, a number of cases of infant botulism have been associated with the ingestion of spore-containing honey. The spectrum of botulism in infants is uncertain but may range from constipation to failure-to-thrive, and has been associated with sudden death. For this reason, it is recommended that honey not be fed to infants under 1 year of age. It may also be prudent to avoid the use of corn syrup.

Of course, infants with intestinal problems may not be able to tolerate highly concentrated formulas. As more concentrated formulas are used with an infant, prolonged diarrhea will signify inability to accept the formula density. If Polycose or Moducal is not accepted, MCT (medium chain triglyceride, available through a pharmacy) or vegetable oil can be tried. Sometimes a combination of supplements, although more difficult for parents to mix, can afford the highest caloric value without causing diarrhea. Concentrated formula can also cause constipation in some infants.

In an infant or toddler accepting some baby or table foods, high-calorie foods including cheese and ice cream should be encouraged. Homemade baby food usually contains less water than the commercial varieties and is, therefore, more dense in calories. Butter, margarine, or oil can be added to foods for extra calories, and powdered skim milk can be added to liquids, yogurt, puddings, and cereal.

Table 5–5 Calorie Supplements for Infants

Supplement	cal/tbsp	Comments
Polycose	23	May increase stool frequency and loosen texture of stools Available at drug stores or by order through pharmacist Easy to mix into formula; can be mixed into entire batch
Moducal	30	Similar to Polycose
Vegetable oil	115	Floats in formula, so to ensure baby gets all of oil, best to put in 1 oz of formula and give as the first part of each feeding

Source: Adapted from *Supplemental Nutritional Support of Babies with Respiratory Distress* (unpublished), Children's Hospital National Medical Center, 1984, with permission of M. Dickie.

Each time the child eats, calorie-dense foods should be offered. For example, crackers with cheese, rather than plain crackers, can be offered for a snack.

If an infant or toddler is unable to take adequate feedings by mouth to produce a positive curve on the growth chart, tube feeding may be considered (see Chapter 6).

Vomiting, Diarrhea, and Constipation

A thorough feeding history and observation should evaluate the frequency of *vomiting* in relationship to amounts, frequency, and types of food as well as to positioning and feeding techniques. (See Chapter 4 for a complete discussion of vomiting.)

Overfeeding of the infant may contribute to vomiting. If overfeeding is suspected on the basis of history and observation, a detailed feeding schedule can be worked out with parents. Parents should also be instructed that it is not necessary to feed the infant in response to every cry. In this regard, continued reinforcement by the professional may be helpful.

Inadequate burping may also cause vomiting. Discussion of the importance of burping should be followed by a demonstration, by the nurse, of proper technique. As part of teaching, parents, or whoever regularly feeds the infant, should give a return demonstration of proper burping. Review and reinforcement of proper techniques over several home visits can be helpful.

Reflux vomiting is described in Chapter 4. Since this disorder can contribute to poor growth, appropriate intervention is important. Reflux vomiting may resolve spontaneously as an infant assumes the upright posture (at 9 to 12 months of age in children without developmental delay). However, if the vomiting is significant in amount or frequency, several steps can be taken to control it. The infant can be positioned prone, with shoulders higher than feet by approximately 30 degrees, for 30 to 60 minutes after each feeding, or longer if necessary. Proper positioning can be accomplished by tipping the mattress in the infant's crib. Alternatively, the child can be placed in an infant or car seat. Frequent small feedings can be used. Formula can be thickened by the addition of small amounts of rice cereal.

If reflux vomiting leads to aspiration, recurrent apnea, esophagitis, esophageal stricture, or prolonged inability to gain weight, surgical intervention may be indicated. A common procedure is the Nisson fundoplication, which wraps the fundus of the stomach around the distal esophagus to tighten the juncture.

Diarrhea and constipation can also be related to nutrition problems and are discussed in Chapter 4.

Medication Effects

Various medications that may be used in the management of the high risk infant can affect nutritional status. Types of medications and their effects are listed in Table 5–6.

Table 5–6 Medications Affecting Nutritional Status

Medication	Effect on Nutritional Status	Intervention
Diuretics	Alter fluid and electrolyte balance	Sodium and potassium supplements may be needed. Monitor for fluid overload or dehydration. Fluid restriction may be necessary.
Phenobarbital	Decreases effectiveness of vitamin D and can alter the calcium and phosphorus metabolism	Monitor serum phosphatase levels every 3–6 months. Vitamin D supplements may be needed.
Dilantin	Alters vitamin D, calcium, and phosphorus metabolism and absorption. Can lead to loss of taste and gum irritation	Monitor serum phosphatase levels every 3–6 months. Good oral hygiene is essential; gum massage may relieve irritation.
Iron	May cause constipation	More fluids or corn syrup in formula may be needed.
Steroids	Increase appetite	Restriction of infant's intake may be needed.

Disorders of Feeding: Skills and Behavior

When feeding difficulties that hinder nutritional intake are suspected, a feeding specialist—often a speech pathologist, occupational therapist, or physical therapist—should be consulted. Following the assessment, therapy to help improve the dysfunction is usually initiated. The intervention should build on any normal patterns the infant has and should proceed at the infant's pace. Whenever a feeding program is developed for an infant, the nurse can work with the therapist both to provide follow-up instruction and demonstration of positions and techniques for the parents as well as to assess the infant's progress. Close coordination between the nurse and therapist will be important to ensure optimal benefits of the intervention program.

A frequent feeding intervention for the high risk infant involves choice of the appropriate nipple for the bottle. If the infant's suck is weak or ineffective, or if the infant tires easily, nipple choice should be evaluated. Proper choice of the type and size of nipple for the bottle-fed infant is important for developing an effective suck and coordination in the suck-swallow-breathe pattern. A soft and small nipple can be used with a very young infant with a weak suck; for an older child, formula flows too rapidly through this nipple, and coordination of suck and swallow

Figure 5–1 Ease of Suck for Commonly Used Nipples

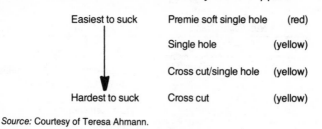

Easiest to suck	Premie soft single hole	(red)
	Single hole	(yellow)
	Cross cut/single hole	(yellow)
Hardest to suck	Cross cut	(yellow)

Source: Courtesy of Teresa Ahmann.

becomes difficult. A cross-cut nipple is more firm and encourages a suck. Nipples are graded for ease of suck as indicated in Figure 5–1. Other nipples, such as the "natural" nipple, can be experimented with as necessary to meet the infant's needs. In addition, for a stressed infant, nonnutritive sucking (e.g., of a pacifier) is much easier than nutritive sucking and can be encouraged.

Other therapeutic techniques can be used to facilitate a smooth suck-swallow-breathe pattern:

- positioning the infant with neck in a neutral midline position, out of hyperextension, or slightly flexed[11]
- promoting jaw stabilization to allow more free movement of the tongue and lips
- facilitating lip activity.

For the lethargic infant, there are several therapeutic possibilities:[12]

- minimizing activity before the meal (e.g., chest therapy, suctioning)
- keeping the infant cool during feedings (e.g., hold slightly away from parent's body)
- using the infant's vestibular system (through movement such as rocking or bouncing) to increase awareness.

For the infant with overt food refusal, therapeutic techniques include the following:[13]

- daily digital stimulation of oral tissues to desensitize lips, gums, and tongue (distinct from feeding time)
- emphasis on gradual acceptance of pleasurable oral experiences
- use of pacifier, if accepted
- consistency in person who feeds the infant.

If the infant with feeding disorders fails to maintain an adequate nutritional status and to evidence growth, tube feeding must be considered. Chapter 6 discusses tube feeding in detail.

FAILURE TO THRIVE

During the first 6 months of life, infants normally gain 15 to 30 grams (½ to 1 oz) per day. Birth weight is doubled by 6 months, tripled by 1 year, and quadrupled by age 2. By the age of 2 years, the premature and full-term infant should exhibit little difference in growth parameters.[14] If an infant or toddler falls below the fifth percentile on the growth curve at any time or shows a consistent deceleration in weight gain over several weeks or months, failure to thrive (FTT) should be suspected.

FTT may be *organic* in origin: genetic short stature, malabsorption, cardiac or respiratory diseases, renal disease, or CNS deficits. *Nonorganic* causes, however, are suspected in as many as 50 percent of children with FTT.[15] FTT is considered nonorganic if no organic causes are found. Nonorganic FTT in infants and toddlers is generally thought to be related to disorders of the parent-infant attachment.[16] (See Chapter 4 for a discussion of attachment.)

If an infant or toddler shows steady deceleration on the growth curve or persistent weight below the fifth percentile, despite attempts to introduce adequate calories, hospitalization should be considered within 1 to 2 months. Hospitalization will allow the opportunity for diagnostic procedures, for observation of weight gain outside the home, and for offering nutritional intervention in an acute situation. If FTT is found to be nonorganic, establishing nutritional recommendations must be augmented by intervention in the parent-infant dyad in order to improve the dysfunctional relationship. Such intervention begins in the hospital but must be continued at home.

The factors affecting parental-infant attachment can be multiple, as discussed in Chapter 4. The nurse should begin intervention by establishing a caring and nurturing relationship with the parents that will encourage them to develop trust and begin to improve self-esteem. Judgmentalism and authority are inappropriate roles for the nurse, whereas concern and friendliness are very important.

Past events and current life stresses should be explored with parents. Feelings about the infant, particularly about any physical deformities, chronic illness, or mental retardation, should be explored. Any positive or negative feelings expressed should be accepted. Suggestions can be offered about solutions to current problems but should be offered in a collaborative, caring manner rather than authoritatively. In this regard, problems should be framed in terms of how to meet the child's needs rather than how to improve the parents' behavior.

More direct nurturing of the parent is also therapeutic. Since building self-esteem in the parent is a goal, the nurse should set small achievable goals at each visit so that there is much opportunity for praise and no opportunity for the parent to fail. Offering positive reinforcement whenever the parent exhibits nurturing behavior toward the infant is critical. In addition, describing and praising all positive interactions and strengths of the parent are helpful.

Role-modeling appropriate care of the child is another aspect of nursing intervention for nonorganic FTT. The feeding observation discussed earlier in this chapter describes observing for clarity of the infant's cues and caregiver response to infant as well as caregiver and infant responses to each other. These areas are of prime importance in intervention. According to Brazelton, it is only when mutual responsiveness is established that weight gain can begin.[17] The nurse can begin to role-model appropriate care by holding the infant close, with eye contact, and smiling. This should be done in the presence of parents for a period of time during each home visit.

While holding the infant, the nurse should observe for any visual or auditory cues and should respond to these by gentle touch and by repeating sounds. As cues are noted, these can be pointed out to parents to increase their awareness of and delight in the child. A feeding can also be given on occasional home visits to role-model interactions during feeding.

In addition to nurturing the parent and role-modeling appropriate care of the child, referral to agencies providing augmentative services may be helpful. Referrals may be made for more in-depth counseling, parent discussion groups, child care education classes, respite care or day care, infant stimulation, or crisis intervention lines that provide phone numbers parents can call at any time to talk.

NOTES

1. The scale should be cleaned with disinfectant between each visit to prevent the spreading of infections, particularly among compromised infants.

2. NCHS growth charts are available from Ross Laboratories, Columbus, Ohio (as adapted from Hammill PVV, Drizd TA, Johnson CL, et al: Physical growth: National Center for Health Statistics percentiles, *Am J Clin Nutr* 32: 607–629, 1979).

3. Dickie M, Children's Hospital National Medical Center, Washington, DC: personal communication, December 1984.

4. Adamow CL, Glassman MS: *Nutritional Assessment of the Handicapped Child*, Washington, DC, American Society for Parental and Enteral Nutrition, 1983, pp 4–5; Pipes P, Carman P: Nutrition and feeding of children with developmental delays and related problems, in Pipes P (ed): *Nutrition in Infancy and Childhood*, St Louis, CV Mosby Co, 1977, p 170.

5. Finnie NR: *Handling the Young Cerebral Palsied Child at Home*, ed 2, New York, EP Dutton Co Inc, 1975.

6. Simon BM, speech-language pathologist, Philadelphia, PA: personal communication, July 1985.

7. Barbero G: Failure to thrive, in Klaus MH, Leger T, Trause MA (eds): *Maternal Attachment and Mothering Disorders*. Johnson & Johnson, 1975, pp 9–11.

8. Barnard K: *Nursing Child Assessment Feeding Scales*, Nursing Child Assessment Satellite Training Project, undated (unpublished). Copies may be ordered from NCAST, WJ-10, University of Washington, Seattle, Washington 98195.

9. Arnon SS, et al: Honey and other environmental risk factors for infant botulism, *J Pediatrics* 94:331–336, 1979.

10. Honey, corn syrups, and infant botulism. *California Morbidity,* no 14, April 13, 1984.

11. Simon BM: personal communication, July 1985; Berg C, Children's Hospital National Medical Center, Washington, DC: personal communication, July 1985.

12. *Ibid.*

13. *Ibid.*

14. Chow MP, et al: *Handbook of Pediatric Primary Care,* ed 2, New York, John Wiley & Sons, 1984, p 1187.

15. Hannaway PJ: Failure to thrive: a study of 100 infants and children, *Clin Pediatr* 9: 99, 1970.

16. *Diagnostic and Statistical Manual III,* Washington, DC, American Psychiatric Association, 1980.

17. Brazelton TB, Koslowski B, Main M: The origins of reciprocity: the early mother-infant interaction, in Lewis M, Rosenblum LA (eds): *The Effect of The Infant on Its Caregiver,* New York, John Wiley and Sons, 1974, pp 49–76.

REFERENCES

Arnon SS, Mitura TF, Damus K, et al: Honey and other environmental risk factors for infant botulism. *J Pediatrics* 94: 331–336, 1979.

Barbero G: Failure to thrive, in Klaus MH, Leger T, Trause MA (eds): *Maternal Attachment and Mothering Disorders.* Johnson & Johnson, 1975, p 9.

Barnard K: *Nursing Child Assessment Feeding Scales.* (Nursing Child Assessment Satellite Training Project.) undated (unpublished). Copies may be ordered from NCAST, WJ-10, University of Washington, Seattle, Washington 98195.

Brazelton TB, Koslowski B, Main M: The origins of reciprocity: the early mother-infant interaction, in Lewis M, Rosenblum LA (eds): *The Effect of the Infant and Its Caregiver.* New York, John Wiley and Sons, 1974, p 49.

Chow MP, Durand BA, Feldman MN, et al: *Handbook of Pediatric Primary Care,* ed 2. New York, John Wiley and Sons, 1984, Chapters 3, 5, and 31.

Connor F, Williamson G, Siepp JM: *Program Guide for Infants and Toddlers with Neuromotor and Other Developmental Disabilities.* New York, Teachers College Press, 1978.

Cupoli J, Hallock JA, Barness LA: Failure to thrive. *Curr Trends Pediatr* 10: 2–43, September 1980.

Darling DB, McCauley RGK, Leonidas JC, et al: Gastroesophageal reflux in infants and children: correlating radiologic severity and pulmonary pathology. *Radiology* 27: 735–740, 1978.

Derivan AT: Disorders of bonding, in Accardo PJ (ed): *Failure to Thrive in Infancy and Early Childhood: A Multidisciplinary Team Approach.* Baltimore, University Park Press, 1982, p 91.

Diagnostic and Statistical Manual III. Washington, DC, American Psychiatric Association, 1980.

Dickie M: *Supplemental Nutrition Support of Babies With Poor Growth.* Washington, DC, Children's Hospital National Medical Center, 1984 (unpublished).

Finnie NR: *Handling the Young Cerebral Palsied Child at Home,* ed 2. New York, EP Dutton Co Inc, 1975.

Fomon SJ: *Nutritional Disorders of Children: Prevention, Screening and Follow-up.* DHEW publication (HSA) 77-5104. US Department of Health, Education and Welfare, 1976.

Hannaway PJ: Failure to thrive: a study of 100 infants and children. *Clin Pediatr* 9: 96–99, 1970.

Honey, corn syrups, and infant botulism. *California Morbidity,* no 14, April 13, 1984.

Kibel MA: Gastroesophageal reflux and failure to thrive in infancy, in Gellis SS (ed): *Gastroesophageal Reflux: Report of the Seventy-Sixth Ross Congress on Pediatric Research*. Columbus, Ohio, Ross Laboratories, 1979, p 39.

Leape LL, Holder TM, Franklin JD, et al: Respiratory arrest in infants secondary to gastroesophageal reflux. *Pediatrics* 60: 924–928, 1977.

Morris SE: *The Normal Acquisition of Oral Feeding Skills: Implications for Assessment and Treatment*. New York, Therapeutic Media Inc, 1982.

Murray CA, Glassman MS: Nutrient requirements during growth and recovery from failure to thrive, in Accardo PJ (ed): *Failure to Thrive in Infancy and Early Childhood: A Multidisciplinary Team Approach*. Baltimore, University Park Press, 1982, p 19.

Palmer FB: Gastroenterology, in Accardo PJ (ed): *Failure to Thrive in Infancy and Early Childhood: A Multidisciplinary Team Approach*. Baltimore, University Park Press, 1982, p 153.

Palmer MM: Oral-motor function in the normal preterm and full-term infant, in *Early Detection and Treatment of the Infant and Young Child with Neuromotor Disorders*. New York, Therapeutic Media Inc, 1983, pp 38–47.

Palmer MM: Oral-motor dysfunction in the premature and term infant, in *Early Detection and Treatment of the Infant and Young Child with Neuromotor Disorders*. New York, Therapeutic Media Inc, 1983, pp 48–60.

Palmer MM: The treatment of oral-motor dysfunction, in *Early Detection and Treatment of the Infant and Young Child with Neuromotor Disorders*. New York, Therapeutic Media Inc, 1983, pp 61–70.

Pipes P, Carman P: Nutrition and feeding of children with developmental delays and related problems, in Pipes P (ed): *Nutrition in Infancy and Childhood*. St Louis: CV Mosby Co, 1977, p 170.

Springer NS, Fricke NL: Endogenous malnutrition following drug therapy, in Palmer S, Eckvall S (eds): *Pediatric Nutrition in Developmental Disorders*. Springfield, Ill, Charles C Thomas, 1978, p 453.

Feeding/Nutritional Assessment
for the Infant

Patient's name _____ DOB _____

Diagnoses _____

Physician or Dietitian prescribing feeding:

_____Phone _____

formula _____cal/oz _____

amount/feed _____frequency _____

how mixed _____

other foods (types, amount and frequency): _____

_____

_____

_____

supplements _____

_____

dietary restrictions _____

_____

_____

_____

HISTORY

birth weight _____ length _____ head circumference _____

feeding history: TPN _____ duration _____

      GT _____ duration _____

      NG _____ duration _____

age at first p.o. feed _____

reflux _____

problems feeding _____

_____

CURRENT FEEDING PATTERNS (Parent Report)

formula _____ cal/oz _____
amount/feed _____ frequency _____
how mixed _____
other foods (types, amount, and frequency): _____
_____
_____

supplements _____
_____

source of Iron _____
medications affecting diet (see accompanying list) _____
_____

TPN _____ GT _____ NG _____
self-feeding skills _____
cues to hunger _____
hungry at feeding time? _____
how long feeding takes _____
position during feed _____
reflux: amount _____ frequency _____
stool: type _____ color _____ frequency _____
problems: sucking _____   chewing _____   swallowing _____
             vomiting _____   diarrhea _____   constipation _____
             food allergy _____   anemia _____
Parental concerns regarding feeding:
_____
_____

PHYSICAL EXAM

overall appearance _____
_____

   actual weight _____ length _____ head circumference _____
NCHS% weight _____ length _____ head circumference _____
weight/length (NCHS%) _____
Present 24 hour intake schedule (obtain *record*, not recall)

Time	Food	Amount	Time	Food	Amount

was this a normal day? _____

total 24-hr volume intake: _____

total 24-hr calorie intake: _____

ideal 24-hr calorie intake (ideal wt(kg)* _____ × 115 cal/kg†): _____

*The weight at the 50th percentile (NCHS) based on actual length.

†May need more if lack of weight gain related to high energy requirements.

FEEDING OBSERVATION

suck _____ suck-swallow _____

coordination with breathing _____

mouth closure on nipple _____

tires with feed _____

Summary of observation (see accompanying guidelines): _____

_____

_____

_____

_____

_____

_____

Assessment: _____

_____

_____

_____

_____

_____

_____

_____

Plan: _____

_____

_____

_____

_____

_____

_____

_____

Completed by _____ Date _____

Nutritional Assessment

Guidelines for Feeding Observation

1. Child's position—safety, contact, comfort, eye-to-eye contact.
2. Parent's response to cues—hunger cue, satiation, distress, pauses.
3. Parent's responsiveness to infant—contingent verbal and facial responses, plays, rocks, talks with infant (note negative interaction).
4. Clarity of infant cues—clear hunger and satiation cues, positive response to feeding.
5. Infant's responsiveness to parents—contingent response to parents' smile or verbalization; infant smiles, verbalizes, or touches parent.
6. Is this feeding normal for this child/was parent uncomfortable because of observer?

Recommended Caloric Intake		*Expected normal weight gain*	
Age(mo)	*cal/kg ideal wt*	*Age*(mo)	*oz/day*
0–6	115	0–3	1
6–12	105	3–6	⅔
12–36	100	6–9	½
		9–12	⅓
		12–24	1½/week

Caloric Content of Foods

Premie formula	24 cal/oz
Regular formula	20 cal/oz
Baby fruit	70–120 cal/jar (pears, applesauce are lowest)
Baby vegetables	40–90 cal/jar (sweet potatoes are highest)
Strained plain meats	90–140 cal/jar
Baby cereal (dry)	10 cal/tbsp
Mixed dinners and desserts	less nutritious/cal

To increase calories

Concentrated formula: 24 cal/oz: 13-oz can of formula concentrate + 9 oz of water
26 cal/oz: add 1½ tbsp polycose to 24 cal/oz mixture
28 cal/oz: add 3 tbsp polycose
30 cal/oz: add 4½ tbsp polycose

Choose high-calorie baby foods
Feed more frequently
Use supplements:
Polycose = 30 cal/tbsp, Vegetable oil or margarine = 40 cal/tbsp

Medications Affecting Diet

Steroids may increase appetite.
Anticonvulsants alter calcium and phosphorus metabolism; monitor serum phosphatase levels.
Zinc and magnesium are important if child has ostomy or frequent diarrhea or vomiting.

Recommended Iron Supplementation

0–6 months: 10 mg/day
6 months–3 years: 15 mg/day

OR

Term infants: 1 mg/kg/day
Preterm infants: 2 mg/kg/day

For Constipation

Karo syrup: 1 tsp/3½ oz of formula for 1 day
             2 tsp/3½ oz of formula on second day if no results

Source: Reprinted with permission of Home Care Program (Ahmann, Lierman, and Peck), Children's Hospital National Medical Center, Washington, D.C.

Appendix 5–B

Nutrition and Feeding of the Healthy Infant

Margaret Wilson, MS, OTR
Elizabeth Ahmann, RN, MS, FNP

The infant having no nutritional problems will require approximately 110 cal/kg (50 cal/lb) per day to maintain normal growth (see Table 5–1). Breast milk or commercial formula with a caloric concentration of 20 cal/oz will supply the infant with all nutritional requirements if iron, fluoride, or both are supplemented as indicated by the health care provider. Feeding time for the healthy infant will provide a warm and close interaction between parent and child, establishing a trusting bond.

The ability to eat can be influenced by early reflexes, movement and positioning of the lips and tongue, jaw control, orofacial anatomic structures, general respiratory changes, sensory awareness of the oral area, and overall body postural tone. Many premature or full-term babies with various neurologic, neuromuscular, or physical impairments may have difficulty with oral motor functioning and consequently with feeding. It is often the nurse, who through careful observation, first becomes aware of feeding difficulties or the potential for oral motor skill delay.

The earliest oral motor skills seen in the normally developing infant are mainly reflexive and are outlined in the accompanying table. As these reflexive skills mature and become more automatic, they are integrated into the child's oral motor repertoire and are no longer simply reflexive. The reflexive and subsequently integrated developmental pattern of sucking, swallowing, and then chewing should also be observed as the infant develops.

Early sucking is characterized by movement of the tongue back and forth from a position between the gums, creating a rhythmic licking motion on the nipple that is synchronized with jaw opening and closing. There is often loss of liquid from the mouth since the lips are only loosely sealed around the nipple. As oral motor control progresses, a rhythmic raising and lowering of the tongue independent of jaw movement, tongue tip elevation, reduced jaw motion, and a firm lip seal around the nipple are noted.

Early on, the sucking pattern triggers swallowing. A smooth coordination of suck-swallow-breathe will be observed in a normal newborn. As the infant develops, jaw stability, lip coordination, and control of tongue movement progress, and swallow eventually becomes independent of suck, allowing cup drinking to begin. Cup drinking can usually be introduced between 6 and 12 months of age.

The introduction of soft and then semisolid foods frequently depends on parental or physician preferences and on the infant's level of hunger. Developmentally, around 5 or 6 months of age, with the maturation of lip and tongue control, the infant progresses from scraping food off a spoon with the upper gums to active participation of the upper lip and tongue in the acceptance of foods. With practice, the infant will also learn to grade the amount of jaw opening needed to get the food from the spoon. By 5 to 6 months, with tongue movements maturing, the healthy infant will progress to accepting solid foods, and at 6 to 7 months, with the improvement of jaw control, to chewing.

The chewing motion of the jaw is initially vertical; it then becomes a side-to-side motion, followed by refined rotary motion, which is usually seen after the first year of life. Over time, the development of grasping and sitting skills encourages self-feeding, and by 2 years of age the infant with no nutritional problems will be cup drinking and self-feeding a wide variety of table foods.

Oral Motor Reflexes

Reflex	Age at Acquisition	Age at Integration	Description
Rooting	Birth	3 months	Turning of face toward a touch stimulus in search of nutrition
Suck-swallow	Birth	2–5 months	Automatic lip closure around food source with several repeated sucks followed by a swallow
Gag	Birth	Diminishes but remains throughout life	Protective mechanism stimulated by touch at back of tongue
Bite	1 month	5–6 months	Rhythmic pattern of bite and release following stimulation of lips or gums

Chapter 6

Home Care of the Infant Requiring Tube Feeding

If an infant cannot accept adequate amounts of formula by mouth, the use of tube feeding to provide sufficient intake may be necessary. Inadequate oral intake by the infant may be due to a variety of problems. For example, infants initially maintained on gavage feedings gain little sucking experience in the nursery;[1] such infants commonly have poorly developed orofacial musculature or, because of lack of appropriate desensitizing oral stimulation, hypersensitive oral tissues, leading to ineffective sucking or food refusal. Infants with cardiac or respiratory compromise may not have the strength to suck the amount of formula necessary for adequate growth. Infants with reflux or other disorders causing frequent vomiting may be unable to retain enough formula to satisfy calorie needs.

In these infants, tube feedings can be used to ensure adequate caloric intake. Depending on the nature and severity of the underlying problem, tube feeding may either supplement or replace oral feedings.

TUBE FEEDING OPTIONS

Parents or caregivers who will be involved in the infant's daily care and feeding should participate with the nurse and the physician in deciding upon the most appropriate methods of tube feeding. They should be informed of the options as well as the risks, benefits, and practical details regarding alternative choices. The infant's needs, parental preferences, and safety factors must all be considered in the choice of a home tube-feeding plan.

There are several methods of tube feeding. Gastrostomy tubes are widely accepted for long-term tube feeding. Nasogastric tubes are relied upon for inter-

Note: Appendixes 6–A and 6–B contain sample home care plans for infants with gastrostomy tubes and nasogastric tubes, respectively.

93

mittent or short-term feeding and are also gaining acceptance for long-term use. Orogastric, nasojejunal, and jejunostomy tubes are used less commonly, and only in special circumstances; they are the least safe for home use. Therefore, only nasogastric and gastrostomy tube feedings are discussed in this chapter.

Nasogastric Tubes

In choosing the appropriate nasogastric (NG) tube for home use, several factors must be considered. First, the size of tube is important. The smaller the lumen of the tube, the more comfortable it is for the child. However, formula passes slowly through a tube with a very small lumen, making feeding times unreasonably long. A lumen size of 8 French is generally adequate for the infant. Second, tubes are made of several types of material; Table 6–1 offers a guide to the advantages and disadvantages of each. Third, it may be helpful to try several tubes to determine the type that the parents are most comfortable inserting. Fourth, if tube feeding is expected to be long-term, the cost of supplies and the likelihood of insurance coverage should be considered in choosing a tube for home use.

Table 6–1 Comparison of Nasogastric Tube Materials

Material	Cost	Reusability	Necessity for Stylet or Guidewire	Comments and Precautions
PVC (polyvinyl chloride)	Least expensive	Reusable 1–2 times only; (no more than 48 hours each time)	No	Insertion facilitated if tube is immersed in ice before use
Polyurethane	Mid-range in cost	Yes, long-term	Comes with or without stylet; some have mercury weight to facilitate insertion	May be expelled from stomach with vomiting or strong cough; position must be carefully assessed prior to feeding
Silastic	Most expensive	Not reusable once it has come out	Stylet needed	Same precautions as for polyurethane

Source: Table prepared with assistance of J. Ward, RN, MA, Children's Hospital National Medical Center, Washington, D.C.

Gastrostomy Tubes

Two types of tubes are commonly used for gastrostomy (G) tube feeding: the Malecot self-retaining gastrostomy tube, which has a basket-type end for holding the tube in place, and a Foley catheter, which has a balloon tip that holds the catheter in place. Generally, the size of tube or catheter is chosen by the surgeon who performs the gastrostomy procedure. Nonetheless, it is important for parents to know the tube size since they will need to obtain a replacement if the tube comes out.

FEEDING APPARATUS

NG or G tube feedings can be administered through several types of apparatus. For bolus feeds, a 30- to 60-cc syringe with a regular tip may be inserted into intravenous (IV) extension tubing. The tubing, in turn, is inserted into the NG or G tube. A plastic clamp can be placed on the IV tubing to regulate or stop the flow during feeding.

An alternative to IV tubing is a specially designed feeding set-up. One type consists of a plastic bottle with a cap connected directly to tubing. This set-up can be used if the family is mixing the formula at home. Another type, practical only for use with a feeding pump, is a plastic bag and tubing set that contains premixed formula. This type is generally used for continuous infusion, rather than for bolus feeds.

The frequency and duration of home tube feeding, as well as ease of flow regulation, the size of the drip chamber, and ease of filling with formula, are factors to consider in choosing a feeding apparatus. The choice should also be determined by family preference, convenience, and cost factors.

If a feeding pump is to be used in the home, the community health nurse may be asked to advise on the best choice. Although a variety of pumps are available, not all are sufficiently accurate to allow the precise control necessary to prevent fluid overload in the infant or young child. In some cases, an IV pump may be an appropriate choice. In any event, care must be taken to choose a pump that will permit a slow rate of infusion. Other considerations include the options of a battery mode and of alarms to signal occlusion in the line and empty container, or both.

Ease of operation is another important factor. The supplier or manufacturer of the chosen pump should provide operating instructions for both the family and the nurse. In order to ensure safe and appropriate operation of the pump these instructions should be reviewed with caregivers verbally, by demonstration, and by their return demonstration. Instructions for routine operation of the pump and for responses to alarms should be reviewed. The family should have the opportunity to practice tube feeding in the hospital with the same pump to be used at home.

HOSPITAL DISCHARGE AND TRANSITION TO THE HOME

If an infant is discharged with tube feedings prescribed, it is important to assess the parents' ability to continue the feedings at home. It is important for the community health nurse to be familiar with the hospital's teaching program, the parents' skills and abilities, and any problems or concerns that may have arisen. Optimally, the parents will have demonstrated full responsibility for feeding for a 24-hour period prior to discharge. In addition, at the time of discharge, it is important that the parents have a list of all the supplies needed for the child's feeding, as well as information about where and how to obtain them.

ROUTINE HOME VISITS

On the first and on every subsequent home visit, the infant's growth parameters should be obtained, and both total daily intake and tube feeding intake determined. It is important to note that if tube feedings are needed for supplemental feeding only, intake through the tube may vary daily with the ability to accept oral feeds.

Vomiting, diarrhea, and abdominal cramping may result from *incorrect tube-feeding techniques*. Inquiry about the occurrence of these symptoms should be a part of every home visit. If any of these symptoms is reported, appropriate changes in feeding rate or in formula type, amount, or concentration should be made; suggested interventions are listed in Table 6–2. Such modifications in the feeding plan can be discussed with the infant's dietitian or primary provider.

Skin care is an important part of routine care for the child being tube-fed. If the infant has an NG tube, the nares should be assessed on each nursing home visit. During the visit parents should be able to demonstrate appropriate assessment and care of the nares. Usually, if the tube is taped securely at both the nares and on the cheek, little irritation will occur. Cleansing with a wet cotton swab and changing the tape regularly will also limit the risk of irritation. A tape that ventilates well, such as Micropore tape, may be helpful. Clear surgical adhesive dressings (e.g., Opsite or Tegaderm) have also been used successfully.[2] If the skin does become irritated, the tube should be moved to the other nostril, and the irritated area cleansed carefully. If necessary, an antibiotic ointment can be applied.

If the infant has a G tube, the insertion site should be inspected on each nursing visit. Parents should be able to demonstrate appropriate care and assessment of the G tube site for irritation, rashes, or granuloma formation. Routine care of the area should be accomplished every one to two days. For routine care, the tape is first removed at the G tube site. The area is cleansed with soap and water on a washcloth; soap without a cream or lanolin base will allow the tape to stick better. A cotton swab may be used on and around the tube to remove any crusting. After

Table 6–2 Common Tube Feeding Problems and Interventions

Problem	*Cause(s)*	*Intervention(s)*
Tube site irritation	Movement of tube back and forth	Tape tube securely.
	Skin irritation under tape	Change position of tape every 1–2 days; assess site for infection or granuloma.
Constipation	Inadequate fluid	Increase water.
	Lack of bulk in the diet	Feed prune juice; add sugar to the feeding; feed puréed fruits or vegetables.
	Inactivity	Encourage activity.
Diarrhea	Feeding too fast	Feed more slowly if gravity feeding; check rate with physician if feeding by pump.
	Formula too concentrated in sugar or salt	Consult dietitian or physician.
	Allergy (intolerance) to an ingredient	
	Side effect of medications given with feedings	Divide medications into smaller, more frequent doses if possible.
	Flu or gastroenteritis	Consult physician.
	Feeding formula contaminated by bacteria, or "spoiled" formula	Stress care in daily cleaning of supplies; clean preparations and refrigeration of feedings; and hanging formula for no more than 4–8 hours.
	Lack of bulk in the diet (This does not really cause diarrhea but can make stools so loose as to cause diaper rash.)	Consult with dietitian about adding a bulky food such as puréed vegetables or fruit.
Abdominal cramping IF SEVERE, CALL PHYSICIAN.	Feeding too fast	Slow the rate of bolus feedings; if using a pump, check the rate: if at the prescribed rate, consult with physician about changing rate.
	Feeding too concentrated	Consult with dietitian.
	Gastrostomy allowing air into the stomach	Consult with physician.

Table 6–2 continued

Problem	Cause(s)	Intervention(s)
Vomiting	Feeding too fast	Feed slower if bolus feeding; consult with physician if feeding by constant drip.
	Feeding tube in the wrong place	Check tube position; tubes in stomach (especially G tubes) may slip out and block the outlet into the intestine.
Aspiration	Tube not inserted fully	STOP FEEDING; CLEAR AIRWAY; call physician. (*Always* check tube placement before feeding.)
	Associated with vomiting	Keep head of bed elevated; position infant on stomach to avoid aspiration.
Plugged tube	Contents not flushed completely through	Prevent by rinsing tube with water after feeding (formula or medications) and before clamping the tube.

Source: Adapted with permission from *Tube Feeding Your Child at Home* by J. Ward, S. Robbins, and L. Riggs, pp. 16–17, Children's Hospital National Medical Center, Clinical Nutrition Group, Washington, D.C., January 1983.

the skin is rinsed and dried thoroughly, it should be inspected carefully. If the skin is intact, the tube can be pulled firmly but gently to assure proper placement. It can then be taped in place. Regularly changing the location of the tape will reduce the risk of irritation. Table 6–3 provides a guide to assessment of possible problems at the G tube site.

THE FIRST HOME VISIT

All aspects of routine visits are, of course, incorporated into the first home visit. In addition, parental preparation to provide safe and appropriate care must be determined. Nurses are further reminded that assessment of the care of the tube-fed infant should be made in conjunction with an evaluation of the infant's nutritional status, including efforts to ensure that nutritional needs are being met. In this connection, a thorough nutritional history should be obtained on the first visit. (Chapter 5 provides a detailed discussion regarding nutrition.)

On the first home visit, assessment of the parents' ability to provide safe and appropriate feeding is important. This is best achieved by observation. If a child

Table 6–3 G Tube Site Care: Possible Problems and Interventions

Problem	*Interventions*
Formula leakage	Check that tube is firmly in place. Cover the area with gauze to protect clothing. Change gauze frequently to prevent maceration of skin. If leakage is heavy, consider placement of larger tube.
Rash or breakdown of skin	Keep area dry; do not apply dressing. Use porous, hypoallergenic tape. Rotate placement of tape daily. For monilial infections, nystatin (e.g., Mycostatin) powder can be dusted on the skin.
Granuloma at G tube site	If small, no intervention is necessary. If problematic, anchor tube over rolled gauze pads to stabilize and reduce irritation at site. Apply silver nitrate carefully.
Tube slips in too far (can cause vomiting or diarrhea)	Check placement of tube regularly with gentle but firm pull. Measure length of tube regularly. Limit risk by anchoring with tape at site and by keeping tube coiled up under clothing.
Tube comes out	Reinsert tube or cover site with gauze and take child to health care provider or emergency facility as soon as possible. Some parents find it helpful to cut off the end of the tube and then insert the tube into the opening. This acts as a stent and keeps the opening the proper size, facilitating reinsertion.

Source: Table prepared with assistance of Liz Riggs, RN, ET, Enterostomal Therapist, Children's Hospital National Medical Center, Washington, D.C.

has an NG tube, the nurse should watch as the parent inserts the tube and *checks its position* prior to a feeding. The position can be checked in two ways: by aspirating for stomach contents and by placing a stethoscope over the infant's stomach and, while quickly injecting 3 cc of air into the NG tube, listening for a popping sound, which indicates correct placement. If not in place, the tube should be removed and repositioned before feeding; a tube placed incorrectly can result in aspiration of formula.

Correct positioning of the infant during tube feedings is important. The infant should be positioned prone, with shoulders higher than feet by at least 30 degrees to facilitate flow of formula through the alimentary tract and to prevent reflux. A sleeping infant can be placed either prone or on the right side, propped by at least 30 degrees. The position should be maintained for 20 to 30 minutes after the feeding.

If the infant is fed by intermittent bolus, feeding should take approximately the same amount of time as for an oral feeding, namely, 20 to 30 minutes. If a pump is not being used, the feeding should run in by gravity. In this case the rapidity of the feeding will be determined by the height of the syringe or bottle. Generally, an appropriate height is 4 inches above the abdomen, although more height may be needed with thicker formulas. The height is important because if the tube is held too high, formula may enter the stomach too fast, causing vomiting, diarrhea, or even overfill with resulting aspiration. If the parent wants both hands free to hold the child, the feeding apparatus can be either hung on a hanger or taped to the wall or crib. Because of the risk of aspiration, it is important that the parent not leave the infant unattended during bolus tube feedings.

If an infant is being fed by continuous infusion, the first visit is an appropriate time to review with parents the instructions for routine operation of the pump and appropriate responses to alarms. The following five principles are important:

1. Positioning, as discussed earlier in this section, will limit the risk of aspiration.
2. To prevent unnecessary infusion of air with the feeding, the drip chamber should be half filled with formula and the entire feeding line completely filled before the tube is attached to the NG or G tube.
3. To prevent spoilage, no more than 4 hours' worth of formula during the day or 8 hours' worth during the night should be hung at one time.[3]
4. Responses to alarms are based on the type of pump; manufacturer instructions should be reviewed with parents.
5. Parents should be within hearing range of the feeding pump alarm; an intercom can be used if the child is in a different room.

The nurse should also assess the parents' confidence in performing the procedures and their comfort in caring for the child during feeding times. It may take time for confidence and comfort to grow, and frequent encouragement during the first several weeks at home can be helpful. During this time, if at all possible, the nurse should be available to visit or to offer phone consultation should any problems arise.

Aspiration is a serious risk with any tube feeding. Steps to prevent aspiration, as well as symptoms and interventions, should be reviewed with parents on the first home visit. During both NG and G tube feedings, appropriate positioning during the feeding (as described previously in this section) is important to prevent aspiration. If at any time during the feeding the child changes color, cannot make noise, or has difficulty in breathing, the feeding should be stopped. With an NG tube, determining proper placement before each feed is also crucial. If the NG tube is accidentally pulled out during the feeding, or if correct placement is uncertain, the parent should reposition the tube before the feeding is resumed and then should remain alert for the signs of aspiration just described. Of course, if aspiration occurs, the physician should be contacted.

SUBSEQUENT VISITS

On each subsequent home visit, it is important to assess the infant's nutritional intake, obtain growth parameters, and, as necessary, observe and review feeding techniques. A history should be obtained about any episodes of vomiting, diarrhea, cramping, or aspiration, and the skin should be assessed for signs of irritation at the nares or at the G tube insertion site. Any parental concerns should also be elicited and addressed. Additional assessment and teaching should address the following issues.

Normalizing the infant's feeding experience, as much as possible, may be important in the prevention of long-term feeding problems. Two aspects of normalization can be reviewed with caregivers. First, in order to assist in maintaining an organized and effective suck and to prevent later oral refusal, caregivers can have the infant suck on a bottle or pacifier during the tube feeding.[4] A pacifier can be used when nutritive sucking is contraindicated or when it is too tiring for the infant. A second aspect of normalizing the feeding experience involves the psychosocial component of feeding. Normal patterns of attachment should be encouraged during each feeding, including holding, cuddling, and talking gently to the infant. (Chapter 5 provides further discussion of the psychosocial component of feeding.)

As a measure to prevent aspiration, checking for *residual stomach contents* prior to a feeding may be important for infants with severe vomiting problems or digestive disorders. As indicated, parents can be instructed in how to check the residual. (It will not be possible, however, to assess accurately stomach residuals when a small-bore NG tube is used.[5]) The nurse should describe and demonstrate the procedure for checking the residual and then watch as caregivers demonstrate the techniques, to assure adequate knowledge.

For checking stomach residuals, the infant should be placed in the supine position. A 20-cc syringe is attached to the end of the tube, and the plunger is pulled; the pull must be gentle to avoid collapsing the tube. Gentle pulling on the plunger is continued until nothing more enters the syringe. The volume of stomach contents in the syringe is called the residual volume; this amount is noted, and then the contents are allowed to flow back into the stomach by gravity. Refeeding the residual prevents loss of fluid and electrolytes. If large volumes of residual remain 1 to 2 hours after a feeding, the next feeding should be delayed. If large-volume residuals persist, a change in formula or in volume of feedings may be indicated.

If medications are given through the feeding tube, or if feedings are intermittent, *clogging of the tube* between feedings may be a problem. Gentle flushing of the tube with several milliliters of water after medications or feedings can prevent this problem. The water should not be forced through the tube; rather, it should be allowed to flow in by gravity. If pressure is necessary to flush the tube, no syringe smaller than 20 cc should be used; smaller syringes exert pressures that can rupture some tubes.[6] If the infant is on a fluid-restricted diet, any water used to flush the tube should be counted as part of the total daily intake. As an alternative method, small amounts of a commercial meat tenderizer (e.g., Accent) dissolved in water or a cola soft drink can be used to clear a clogged tube.[7]

ONGOING CONCERNS

The child's normal daily activities need not be curtailed owing to the use of an NG or G tube. In order to prevent accidental detachment during play, NG or G tubes can be taped securely to the skin or wrapped inside clothing. Other than careful positioning during and after feeding, the infant can be allowed full freedom of movement. The child with a G tube should not be uncomfortable in the prone position, and play in this position should be encouraged. Bathing and tub play are also safe for the infant with the G tube, although parents may need encouragement to be comfortable with this activity.

NOTES

1. Bernbaum JC, Pereira GR, Watkins JB, et al: Nonnutritive sucking during gavage feeding enhances growth and maturation in premature infants, *Pediatrics* 71: 41–45, 1983.

2. Ward J, Children's Hospital National Medical Center, Clinical Nutritional Group, Washington, DC, personal communication, December 1984.

3. Ward J, Robbins S, Riggs L: *Tube Feeding Your Child at Home*, Washington, DC, Children's Hospital National Medical Center, 1983, p 8; Folk CC, Courtney ME: Home tube feedings: general guidelines and specific patient instructions, *Nutr Supp Serv* 2: 19, June 1982. Page and Clibon, on the other hand, suggest that 6 hours is the longest formula should be left hanging at room temperature (Page CP, Clibon V: A method of enterally feeding defined formula diet, *Am J Intrav Ther Clin Nutr*, January 1982, p 29.

4. In a study of premature infants, at a mean age of 10 days, nonnutritive sucking was found to accelerate the maturation of the sucking reflex, decrease intestinal transit time, and cause a more rapid weight gain (see Bernbaum JC: Nonnutritive sucking.)

5. Rogers L, Moss JP, Wright RA: New developments in enteral feeding techniques, *Nutr Supp Serv* 2: 19, October 1982.

6. Folk CC, Courtney ME: Home tube feedings, p 19.

7. Ward J: personal communication, December 1984.

REFERENCES

Bayer LM, Scholl DE, Ford EG: Tube feeding at home. *Am J Nurs*, September 1983, pp 1321–1325.

Bernbaum JC, Pereira GR, Watkins JB, et al: Nonnutritive sucking during gavage feeding enhances growth and maturation in premature infants. *Pediatrics* 71: 41–45, 1983.

Folk C, Courtney ME: Home tube feedings: general guidelines and specific patient instructions. *Nutr Supp Serv* 2: 18–22, June 1982.

Konstantinides NN, Shronts E: Tube feeding: managing the basics. *Am J Nurs*, September 1983, pp 1312–1320.

Leong ET: Care of the tube feeding patient: chance or choice. *Nutr Supp Serv* 1: 32–34, July 1981.

Metheny NL: 20 ways to prevent tube feeding complications. *Nursing '85*, January 1985, pp 47–50.

Murphy L, Hostetler C: Tube feeding reconsidered. *NITA* 4: 409–413, November/December 1981.

Page CP, Clibon V: A method of enterally feeding defined formula diet. *Am J Intrav Clin Nutr*, January 1982, pp 9–20ff.

Piepmeyer J, Lichtenstein V, Moussavian SN, et al: *Tube Feeding at Home*. Evansville, Ind, Mead-Johnson Nutritional Division, 1982.

Rogers L, Moss JP, Wright RA: New developments in enteral feeding techniques. *Nutr Supp Serv* 2: 17–20, October 1982.

Ward J, Robbins S, Riggs L: *Tube Feeding Your Child at Home*. Washington, DC, Children's Hospital National Medical Center, January 1983 (unpublished).

Children's Hospital National Medical Center Home Care Team

Plan of Treatment

Page _____

Date _____ Case Manager _____

Name _____ Hosp# _____ DOB _____

PROBLEM: **G-TUBE FEEDING**

GOALS/OBJECTIVES	METHODS	STAFF/REVIEW
Child will receive prescribed G-tube feeding.	Assess G-tube feeding plan at each visit; confer with primary care provider and dietitian as needed.	
	Assist to obtain needed supplies.	
Caregivers will demonstrate ability to give feeding in appropriate manner via tube.	Observe caregivers administer formula via tube; teach/reinforce skills and safety precautions as needed.	
If continuous infusion pump used, caregivers to describe pump use and appropriate response to pump alarms.	Assess knowledge and teach/reinforce skills and safety precautions as needed.	

GOALS/OBJECTIVES	METHODS	STAFF/REVIEW
Child will be held close and cuddled or otherwise attended to, during feeding.	Assess attachment behavior during feeding and encourage as necessary.	
Child will suck during tube feeding if indicated.	Assess caregivers efforts to encourage sucking. Reinforce as necessary.	
Caregivers will demonstrate appropriate routine stoma care and will describe signs of excoriation and appropriate interventions.	Assess stoma site at each visit. Observe caregivers providing routine stoma care. Assess knowledge of signs of excoriation and interventions. Teach/ reinforce as needed. Contact surgeon or primary care provider as needed re: excoriation/ granuloma formation.	
Caregivers will correctly describe technique for reinsertion of G-tube and for assessment of correct position.	Assess knowledge. Teach/ reinforce as necessary.	
Caregivers will describe/ demonstrate appropriate plan for cleaning supplies.	Assess knowledge. Teach/ reinforce as necessary.	

Source: Reprinted with permission of Home Care Program, (Ahmann, Lierman, and Peck), Children's Hospital National Medical Center, Washington, D.C.

Children's Hospital National Medical Center Home Care Team

Plan of Treatment

Page _____

Date _____ Case Manager _____
Name _____ Hosp# _____ DOB _____

PROBLEM: **NASOGASTRIC FEEDING**

GOALS/OBJECTIVES	METHODS	STAFF/REVIEW
Child will receive prescribed NG feeding.	Assess NG feeding plan at each visit; confer with primary care provider and dietitian as needed.	
	Assist to obtain supplies needed.	
Caregivers will demonstrate appropriate safe technique for passage of tube and for assessment of correct position.	Observe caregivers pass tube and check position. Teach/reinforce skills as needed.	
Caregivers will demonstrate ability to give feeding in appropriate manner via tube.	Observe caregivers administer formula via tube; teach/reinforce skills and safety precautions as needed.	

GOALS/OBJECTIVES	METHODS	STAFF/REVIEW
If continuous infusion pump used, caregivers to describe use of pump appropriate response to pump alarms.	Assess knowledge and teach/reinforce as needed.	
Caregivers will describe s/sx of appropriate interventions.	Assess knowledge and teach/reinforce as needed.	
Child will be held close and cuddled or otherwise attended to, during feeding.	Assess attachment behavior during feeding and encourage as necessary.	
Child will suck during tube feeding if indicated.	Assess caregivers efforts to encourage sucking. Reinforce as necessary.	
Child's nares will be without excoriation. Caregivers will demonstrate ability to assess nares for excoriation and will describe appropriate care measures.	Assess nares each visit. Teach/reinforce care as needed. Contact primary care provider prn re: excoriation.	
Caregivers will describe/ demonstrate appropriate plan for cleaning supplies.	Assess knowledge. Teach/ reinforce prn.	

Source: Reprinted with permission of Home Care Program (Ahmann, Lierman, and Peck), Children's Hospital National Medical Center, Washington, D.C.

Chapter 7

Home Care of the Infant with Respiratory Compromise

This chapter discusses principles and procedures applicable to respiratory compromise of any etiology. The general principles are illustrated by frequent reference to bronchopulmonary dysplasia, a lung disease commonly associated with prematurity.

DESCRIPTION OF THE PROBLEM

Many preterm infants are born with lungs insufficiently developed for ventilation and oxygenation in the absence of mechanical support and supplemental oxygen. However, with use of these measures, the lungs are subjected to high airway pressures and high concentrations of oxygen over a prolonged period of time. In the lung tissue of premature infants, these treatment modes can cause pathophysiologic changes, leading to diminished pulmonary function. The resulting complex of pathologic changes in the lungs of these infants is called bronchopulmonary dysplasia (BPD).

The changes of BPD do not, of course, occur all at once. Changes that occur in the lung over time can include anatomic changes, resultant physiologic changes, and ultimately alterations in pulmonary function. In some cases, the pulmonary disorder can also lead to cor pulmonale. Even when the lungs are growing and new portions develop, pulmonary physiology and function remain abnormal. Some studies suggest that most children who have BPD will have abnormal findings on chest x-ray films and pulmonary function tests until they are 6 to 9 years of age.[1]

In planning home care for an infant with BPD, the following problems, for which summary treatment descriptions are provided, may need to be addressed:

Note: Appendix 7–A contains a standard home care plan for the infant with respiratory compromise. Appendix 7–C contains a home care plan for the infant with cardiac compromise.

1. *hyperreactive airways disease and small airways disease:* The use of oral or nebulized bronchodilators may be necessary.
2. *hypoxemia:* Short- or long-term oxygen therapy may be required (see Chapter 9).
3. *retained secretions:* Chest therapy, suctioning, and humidity are indicated treatments.
4. *infections:* Pneumonias may occur every two to three months in the first year and may require rehospitalization to treat.
5. *Cor pulmonale and fluid retention:* Treatment with administration of digoxin, diuretics, and sodium chloride and fluid restriction may be necessary. (Cor pulmonale is discussed in more detail later in the chapter.)

HOSPITAL DISCHARGE AND TRANSITION TO THE HOME

When the infant with respiratory compromise is discharged from the hospital, coordination between the community health nurse and the hospital staff is important to ensure continuity of care for the infant and family. The nurse should obtain information about the infant's hospital course, baseline vital signs, discharge medications, care instructions, and plans for follow-up. In addition, information regarding parents' knowledge about the infant's condition and care, their level of confidence with providing care, and any further teaching and support measures recommended by hospital staff can assist in development of an appropriate home care plan.

Coordination prior to discharge is also important to ensure that *emergency preparations* have been made. One important emergency preparation is having a telephone in the home. If a telephone cannot be obtained, an alternate plan for getting help in an emergency should be worked out. For example, if a neighbor is available during the day, the infant can be "football carried" to the neighbor's home during CPR, and the rescue squad called by the neighbor. It must be stressed, however, that this plan is not optimal, and every effort should be made to obtain a telephone in the infant's home.

A second emergency preparation involves notification of the telephone and electric companies that the family needs to be on a priority service list. This means that the companies will notify the family of any anticipated interruptions of service. Similarly, prior personal contact with rescue squad and emergency facility personnel and provision of written information to these agencies can help to ensure prompt and appropriate emergency interventions, if necessary. Appendix A at the end of this book contains sample form letters that can be used for each of these notifications.

As an additional preliminary step, the nurse should review emergency precautions with the parents. These precautions include posting CPR guidelines at the

Exhibit 7–1 Emergency Information Listing

Post this information near each telephone in the home:

1. Rescue squad number   _____

2. Emergency facility number   _____

3. Physician number: day   _____

   evening   _____

4. Nurse number   _____

5. Equipment supplier number   _____

6. Electric company emergency number _____

7. Home address   _____

                                _____

8. Nearest intersection   _____

9. Home phone   _____

infant's bedside and also a list of emergency telephone numbers and other important information near all telephones in the home, as shown in Exhibit 7–1. The home address and closest intersection or cross street should be included in case a babysitter must make an emergency call or parents panic and forget.

ROUTINE HOME VISITS

On every home visit, temperature, pulse, and respiratory rate—should be obtained and recorded. Each infant will have unique baseline values for these vital signs. It should be noted that the respiratory rate may increase after feeding, with changes in position, with activity, or with crying, and that the respiratory rate and pulse will usually be lower during sleep times. However, values above or below the infant's baseline values, when not attributable to activity or emotional stress, may signify respiratory or cardiac compromise. Caregivers themselves may wish to learn assessment of vital signs, particularly if they live in a rural area far from medical assistance.

Lung auscultation should be performed on each home visit. The stethoscope should be placed directly and firmly on the skin of the infant's chest to avoid the sound of skin or clothes rubbing. Auscultation should proceed from side to side and from top to bottom over the anterior, posterior, and lateral chest wall areas.

Table 7–1 Adventitious Lung Sounds Common in BPD

Sound	Description
Wheezes	Continuous sounds or vibrations produced by airflow through smaller airways that are narrowed by constriction, mucosal swelling, secretions, and so on Generally high-pitched More prominent during expiration, but may also be heard during inspiration If mild, may clear with coughing
Rhonchi	Continuous sounds or vibrations produced by airflow through larger airways that are narrowed by mucosal swelling, secretions, and so on Generally low-pitched More prominent during expiration, but may also be heard during inspiration If mild, may clear with coughing
Rales	Discrete, discontinuous, bubbling sounds produced by moisture in the airways May be fine or coarse Usually heard during inspiration, and sometimes only in the dependent portions of the lung. (Note that in the infant, the dependent areas may not necessarily be the lower lobes.) If mild, may clear with coughing

Source: Bates B: *A Guide to Physical Examination*, ed 2. Philadelphia, JB Lippincott Co, 1973, p 134.

Auscultation from side to side allows comparison of sounds in one lobe or area with those in the contralateral lobe or area. The general quality of breath sounds, as well as the presence or absence of adventitious sounds, should be noted, as indicated in the following descriptions:

- quality: During auscultation, the lengths of the inspiratory and expiratory phases should be compared. With BPD, the expiratory phase may be relatively prolonged. Decreased breath sounds and poor movement of air, in any or all lobes, may signal distress.
- adventitious sounds: All lobes of the lung should be auscultated to assess for wheezes, rhonchi, and rales; these sounds are described in Table 7–1. *Wheezes* may be noted in the infant with hyperreactive airways disease and may be more pronounced during an exacerbation. *Rhonchi* are common in the infant with BPD and may signify increased or thickened secretions. *Rales* may signify pneumonia or edema and fluid overload.

There is some disagreement among published definitions of the terms wheezes, rhonchi, and rales.[2] Therefore, for the purpose of effective communication with physicians and others involved in the care of the infant, it is important that the nurse use a consistent system of nomenclature and be able to describe clearly the adventitious sounds noted.

Each infant will have some unique characteristic lung sounds; auscultation during several visits will allow the establishment of a relative baseline. If caregivers desire, they can be taught to auscultate the lungs and to differentiate lung sounds.

Signs and symptoms of respiratory distress should also be assessed on each visit. The infant's alertness and level of activity are important indicators of overall status. Retractions, nasal flaring, pallor, cyanosis, edema, or diaphoresis may signal distress. Irritability and loss of appetite should also be noted. Caregivers should be instructed to look for these signs and symptoms; they should also be given guidelines, developed in conjunction with the physician, identifying circumstances that require medical advice.

In addition, on each home visit, the infant's *respiratory secretions* should be assessed for amount, consistency, color, and odor. An increase in amount or viscosity of secretions, a yellow-green color, or a foul odor may signify infection. Caregivers should be instructed to contact the infant's physician should they notice any of these changes. (Measures that can be taken to limit the risk of infection are discussed later in this chapter.)

A further aspect of the infant's care that should be explored on each home visit is the *medication regimen*. The nurse should regularly both question the parent about and observe the infant for any medication side effects (see Appendix 7–B). Parental awareness of the purpose of each medication and of medication side effects is also important. Written information may assist caregivers in learning and remembering these details.

THE FIRST HOME VISIT

On the first home visit, all aspects of the routine home visit should be addressed. In addition, parental provision of safe and appropriate care of the infant with respiratory compromise must be determined.

On the first visit, and subsequently as necessary, all *medications* should be reviewed. Infants with BPD (or other respiratory compromise) may be on any combination of bronchodilators, digoxin, diuretics, electrolytes, and steroids (see Appendix 7–B). The dose and concentration on each bottle should be carefully compared with those prescribed. Since small errors can have a significant effect on an infant, the parents' ability to measure prescribed doses correctly should also be assessed. In this connection, labeling syringes for each medication with a piece of tape marking the dosage line can often aid in ensuring accuracy.

Medication schedules should also be reviewed with parents on the first home visit. Schedules may be complex since some infants with multiple problems may be on as many as 10 to 12 medications a day. Medication schedules at home should be tailored, as much as possible, to the family's daily schedule; minimizing night-time doses and grouping medications at several times during the day can be very helpful. If the schedule is still unreasonable, it may be appropriate to ask the physician to consider altering the frequency of doses or perhaps eliminating some medications if the infant has been stable for some time. Some parents may be assisted by a medication checklist, as illustrated in Exhibit 7–2.

Parental techniques for administering nebulized medications should also be assessed, and the appropriate technique reviewed as necessary. Nebulized medications can be administered through a hand nebulizer or a compressor-powered nebulizer. The compressor will provide the prolonged administration time that may be most effective in the very narrow airways of the infant.

For administration of nebulized medications with a compressor, the medication is inserted into the cup with the prescribed diluent, and the mask, T piece, or other delivery device is attached. The tubing is then attached to both the nebulizer and the source of air or oxygen. Baseline values for vital signs are obtained for the purpose of comparison with values obtained both several minutes after commencement of treatment and at the conclusion of treatment. (A pulse of more than 230 in infants, or more than 200 in older children, or persistent tachycardia indicates a need to contact the physician.[3]) Coughing and suctioning are encouraged during treatments as necessary. The treatment is continued until all of the solution has been inhaled, generally for 10 to 20 minutes. Some infants, however, may need rest periods partway through treatment. If the infant is also receiving oxygen, the oxygen distributor or respiratory therapist may be able to arrange an equipment set-up allowing the oxygen and the nebulized medication to be delivered simultaneously.

In addition to giving medications to the infant with BPD, parents must provide regular *chest therapy* to ensure that secretions are not retained in the lungs. On the first home visit, the nurse should observe the parents while they administer chest therapy and, as necessary, should provide instruction in the appropriate positions, techniques, and schedule. Discussion followed by demonstration and parents' return demonstration may facilitate optimal routine performance of chest therapy.

Accurate positioning during chest therapy is necessary to encourage the drainage of secretions from each lobe of the lung. (Positions are illustrated in Figure 7–1.) Percussing, or clapping with a cupped hand, will assist in loosening secretions; percussing for 1 minute in each position is generally recommended. Chest therapy is provided as frequently as needed to clear secretions, usually after nebulizer treatments or before feeds, or both. Chest therapy should be more frequent if the infant has a cold or respiratory distress with either increased or more viscous secretions.

Exhibit 7–2 Sample Weekly Medication Checklist

TIME	MEDICATION	SUN	MON	TUES	WED	THURS	FRI	SAT
6am	Quibron 5.5cc							
	Metaprel Aerosol 0.15cc in 2.5cc NS*							
7am	Aldactazide 1.5cc							
	Sodium Chloride 10cc							
11am	Quibron 5.5cc							
	Prednisone 3mg							
	Ammonium Chloride 4cc							
	Phenobarbital 4cc							
12noon	Metaprel Aerosol 0.15cc in 2.5cc NS							
3pm	Sodium Chloride 10cc							
	Potassium Chloride 3cc							
5pm	Quibron 5.5cc							
6pm	Metaprel Aerosol 0.15cc in 2.5cc NS							
11pm	Quibron 5.5cc							
	Prednisone 3mg							
	Ammonium Chloride 4cc							
	Phenobarbital 4cc							
	Aldactazide 1.5cc							
	Sodium Chloride 10cc							
12mn	Metaprel Aerosol 0.15cc in 2.5cc NS							

*NS = normal (physiologic) saline.

Figure 7–1 Chest Therapy Positions

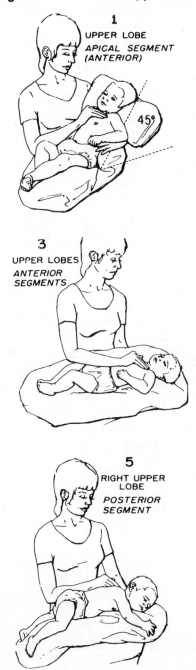

1
UPPER LOBE
*APICAL SEGMENT
(ANTERIOR)*
45°

2
UPPER LOBE
*APICAL SEGMENT
(POSTERIOR)*
45°

3
UPPER LOBES
*ANTERIOR
SEGMENTS*

4
LOWER LOBES
*APICAL
SEGMENTS*

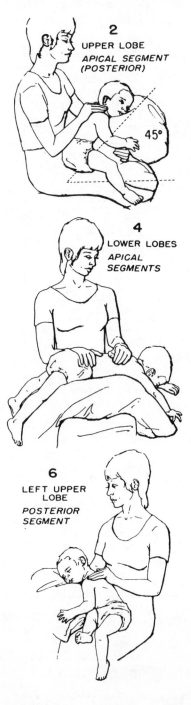

5
RIGHT UPPER
LOBE
*POSTERIOR
SEGMENT*

6
LEFT UPPER
LOBE
*POSTERIOR
SEGMENT*

Figure 7–1 continued

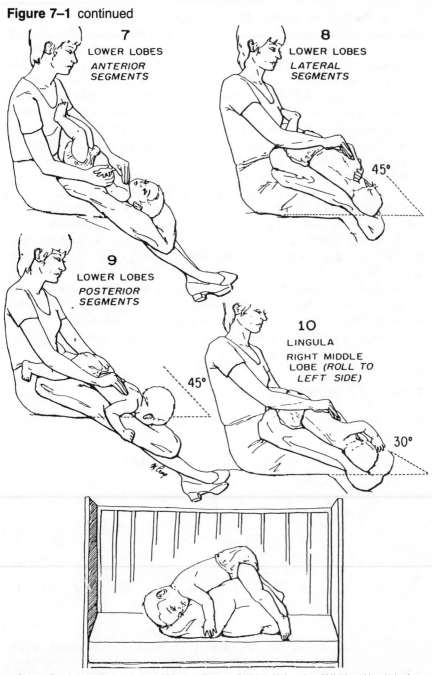

7
LOWER LOBES
*ANTERIOR
SEGMENTS*

8
LOWER LOBES
*LATERAL
SEGMENTS*

45°

9
LOWER LOBES
*POSTERIOR
SEGMENTS*

45°

10
LINGULA
RIGHT MIDDLE
LOBE *(ROLL TO
LEFT SIDE)*

30°

Source: Reprinted with permission of Physical Therapy Division, University of Michigan Hospitals, Ann Arbor, Mich.

Suctioning is another component of care important for the infant with BPD or other respiratory compromise. Caregivers' suction techniques should be assessed for both adequacy and safety, and instructions should be offered as necessary in appropriate techniques. Suctioning should always follow chest therapy. In addition, suctioning should be done when secretions fill the oropharynx or nasopharynx; when secretions increase in amount or viscosity; when the presence of fluids is audible; or when the infant exhibits either respiratory distress or poor color. Saline drops can be instilled prior to suctioning to loosen secretions.

For some infants with a strong cough, a bulb syringe will be adequate for suctioning (see Figure 7–2). For this procedure, the syringe is squeezed before insertion into the nose or mouth and then slowly released to withdraw secretions. The syringe should be cleaned with a saline solution between each use.

Many infants will need deeper catheter suctioning to remove secretions. If a suction machine is in the home, its proper functioning should be determined on the first home visit. For this procedure, the catheter is first connected to the machine and then inserted gently through the nostril with no suction applied. The catheter may be inserted until a cough reflex is stimulated. Suction is applied with gentle rotation and slow withdrawal of the catheter for no more than 5 seconds; harsh suctioning is avoided because of potential bleeding and tissue damage. The infant should be allowed at least 3 to 5 breaths, and color should be regained, between each pass of the catheter. The catheter is cleaned with saline between each pass,

---

Figure 7–2 Portable Mouth Suction and Bulb Syringe

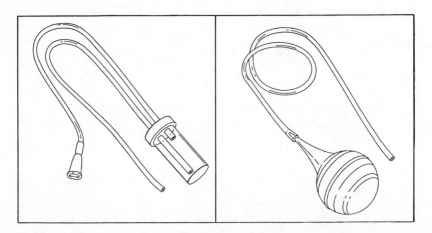

Source: Reprinted from *Home Care of Your Child with a Tracheostomy: A Parent Handbook* by P. Hennessy (Ed.), p. 9, with permission of Children's Hospital National Medical Center, Washington, D.C., © 1983.

and suctioning is repeated until the oronasopharynx is clear, but for no more than three passes.[4] A DeLee, or mouth, suction device should always be available in case of electrical failure, and caregivers should understand its use, as well as that of the suction machine. (The DeLee syringe is illustrated in Figure 7–2.)

SUBSEQUENT HOME VISITS

Home visits should generally begin by addressing any problems or concerns identified by parents. At the same time, however, the nurse should have a plan in mind for ongoing assessment and teaching. The plan should address not only those areas described for the first home visit and routine visits but also the following specific aspects of care.

Infants with BPD, particularly if the disease is moderate to severe, are at high risk for frequent *infections* throughout their first 1 to 1½ years of life. This risk should be discussed with parents, in part to eliminate or minimize unnecessary guilt if rehospitalization does become necessary. In addition, simple principles for limiting the risk of infection can be reviewed. These principles include limiting the infant's exposure to persons with an upper respiratory infection, and cleaning respiratory care equipment regularly and thoroughly (as discussed in Appendix A at the end of this book). Of course, nurses should advise parents to observe the infant routinely for early signs of an infection: a change in secretions, respiratory pattern, or respiratory rate; irritability; and a loss of appetite. The physician should be notified if these signs are observed.

The nurse should also assess parental knowledge of the *signs and symptoms of respiratory distress*: tachypnea, nasal flaring, retractions, tachycardia, and cyanosis. Signs and symptoms should be reviewed as necessary, and as discussed earlier in this chapter, caregivers should be given guidelines detailing what signs and symptoms indicate the need for medical consultation. Plans for emergency interventions should be assessed, and assistance provided as necessary in developing appropriate plans. As part of emergency planning, CPR technique should be reviewed regularly. Verbal recall is best supplemented by caregiver demonstration to assure correct technique.

Teaching on subsequent home visits should also be directed toward helping parents become knowledgeable about their infant's condition. Their knowledge of pulmonary anatomy and physiology and of the pathophysiology, clinical manifestations, and clinical course of BPD, as well as the reason for each intervention (e.g., chest physiotherapy, suctioning), should be assessed. Any gaps in knowledge or understanding can be filled by teaching that uses discussion, drawings, written materials, and repetition, as necessary. In general, a knowledgeable caregiver is a more confident caregiver.

Since nutrition and growth are often problem areas for infants with BPD, the nurse should perform an assessment of *nutritional intake and growth parameters* on all home visits. Because of the work of breathing, as well as feeding difficulties that may result from respiratory compromise, ensuring adequate calorie intake to promote growth may be a challenge. Parents will often be very concerned about poor growth patterns. The nurse should both assure them that slow growth is not uncommon with BPD and assist them to do whatever possible to encourage optimal nutritional intake in the infant. Chapters 5 and 6 provide an in-depth discussion of nutrition and feeding.

The initial weeks after hospital discharge are generally the most anxiety-provoking for parents of an infant with respiratory compromise. Bonding may have been disrupted owing to prolonged hospitalization; degree of concern for the infant's safety and health is high; and fear of making mistakes in the infant's care is pronounced. Encouragement and support by the nurse during the initial weeks at home can help to build confidence in parents.

COR PULMONALE

Cor pulmonale is a form of heart disease, in which the right ventricle becomes enlarged. Cor pulmonale can result from underlying pulmonary disease. Home care of the infant with cor pulmonale is based on plans for appropriate respiratory management, prevention of infection, and cardiac management. If cor pulmonale is present without congestive heart failure (CHF), cardiac management is aimed at reducing the overload of the right ventricle and improving its functioning. Diuretics and digoxin may be used, and fluid restriction may be necessary in some cases. The reader is referred to other resources for an in-depth discussion of care of the infant with cardiac compromise. However, two aspects of care must be stressed here: medication administration and observation for signs and symptoms of CHF.

Exact measurement of medications is essential with infants owing to the small margin between therapeutic and toxic doses of both digoxin and diuretics. Observing parents administer medications on one or more visits provides the opportunity to access accuracy of dosage measurements. Unless the infant's cardiac condition is very unstable, it is generally unnecessary to have parents check the apical pulse prior to digoxin administration.[5] However, guidelines for digoxin administration (see Exhibit 7–3) and *signs of digoxin toxicity* should be reviewed. In infants and young children, the earliest sign of digoxin toxicity is usually vomiting, often with nausea and anorexia. Although extracardiac signs can occur, they are less easily assessed in this age group.

The infant with cor pulmonale is always at risk of developing CHF. CHF occurs when the heart is unable to pump sufficient blood to the systemic circulation to meet the metabolic demands of the body. CHF can lead to, but is distinct from, true myocardial failure. Because of the risk of CHF, the nurse should observe for signs and symptoms at each home visit; these are listed in Exhibit 7–4. In addition, the nurse should assess parental knowledge of these signs and symptoms and then

Exhibit 7–3 Guidelines for Administering Digoxin

1. Give digoxin at regular intervals, usually every 12 hours, such as 8 AM and 8 PM.
2. Plan the times so that the drug is given *1 hour before* or *2 hours* after feedings.
3. Use a calendar to mark off each dose that is given, or post a reminder, such as a sign on the refrigerator.
4. Have the prescription refilled *before* the medication is completely used.
5. Administer the drug carefully by slowly squirting it on the side and back of the mouth.
6. Do not mix it with other foods or fluids, since refusal to consume these results in inaccurate intake of the drugs.
7. If the child has teeth, give him water after administering the drug; whenever possible, brush the teeth to prevent tooth decay from the sweetened liquid.
8. If a dose is missed and more than 6 hours has elapsed, withhold the dose and give the next dose at the regular time; if less than 6 hours has elapsed, give the missed dose.
9. If the child vomits within 15 minutes of receiving the digoxin, repeat the dose *once*; if more than 15 minutes has elapsed, do not give a second dose.
10. If more than two consecutive doses have been missed, notify the physician.
11. Do not increase or double the dose for missed doses.
12. If the child becomes ill, notify the physician immediately.
13. Keep digoxin in a safe place, preferably a locked cabinet.
14. In case of accidental overdose of digoxin, call the nearest poison control center immediately.

Source: Reprinted from *Nursing Care of Infants and Children*, 2d ed., by L.F. Whaley and D.L. Wong, p. 1325, with permission of The C.V. Mosby Company, © 1983.

Exhibit 7–4 Clinical Manifestations of CHF*

Cardiovascular	Respiratory
Tachycardia (sleeping, apical pulse of 140–160)	Tachypnea
Precordial impulse	Dyspnea, orthopnea
Gallop rhythm	Retractions
Nasal flaring	Enlarged liver
Periorbital edema	Grunting respirations
Rapid weight gain	Fine rales
Peripheral cyanosis	
Distended neck veins (rare)	

Related
Feeding difficulties, anorexia
Diaphoresis
Oliguria
Irritability
Fatigability

*Some of these signs in isolation may resemble characteristics of the underlying respiratory problem; therefore, it is important to perform an overall assessment of the infant.

provide augmentative education as needed. Parents should also be instructed to seek medical attention at the first signs of CHF. Although mild CHF may be managed at home in some cases, CHF will generally require hospitalization during the acute phase.

NOTES

1. Various studies of infants surviving hyaline membrane disease (HMD), BPD, or idiopathic respiratory distress syndrome (IRDS) indicate that clinical symptoms or radiographic changes, or both, may be noted for up to 6 to 9 years: Lamarre A: Residual pulmonary abnormalities in survivors of idiopathic respiratory distress syndrome, *Am Rev Resp Dis* 108: 60, 1973, Taussig LM, Lemen RJ: Chronic obstructive lung disease, *Adv Pediatr* 26: 384, 1979; and Thurlbeck WM: Postnatal growth and development of the lung, *Am Rev Resp Dis* 111: 803–844, 1975.

2. For example, the definitions in Table 7–1 are generally in agreement with those suggested by the American College of Chest Physicians and American Thoracic Society Joint Committee on Pulmonary Nomenclature, except that the Joint Committee does not distinguish between wheezes and rhonchi; see American College of Chest Physicians and American Thoracic Society Joint Committee on Pulmonary Nomenclature: Pulmonary terms and symbols, *Chest* 67: 583–586, 1975.

3. Procedure for administering nebulized medications, in *Policy and Procedure Manual, IV*, Washington, DC, Children's Hospital National Medical Center, Division of Nursing and Operations, Home Care Program, undated (unpublished).

4. Procedure for nasal & oral suctioning, in *Policy and Procedure Manual, IV*, Washington, DC, Children's Hospital National Medical Center, Division of Nursing and Operations, Home Care Programs, undated (unpublished).

5. Clare M, Children's Hospital National Medical Center, Washington, DC: personal communication, 1985.

REFERENCES

American College of Chest Physicians and American Thoracic Society Joint Committee on Pulmonary Nomenclature: Pulmonary terms and symbols. *Chest* 67: 583–593, 1975.

Avery ME, Fletcher BD, Williams RG: *The Lung and Its Disorders in the Newborn Infant*, ed 4. Philadelphia, WB Saunders Co, 1981, pp 263–274.

Bates B: *A Guide to Physical Examination*, ed 2. Philadelphia, JB Lippincott Co, 1979.

Bell CW: Blodgell D, Goike CA, et al: *Home Care and Rehabilitation in Respiratory Medicine*. Philadelphia, JB Lippincott Co, 1984.

Brashear RE, Rhodes ML (eds): *Chronic Obstructive Lung Disease*. St Louis, CV Mosby Co, 1978.

Brunner LS, Suddarth DS (eds): *The Lippincott Manual of Nursing Practice*, ed 3. Philadelphia, JB Lippincott Co, 1982, Chapters 9, 41.

Daly WJ: Pathogenesis and treatment of cor pulmonale, in Brashear RE, Rhodes ML (eds): *Chronic Obstructive Lung Disease*. St Louis, CV Mosby Co, 1978, p 177.

Ehrenkranz RA, Warshaw JB: Chronic lung disease in the newborn, in Stern L (ed): *Diagnosis and Management of Respiratory Disorders in the Newborn*. Reading, Mass, Addison-Wesley Publishing Co, 1983, pp 84–109.

Graham G, Ross E: *Heart Disease in Infants and Children*. Chicago, Year Book Medical Publishers Inc, 1980.

Lamarre A: Residual pulmonary abnormalities in survivors of idiopathic respiratory distress syndrome. *Am Rev Resp Dis* 108: 57–61, 1973.

Moller JH, Neal WA: *Heart Disease in Infancy.* New York, Appleton-Century-Crofts, 1981.

Nursing '82 Drug Handbook. Springfield, Pa., Intermed Communications Inc, 1982.

Physicians' Desk Reference, ed 39. Oradell, NJ, Medical Economics Co Inc, 1985.

Pinney MA, Cotton EK: Home management of broncho-pulmonary dysplasia. *Pediatrics* 58: 856–859, 1976.

Policy and Procedure Manual, IV. Washington, D.C., Children's Hospital National Medical Center, Division of Nursing and Operations, Home Care Program, undated (unpublished).

Taussig LM, Lemen RJ: Chronic obstructive lung disease. *Adv Pediatr* 26: 343–416, 1979.

Voyles JB: Broncho-pulmonary dysplasia. *Am J Nurs*, March 1981, pp 510–514.

Whaley LF, Wong DL: *Nursing Care of Infants and Children*, ed 2. St Louis, CV Mosby Co, 1983, Chapter 35.

Children's Hospital
National Medical Center
Home Care Team

Plan of Treatment

Page _____

Date _____ Case Manager _____

Name _____ Hosp# _____ DOB _____

PROBLEM: **RESPIRATORY COMPROMISE**

GOALS/OBJECTIVES	METHODS	STAFF/REVIEW
Child to be at minimal risk for respiratory distress.	Assess pulse and respiratory rate each visit.	
	Auscultate lungs.	
	Observe for signs/ symptoms of respiratory distress.	
	Assess for appropriate use of medications, including nebulized treatments if prescribed; review/teach as necessary.	
	Assist caregivers in arranging a workable medication schedule.	
	Assess for side effects of medications and teach caregivers the same.	
	Assess caregivers' skill with chest therapy; teach/ review as needed.	

GOALS/OBJECTIVES	METHODS	STAFF/REVIEW
	Assess caregivers' skill with suctioning; teach/ review as needed.	
	Observe for signs of fluid retention.	
	If fluid restriction prescribed, review daily fluid intake each visit. Teach caregivers reason for fluid restriction and signs of retention.	
Caregivers to verbalize an understanding of BPD.	Assess knowledge of pulmonary anatomy/ physiology, patho-physiology of BPD, clinical manifestations, and clinical course of BPD. Teach/reinforce as needed.	
Caregivers to verbalize signs/symptoms of respiratory distress and to have appropriate plans for intervention.	Assess knowledge of signs/symptoms of respiratory distress. Teach/review as needed.	
	Assess plans for emergency intervention and assist in developing as needed.	
	Ensure that phone and electric companies, rescue squad and emergency departments are aware of child's status.	
	Assess caregivers' ability to provide CPR competently; teach/review regularly.	

GOALS/OBJECTIVES	METHODS	STAFF/REVIEW
	Review with caregivers the indications for calling doctor and/or rescue squad.	
Infant will be at limited risk for congestive heart failure.	Assess pulse and respiratory rate each visit.	
	Assess for signs and symptoms of cardiac failure each visit.	
	If medications prescribed, assess for appropriate use and observe for side effects/toxic effects.	
	Teach precautions to prevent infection and importance of early intervention if signs of infection develop.	
Caregivers will verbalize accurate knowledge of s/sx congestive heart failure.	Assess knowledge and teach/review prn.	
Caregivers will be prepared for possibility of frequent hospitalizations.	Educate and provide emotional support related to possible need for frequent hospitalizations.	
Child to have regular and prn follow-up by physician managing pulmonary status.	Encourage regular and prn appointments.	
	Communicate/coordinate with managing physician(s) on a regular basis and as needed for problems.	

Source: Reprinted with permission of Home Care Program (Ahmann, Lierman, and Peck), Children's Hospital National Medical Center, Washington, D.C.

Medications Used
in the Management of BPD

MEDICATION*	USE	COMMON SIDE EFFECTS
Bronchodilators	For bronchospasm or hyperreactive airways disease (several bronchodilators may be used in combination)	
Xanthine derivatives Aminophylline Theophylline Oxytriphylline Dyphylline		Restlessness, dizziness, insomnia, palpitations, tachycardia, nausea, vomiting, anorexia
Adrenergic antagonists Ephedrine Metaproterenol Terbutaline Albuterol		Insomnia, nervousness, tremor, palpitations, tachycardia
Adrenergic nebulized bronchodilators Epinephrine Isoproterenol Isoethamine (may be combined with other agents)		Insomnia, nervousness, tremor, hypertension, palpitations, tachycardia, especially during treatment

MEDICATION*	USE	COMMON SIDE EFFECTS
Digitalis	For cor pulmonale complicating BPD	Fatigue, muscle weakness, agitation, blurred vision, anorexia, nausea, cardiotoxicity
Diuretics	For fluid retention with cor pulmonale	Dehydration, electrolyte imbalances
Electrolytes	For electrolyte replacement during diuretic therapy, as indicated (sodium and potassium are those commonly required)	
Sodium		Gagging (because of taste), vomiting
Potassium		With overdosage leading to hyperkalemia, cardiotoxic effects, as well as nausea, vomiting, and abdominal pain

*For specifics on a particular medication, or for full range of side effects, contraindications, and drug interactions, consult the *Physicians' Desk Reference*, listed in References for this chapter.

Children's Hospital
National Medical Center
Home Care Team

Plan of Treatment

Page _____

Date _____ Case Manager _____

Name _____ Hosp# _____ DOB _____

PROBLEM: **CARDIAC COMPROMISE**

GOALS/OBJECTIVES	METHODS	STAFF/REVIEW
Child will be at limited risk for cardiac failure.	Monitor vital signs; and monitor for signs and symptoms of cardiac failure each visit.	
If medications prescribed, caregivers will demonstrate correct administration of medications, will state knowledge of purpose side effects and toxic effects.	Monitor for side effects/ toxic effects each visit. Assess caregivers for correct administration of prescribed medications. Stress critical nature of exact doses. Review medication schedule for appropriacy to family schedule Assess knowledge of medications including purpose, side effects and toxic effects; teach/review prn.	

GOALS/OBJECTIVES	METHODS	STAFF/REVIEW
Caregivers will verbalize accurate knowledge of signs/symptoms of cardiac failure.	Assess knowledge and teach/review prn.	
Caregivers will state suitable plans for emergency intervention.	Emphasize posting cardiologist phone number for easy access.	
	Assess caregivers' plans for emergency intervention; assist in developing prn.	
	Ensure that appropriate rescue squads/emergency rooms have been notified of child's status.	
Child will be at limited risk of infection.	Teach caregivers that cardiac failure can be precipitated by an infection.	
	Review precautions to prevent infection (avoid exposure to persons with infections, handwashing).	
	Stress the importance of early intervention should any signs of infection develop.	
Child will demonstrate acceptable growth patterns.	Assess growth parameters and nutritional status on regular basis.	
	Assess feeding patterns for use of soft nipple with large hole and small frequent meals; reinforce, if necessary.	

GOALS/OBJECTIVES	METHODS	STAFF/REVIEW
	If persistent inadequate growth, confer with dietitian/pediatrician/ cardiologist re: increased calories and/ or tube feeding, prn.	
Child will have regular cardiology follow-up.	Encourage regular appointments with cardiologist.	
	Coordinate/communicate with cardiologist prn.	

Source: Reprinted with permission of Home Care Program (Ahmann, Lierman, and Peck), Children's Hospital National Medical Center, Washington, D.C.

Chapter 8

Home Care of the Infant on an Apnea Monitor

Infants may require apnea monitoring as a part of the management of a variety of problems: respiratory compromise of various causes; tracheostomy use; a family history of apnea or sudden infant death; and documented apnea. Apnea is relatively common in premature infants, and will be discussed in some detail in this chapter. However, the principles and procedures related to use of the apnea monitor are applicable when the monitor is used for any reason.

DESCRIPTION OF THE PROBLEM

Aranda and colleagues have described *apnea* as "the cessation of breathing for more than 20 . . . or 30 sec. . . . [Apnea] is observed in 25% of neonates weighing less than 2500 g at birth . . . the incidence varies inversely with fetal maturity to as high as 84% in preterm neonates weighing less than 1000 g at birth."[1]

Apnea should be differentiated from *periodic breathing,* a frequent and normal finding in premature infants. Periodic breathing, as defined by Korones, "is characterized by sporadic episodes in which respirations cease for up to 10 seconds. Periodic breathing is not associated with cyanosis or bradycardia. . . . [whereas] apneic episodes . . . are of longer duration [and] often cause generalized cyanosis."[2]

Apnea can be classified as central, obstructive, or mixed. In *central* apnea, no movement of the abdominal or thoracic respiratory muscles occurs, and airflow is absent. In *obstructive* apnea, there is movement of respiratory muscles but no air exchange. *Mixed* apnea is a combination of central followed by obstructive apnea.

Note: Appendix 8–A contains a standard home care plan for the infant on an apnea monitor. Appendix 8–B contains a home assessment form that may be useful in data collection and record keeping.

All three types of apnea can occur in premature infants as well as term infants. The long-term prognosis for each type is uncertain. A number of factors can contribute to or provoke apneic spells:

- extreme immaturity
- hypoxia or hypoxemia related to airway obstruction, pulmonary disease, anemia, or congestive heart failure
- CNS disorders including intraventricular hemorrhage (IVH), seizures, and other pathologic conditions
- metabolic alterations disturbing central nervous system metabolism, including hypoglycemia, hypocalcemia, hyperbilirubinemia, and acidosis
- infections (including colds) and fevers
- Valsalva maneuvers
- vasovagal stimulation (e.g., insertion of a feeding tube).

Apneic episodes may be accompanied by bradycardia, a rise and subsequent fall in blood pressure, decreased peripheral blood flow, hypoxemia, and hypotonia. Prolonged apnea without intervention can lead to respiratory arrest, brain damage, and death.

Sudden infant death syndrome (SIDS) and apnea are not synonymous, although apnea may increase the risk of sudden death. SIDS is defined as the sudden, unexpected death of a previously healthy infant, the cause of which remains unexplained despite careful postmortem studies.[3] By contrast, apnea—particularly sleep apnea—is rarely fatal. Although no clear cause has been determined for SIDS, numerous factors have been associated with a high risk of SIDS: socioeconomic, ethnic, and prenatal and perinatal factors; maternal blood type; infections; gender (male infants are more frequently affected); hypoxia; impaired ventilatory control; altered breathing patterns; and, in some instances, cardiac arrhythmias.[4]

The term "near-miss SIDS" is sometimes used to refer to an apneic episode during sleep in an apparently healthy infant that is accompanied by changes in color and tone and requires prolonged vigorous shaking or mouth-to-mouth resuscitation to restore breathing.[5] Infants with a history of "near-miss" episodes or with a family history of SIDS should be managed similarly to infants with documented apnea.

The management of apnea includes three components. First, proper positioning is used to prevent gastroesophageal reflux and to accommodate any anatomic abnormalities. Second, cardiorespiratory monitoring assists in alerting parents to apneic episodes. (However, alarms often will not be triggered by episodes of obstructive apnea.) Third, appropriate intervention—ranging in degree from tactile stimulation for mild apneic episodes to vigorous resuscitation for severe episodes lasting 30 seconds or longer—is used to restore breathing.

Home care of infants with apnea, or those being monitored for other conditions, is an increasingly common mode of management. The community health nurse must be prepared to assist and support families in providing appropriate home care for the infant requiring an apnea monitor.

HOSPITAL DISCHARGE AND TRANSITION TO THE HOME

Coordination with hospital staff at the time of discharge from the hospital is important. The nurse should ascertain what monitor is to be used and learn the prescribed settings on that machine. The pattern of the infant's apneic episodes in the hospital (frequency, duration, associated symptoms, need for resuscitation, and precipitating factors) should be identified. In addition, the home care nurse should know what the parents have been taught about apnea, the infant's condition, monitoring, responses to monitor alarms, CPR, home record keeping, follow-up schedule, and criteria for discontinuing the monitor, as well as what fears and concerns parents have expressed. This information will enable appropriate planning for follow-up teaching and support. The home care nurse may be asked to offer advice on the selection of an appropriate monitor and an equipment vendor. In this regard, the nurse should be aware that impedance monitoring is generally considered the safest and most accurate approach, and will be discussed in this chapter. Factors to consider in choice of a monitor are discussed in Appendix 8–C. Factors important in choosing an equipment vendor are discussed in Chapter 2.

Before discharge, it is also important to ensure that *emergency preparations* have been made (see Chapter 7). In addition, plans for safely transporting the infant home should be reviewed step by step with the parents. The monitor should be used during transport since infants are often lulled to sleep by the vibrations in the car. Rechargeable monitors can run for several hours without an electrical outlet; a battery pack is available for other monitors. If the infant's monitor is not portable, parents should be instructed in how to hand-monitor.

During transport, one adult should always be available to attend to the infant should an apneic episode occur. Either the infant should be transported by cab or bus, or the parent should be accompanied by a relative or friend who will drive. If only one adult is available during an emergency, there must obviously be an exception to the two-adult rule. However, in such a situation, the infant's car seat should be placed in the front seat of the car; the driver should drive in the right-hand lane, so that safe stopping is possible if resuscitation becomes necessary en route; and interstate highways or other high-speed roads should be avoided.[6]

ROUTINE HOME VISITS

On every home visit, pulse and respiratory rate should be obtained and documented. If the monitor has a digital read-out, its accuracy should be ascertained. The infant's color and respiratory patterns should also be observed and recorded. The normal color changes related to sleep, feeding, room air temperature changes, and stooling should be discussed with parents. At the same time, they should be reminded that frequent short apneic episodes, even those not severe enough to set off monitor alarms, can lead to hypoxia and subsequent pallor, cyanosis, and hypotonia. The presence or absence of these symptoms should be noted and documented on each visit; if persistent or recurrent, a medical evaluation is indicated.

On each home visit, history of the frequency and duration of any apnea or bradycardia alarms should also be obtained. The infant's status during alarms, any preceding symptoms, and the degree of stimulation needed for arousal should also be reviewed. Parents should be encouraged to keep a complete record of all apnea events. A convenient form for this purpose is provided in Exhibit 8–1.

Caregivers should be taught about factors other than apnea that may cause alarms and should be instructed to be alert for indications of the need for medical evaluation of the infant. Increasingly frequent bradycardia alarms as the infant grows older may indicate the need to change the monitor settings. Alarms may also result from normal bradycardias caused by stretching, hiccupping, passing gas or a bowel movement, prolonged crying, and, in some cases, feeding. Alarms may also be more frequent if the infant has a cold or fever, and after immunization. Frequent bradycardia alarms may also, however, signify the occurrence of many short apneas that are too short to be noted on the monitor but are leading to hypoxia. For each infant, the criteria for concern are determined in conjunction with the physician and should take into consideration the frequency and duration of alarms and specific associated symptoms. Parents should also be encouraged to telephone the nurse or doctor any time they have concerns about the alarms or the infant's status.

THE FIRST HOME VISIT

All aspects of routine home visits should be accomplished on the first visit. In addition, the nurse should determine that parents are prepared to provide safe and appropriate care. Emergency precautions should be reviewed, and the equipment inspected and its appropriate use assured. Rehearsal of responses to monitor alarms and review of CPR procedures are additional components of a thorough first home visit.

Exhibit 8–1 Sample Apnea Record Form

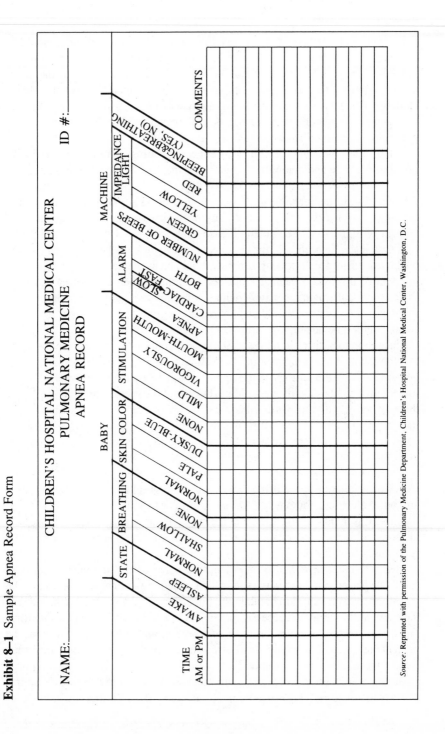

CHILDREN'S HOSPITAL NATIONAL MEDICAL CENTER
PULMONARY MEDICINE
APNEA RECORD

NAME: _____   ID #: _____

Source: Reprinted with permission of the Pulmonary Medicine Department, Children's Hospital National Medical Center, Washington, D.C.

Parents' ability to count accurately the pulse and respiratory rate should be assessed. Safety precautions should be reviewed, including never bathing the infant with the monitor on because of the risk of shock, and minimizing the risk of strangulation by threading the monitor wires out the lower end of the child's clothing. The nurse should also review emergency precautions with parents, such as posting CPR guidelines and emergency telephone numbers in the home. These precautions are described in more detail in Chapter 7.

If the infant has reflux leading to frequent vomiting, parents should also be asked to describe and demonstrate *reflux precautions*. The baby should be positioned in an infant seat inclined by 35 to 45 degrees, or prone with shoulders higher than feet by 30 degrees, during feedings and for 45 to 60 minutes thereafter. Feedings can also be thickened slightly with rice cereal. The frequency and amount of reflux should be noted on each visit. (See also Chapters 4 and 5.)

A systematic inspection of the *equipment and supplies* in the home is important on the first visit. The following supplies should be available: lead wires (two sets minimum), disposable patches (four sets minimum), belt and permanent electrodes (optional), monitor manual with troubleshooting guide, and battery pack (optional). The monitor should be plugged into a grounded outlet, or a grounding adapter should be added.

Since monitors differ in their sensitivity and controls, it is important to check that the monitor recommended in the treatment plan is the model actually in the home. Checking the settings on the monitor, if these are not set internally, is also important. Parents should be encouraged to check the settings regularly to assure that they agree with those prescribed. If there are other children in the house, the monitor should be kept out of their reach. A child-proof panel may also be used to cover the knobs. (These are generally available from the manufacturer or supplier.)

The monitor should be placed on a hard surface at the infant's bedside with 8 inches of ventilation space behind and above it. It should not be placed on top of any other electrical equipment. An extension cord should not be used with the monitor. It is important to ensure that the monitor alarms can be heard throughout the home; if they cannot, either a remote alarm or an inexpensive intercom system is recommended.

Electrode placement is also important to observe on the first visit. Electrodes should be placed symmetrically as indicated in Figure 8–1. The electrodes may be repositioned to prevent skin breakdown, but they must always contact the sides of the chest wall in order to sense the movement of breathing. Electrodes should be replaced as their attachment becomes less secure, and at least every 2 days. To prevent inaccurate monitoring, an electrode belt should not be used until the infant weighs more than 8 to 10 pounds.

As preparation for emergencies, parents should be asked to describe the appropriate response to each type of monitor alarm: apnea, bradycardia, and loose-lead.

Figure 8–1 Placement of Apnea Monitor Electrodes or Belt

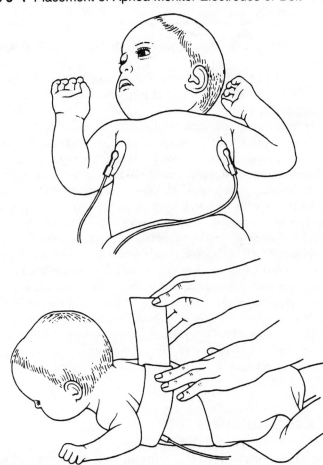

Source: Reprinted from Home Care and Rehabilitation in Respiratory Medicine by C.W. Bell et al., p. 261, with permission of J.B. Lippincott Company, © 1984.

This aspect of the child's care, as well as CPR, should be reviewed with anyone who will care for the infant, including babysitters. The steps in *response to an apnea alarm* are as follows:

1. Observe the baby for respiratory movement.
2. If respiratory movement is *not* noted, or the baby appears lethargic, attempt to stimulate breathing by calling loudly to and then touching the baby, starting with a gentle touch and proceeding to a vigorous touch if necessary.[7]

3. If there is no response, proceed with mouth-to-mouth resuscitation and CPR if necessary.

In *response to a bradycardia alarm,* stimulating the infant should be sufficient in most cases.

In addition to apnea and bradycardia alarms, parents should know how to respond to a *loose-lead alarm.* This alarm may indicate any of the following: a loose electrode patch, a dirty electrode, oil on baby's skin, a loose belt, detachment of wires from electrode or cable, malfunctioning wires, defective cable, or, more rarely, a monitor malfunction. Responses to loose-lead alarms depend on the specific monitor; a manufacturer's handbook or troubleshooting guide is usually supplied with each monitor. Review of these materials with parents can encourage a more thorough understanding of the working of the monitor and troubleshooting strategies. Parents should be encouraged to contact the nurse, physician, or equipment supplier if needed as questions arise.

It is helpful to reassure parents that most infants will not require CPR. Nonetheless, maintenance of CPR skills, with regular review, is crucial. Each person who will care for the infant should be asked to describe and demonstrate CPR; the nurse should observe for correct procedure and timing. In addition, it is important that each caregiver practices when and how to call for help and how to manage both CPR and calling the rescue squad (e.g., "football carrying" the infant or dragging the infant along the floor). Previous practice makes coping with actual events less frightening. If teaching or review of CPR techniques is necessary, discussion followed by demonstration and return demonstration by parents, repeated as necessary, is recommended.

SUBSEQUENT HOME VISITS

Visits should generally begin by addressing any problems or concerns identified by parents. At the same time, the nurse should have a plan in mind for ongoing assessment and teaching. The plan should address not only those areas described for the first and routine home visits but also the following aspects of care.

Many parents are concerned about *skin care.* Electrode patches can generally be left in place for two days. The skin can be cleansed with soap and water as usual, but no oils or lotion should be applied in the area of the patches or the patches will not function properly. Some baby bath products also leave a film on the skin and may lead to inappropriate alarms. If the skin under the patches becomes irritated, patches can be moved as described earlier in this chapter.

It is important to assess parental knowledge about both the child's condition and the reason for monitoring. If gaps in understanding are identified, instruction using discussion and written materials should be repeated as necessary. A thorough understanding of the condition and the reasons for monitoring will encourage optimal compliance with a difficult care regimen.

For the family of a child on an apnea monitor, *daily patterns* and normal household chores must often be reorganized to accommodate the need to be within earshot of the monitor. Vacuuming, going to get the mail, going to the basement to do the laundry, and showering, for example, are not safe when only one parent is home with a monitored infant. The family may need assistance in identifying previous daily patterns and in developing new ways to accomplish daily tasks and responsibilities without jeopardizing the infant's safety. At the same time, parents and other family members should be encouraged to maintain involvement in their usual activities and to avoid becoming isolated, neglecting the affected child's siblings, or treating the baby as an invalid. (See also Chapter 18.)

The family may need assistance in finding qualified babysitters, because the child must never be left with someone unfamiliar with the monitor or who does not know CPR. Some options for babysitting and respite care are discussed in Chapters 2 and 20. Although parents may be anxious about leaving the child at first, it is important to offer ongoing encouragement and support for them to take a break. The strain of constant care and anxiety can wear heavily both on individual caregivers and on their interpersonal relationships.

Because having a child at home on a monitor can be very anxiety-provoking, parents should know who can be contacted, on a 24-hour basis, if problems arise. In addition, frequent visits and ready availability of the community health nurse can ease the transition from hospital to home.

DISCONTINUING USE OF THE MONITOR

The decision to discontinue monitoring an infant is a very individual matter. For a child with documented apnea, five general criteria for discontinuation have been described by Ariagno:[8]

(1) The infant has been free of "life-threatening" events requiring prolonged vigorous stimulation or resuscitation for at least three months, or for two months if there have been no critical problems since the presenting episode.

(2) The infant has not experienced a real monitor alarm for at least two months, on an apnea setting of 20 seconds and a heart rate setting of 60 beats/minute.

(3) During the asymptomatic period, the infant must have experienced the stress of an upper respiratory tract infection, DPT [diphtheria-pertussis-tetanus] immunization, or another illness without recurrence of symptoms.

(4) Clinical evaluation including neurological, developmental and physical examinations shows that initial and any other reasons for monitoring have been resolved.

(5) The infant has shown no abnormalities on cardiorespiratory recordings, if these were present at the time of the child's initial evaluation.

In addition, two normal sleep tests spaced at 2- to 3-month intervals are often recommended.

Even when no further medical reason exists for monitoring, some parents may be reluctant to relinquish the monitor. Despite initial anxiety, most parents come to rely on the monitor for a sense of safety and security. A weaning program, allowing time to relinquish the monitor, may be necessary. Caregivers should also be helped to recognize the infant's stable condition and to view the infant as no longer "at risk."

ONGOING CONCERNS

In some cases, the parents of a child requiring an apnea monitor may have concerns both about having more children and about whether subsequent children would also need monitoring. Parents should be encouraged to explore these concerns, with medical and nursing input offered as questions arise.

NOTES

1. Aranda JV, Trippenbach T, Turmen T, et al: Apnea and control of breathing in newborn infants, in Stern L (ed): *Diagnosis and Management of Respiratory Disorders in the Newborn,* Reading, Mass, Addison-Wesley Publishing Co, 1983, p 135.

2. Korones SB: *High Risk Newborn Infants,* ed 3, St Louis, CV Mosby Co, 1981, p 155.

3. *Medical Examiners' and Coroners' Handbook on Death Registration and Fetal Death Reporting,* DHEW publication (HSA) 78–1110, US Department of Health, Education and Welfare, Public Health Service, 1978, p 3.

4. Kelly DH, Shannon DC: Sudden infant death syndrome and near sudden infant death syndrome: a review of the literature, 1964 to 1982, *Pediatr Clin North Am* 29: 1241–1255, October 1982.

5. Kelly DH, Shannon DC and O'Connell K: Care of infants with near-miss sudden infant death syndrome, *Pediatrics* 61: 511, 1978.

6. Liebold S, Apnea Clinic, Children's Hospital National Medical Center, Washington, DC: personal communication, 1985.

7. Gentle to vigorous touching rather than shaking has been recommended in order to avoid the risk of the "shaken baby syndrome," Duncan J, Department of Pediatrics, Mercy Hospital and Medical Center, San Diego: personal communication, 1985.

8. Ariagno RL: Evaluation and management of infantile apnea, *Pediatr Ann* 13: 217, March 1984.

REFERENCES

Aranda JV, Trippenbach T, Turmen T, et al: Apnea and control of breathing in newborn infants, in Stern L (ed): *Diagnosis and Management of Respiratory Disorders in the Newborn*. Reading, Mass, Addison-Wesley Publishing Co, 1983, pp 134–157.

Ariagno RL: Evaluation and management of infantile apnea. *Pediatr Ann* 13: 210–217, March 1984.

Blodgett D: Infant monitoring at home, in Bell CW, Blodgett D, Goike CA, et al.: *Home Care and Rehabilitation in Respiratory Medicine*. Philadelphia, JB Lippincott Co, 1984, pp 257–265.

Daily WJR, Klaus M, Meyer HBP: Apnea in premature infants: monitoring, incidence, heart rate changes, and effect of environmental temperature. *Pediatrics* 43: 510–518, 1969.

DiMaggio GT, Schultz AH: The concerns of mothers caring for an infant on an apnea monitor. *MCN: The American Journal of Maternal/Child Nursing* 8: 294–297, Jul/Aug 1983.

Healthdyne Infant Monitor (Model 16900): Home Operators Manual. Marietta, Ga, Healthdyne, 1982. (Available from Healthdyne, 2253 Northwest Parkway, Marietta, Georgia 30067.)

Kelly DH, Shannon DC: Sudden infant death syndrome and near sudden infant death syndrome: a review of the literature, 1964 to 1982. *Pediatr Clin North Am* 29: 1241–1261, October 1982.

Kelly DH, Shannon DC, O'Connell K: Care of infants with near-miss sudden infant death syndrome. *Pediatrics* 61: 511–518, 1978.

Korones SB: *High Risk Newborn Infants*, ed 3. St Louis, CV Mosby Co, 1981.

Medical Examiners' and Coroners' Handbook on Death Registration and Fetal Death Reporting. DHEW publication (HSA) 78–1110). US Department of Health, Education and Welfare, Public Health Service, 1978.

Oxygen Therapy Services Inc: *Home Monitoring Program: Important Instructions and Information*. (Available from Oxygen Therapy Services, Inc., 6623 Mid Cities Avenue, Beltsville, Maryland 20705.) Washington, DC, National Medical Home Care, undated (unpublished).

Steinschneider A: Prolonged apnea and the sudden infant death syndrome: clinical and laboratory observations. *Pediatrics* 50: 646–654, 1972.

Steinschneider A, Weinstein SL, Diamond E: The sudden infant death syndrome and apnea/obstruction during neonatal sleep and feeding. *Pediatrics* 70: 858–863, 1982.

Volpe JJ, Koenigsberger R: Neurologic disorders, in Avery GB (ed): *Neonatology: Pathophysiology and Management of the Newborn*, ed 2. Philadelphia, JB Lippincott Co, 1981, pp 910–963.

Webb LZ, Duncan JA: Selecting the right home apnea monitor. *Pediatr Nurs*, May/June 1983, pp 179–182.

Children's Hospital
National Medical Center
Home Care Team
Plan of Treatment

Page_____

Date_____   Case Manager_____

Name_____   Hosp#_____   DOB_____

PROBLEM: **APNEA MONITOR**

GOALS/OBJECTIVES	*METHODS*	*STAFF/REVIEW*
Child will be at minimal risk of life threatening apnea episodes.	Obtain AP and RR each visit. Observe for pallor, cyanosis, shallow respirations, hypotonia. Assess caregivers for placement of electrodes, safe use of monitor; teach/review as necessary. Assess frequency of monitor use during all sleep times and when infant is out of sight. Assess number, type, and duration of alarms and associated symptoms each visit. Encourage family to keep careful record.	

144

GOALS/OBJECTIVES	METHODS	STAFF/REVIEW
	Assess caregivers for appropriate response to each type of monitor alarm; teach as necessary.	
	Review possible causes of alarms with family.	
	Assist family to recognize when to contact physician or apnea monitor supplier re: concerns.	
Caregivers to verbalize knowledge about apnea and purpose of monitor.	Assess knowledge about apnea and purpose of monitor. Teach/ reinforce as needed.	
Caregivers to develop appropriate plans for emergency intervention.	Assess caregivers' knowledge of when intervention is necessary. Teach/review as needed.	
	Assess plans for emergency intervention and assist in developing as needed.	
	Assess caregivers' ability to provide CPR competently; teach/ review regularly.	
	Review with caregivers the indications for calling doctor/rescue squad.	
Child to be free from skin breakdown.	Observe area of electrode placement for skin breakdown.	

GOALS/OBJECTIVES	METHODS	STAFF/REVIEW
	Review with caregivers skin care (including *no* oils or lotions) and movement of patches, prn.	
Caregivers to adjust activities of daily living to allow for hearing monitor at all times.	Assess effect of home monitoring on caregiver's daily schedules.	
	Assist family to develop new patterns of family member responsibilities, if needed.	
	Assist in developing safe travel plans, prn.	
If child has reflux, caregivers demonstrate appropriate reflux precautions.	Observe for use of appropriate reflux precautions; teach/ reinforce as needed.	
Infant to have regular and prn follow-up by managing physician.	Encourage regular and prn appointments/ attention to need to change alarm parameters as infant grows.	
	Communicate/ coordinate with managing physician(s) on a regular basis and as needed for problems.	

Source: Reprinted with permission of Home Care Program (Ahmann, Lierman, and Peck), Children's Hospital National Medical Center, Washington, D.C.

Children's Hospital
National Medical Center
Home Care Program
Initial Home Assessment
for Child with an Apnea Monitor

Name_____ Hosp#_____ DOB_____

Primary caretaker_____ Back-up caretaker_____

Address_____ Address_____

_____ _____

Telephone_____ Telephone_____
Date of hospital discharge_____ Start of service date_____
Diagnoses_____

_____

Reason for apnea monitor:_____
Physician managing:_____
                    Telephone_____ Page_____
Type of monitor_____
Parameters: Apnea delay__ Cardiac High_____ Cardiac Low_____
Equipment supply company_____
    Telephone_____ 24-hour service telephone_____
Funding for equipment_____

EVERY VISIT: Assess number of apnea alarms, number of bradycardia alarms, number of "beeps" per alarm, patient status during alarms, frequency of use of monitor. Obtain AP, RR; and observe for pallor and cyanosis.

I. Equipment

	Date observed	N/A	Comments
Monitor type			
Leads (min. 2 sets)			

Patches (min. 2 sets)	
Belt	
Patches for belt	
Battery pack (opt)	
Monitor manual or troubleshooting guide	

II. Emergency notifications

	Date sent	N/A	Comments
Letter to Telephone Co.			
Letter to Electric Co.			
Letter to Rescue Squad			
Personal contact with Squad (opt)			
Letter to nearest emergency room			
Family given ER card			

III. Emergency information posted

	Date observed	N/A	Comments
Rescue squad number			
Physician's number day/evng/wknd			
Equipment Supply Co. number			
Power Co. emergency number			
CPR guidelines			
Patient's name & address (opt)			

IV. Emergency care
Mandatory for Primary Caretaker and Recommended for Back-up Caretakers

	Primary Caretaker Date	Back-up Caretaker Date	Comments
Describes response to alarms:			
a. Apnea			
b. Bradycardia			

c. Tachycardia

Describes emergency plan for:
a. Respiratory failure

b. Power failure

Demonstrates CPR:

Demonstrates use of ambu bag:

V. Routine care

	Primary Caretaker Date	Back-up Caretaker Date	Comments
State reason for apnea monitor			
Demonstrates set-up of leads and patches			
Demonstrates correct use of monitor			
States correct monitor settings			
States prescribed frequency of use of monitor			
Describes and demonstrates reflux precautions (opt)			

VI. Safety precautions

	Date reviewed	N/A	Comments
Monitor on hard surface			
Ventilation space on top			
Parents can hear from all locations			
Microwave/CB/color TV interference			
No use of extension cord			
8″ from wall in back			
Not on electrical equipment			
Parents cannot turn off during sleep			

Wires threaded out lower end of
  clothes
_____

Not to use in water
_____

Comments:_____
_____

Caretaker description of planning daily tasks to enable hearing monitor
(e.g. vacuuming)

Primary caretaker:_____
_____
_____
_____
_____
_____

Back-up caretaker:_____
_____
_____
_____
_____
_____

VII. Describe caretaker/child interaction (overall interaction and with respect to monitor use)

_____
_____
_____
_____
_____
_____
_____

VIII. Describe caretaker's overall confidence and concerns about apnea monitor

_____
_____
_____
_____

IX. Assessment of problems identified

_____

_____

_____

_____

_____

X. Plan to address problems identified

_____

_____

_____

_____

_____

_____   _____
Signature   Date completed

Source: Reprinted with permission of Home Care Program (Ahmann, Lierman, and Peck), Children's Hospital National Medical Center, Washington, D.C.

Appendix 8–C

Selection of an Apnea Monitor

The selection of the most appropriate monitor for an individual infant and family depends on their situation and reasons for monitoring. In evaluating which monitor among several is best for an infant and family, the nurse considers:

TYPE: Is it an apnea or an apnea and bradycardia monitor? The type of monitor used is usually determined by the physician after identification of the cause of the apnea.

SIZE: How large is the equipment? Determine if size will limit home use of a monitor.

WEIGHT: How heavy is the monitor? Determine if weight will limit a monitor's use in the home.

PORTABILITY: How movable is the monitor? This aspect may be more important for some parents, such as working parents with out-of-the-home babysitting.

TYPES OF ALARMS: What types of alarms does the monitor have? Common alarms sound in response to apnea, bradycardia, apnea and bradycardia, tachycardia loose lead, and weak battery signals. Evaluate what types of alarms are best for each infant and family.

ALARM SIGNALS: What kinds of alarms does the machine have? Some monitors have visual alarms, others have auditory and some have both. Evaluate how loud they are and how easily seen. For parents with deficits in either of these areas, this aspect may be critical. Does the monitor have a memory alert system? This system lets the provider know if an apneic and/or bradycardic event has occurred. If the infant begins to breathe again or if the heart rate picks up after the alarms have been activated, the audible alarm is silenced. However, the visual alarm will remain "on" until the reset button is pushed, informing the provider of the type of event.

SENSITIVITY: How sensitive is the machine? Is this variable factory preset, set by another piece of equipment, automatic, or dialed in by the human hand? Sensitivity can be a critical parameter in home use. Inappropriate activating of the alarms can lead to family noncompliance.

POWER SOURCE: Evaluate whether an electric or battery-powered monitor is better for the family and the specific community. In areas of frequent power outages, battery back-up must be considered. Does the system have a battery recharger?

COMPLEXITY OF USE: How easy is the monitor to use? Is the equipment easy for the parents to use? Can the family be taught to "trouble-shoot" the monitor? As this aspect varies from individual to individual, it requires careful assessment.

SERVICING: Is there a service technician available 24 hours a day? Are there regular service calls by the technician for periodic assessment of monitor functioning? Consider the background of the technicians: are they medically trained, for example as respiratory therapists? Or are they trained as salespersons as well as monitor technicians? Determine if this aspect influences the situation.

ATTACHMENTS: What monitoring attachments are required? Is a belt used with fixed or movable electrodes? Or are electrodes placed directly on the infant's skin? Are these electrodes wet or dry? Assess the effect of these attachments on the infant's skin, movement, and other aspects of daily care and living.

COSTS: How much is the purchase or rental of the monitor? Prices vary among types of equipment. It is important not to let cost of the monitor dictate the type used. Funding is available through several sources. Private and State insurance companies including CHAMPUS will often pay part or all of home monitoring costs. State Children's Service Bureaus provide financial assistance if eligibility requirements are met. Philanthropic organizations also provide monies depending on the individual situation.

FLEXIBILITY: How flexible is the home monitor? Can the monitor record 24-hour tracings of heart and respiratory rates in the home; these pneumocardiograms are often used to monitor treatment. If they can be done in the home on the monitor the parents are already using, the need for additional equipment and possible hospitalization is eliminated.

RELIABILITY: It is important to assess reliability of the monitor. Evaluate manufacturer testing and field experience. Determine if there have been any lawsuits regarding the monitoring equipment.

INSTRUCTIONS: Review monitor instructions. Are they adequate and clear?

SUPPLIER: Determine location of monitor company's headquarters. Validate availability of monitors in specific geographic areas and delivery time-frame involved.

Source: Reprinted from "Selecting the Right Home Apnea Monitor," *Pediatric Nursing,* p. 179, by L.Z. Webb and J. Duncan, with permission of Anthony J. Janetti, Inc., © May/June 1983.

Chapter 9

Home Care of the Infant Requiring Oxygen Therapy

Some infants with pulmonary or cardiac disorders will require oxygen therapy at home. This chapter discusses the choice of oxygen system as well as factors relevant to both hospital discharge and home care of the infant requiring oxygen therapy.

CHOICE OF OXYGEN SYSTEM

The following factors influence the choice of oxygen equipment for use in the home: prescribed liter flow or concentration, portability (and duration of portability needed), the need for continuous versus intermittent use, and humidity needs.

Oxygen Concentrators

An oxygen concentrator separates oxygen from the ambient (room) air. Concentrators generally provide only low-flow oxygen. They provide humidity through the attachment of a bubble humidifier.

Concentrators are cost-effective if used for continuous low-flow oxygen delivery.[1] They cannot, however, be used with Venturi masks or medication nebulizers; the back-pressure from these devices retards the flow of oxygen from the concentrators. An oxygen concentrator is bulky, and the home should be assessed for available space prior to a decision to use one. If a concentrator is used, cylinder oxygen should be made available for portability and for back-up in case of power failure or equipment malfunction.

Note: Appendix 9–A contains a standard home care plan for the infant requiring oxygen therapy at home. Appendix 9–B contains a home assessment form that may be useful in data collection and record keeping.

Liquid Oxygen

Liquid oxygen can be used with any low-flow oxygen delivery device. It may be the most cost-effective method of oxygen delivery for low to moderate continuous-flow use.[2] Some liquid oxygen units may not, however, provide the pressure and flow required to operate a Venturi mask or nebulizer. In addition, a source of humidity must be added to the liquid system. The system can be augmented by using relatively lightweight, easily carried portable units, which can be refilled as needed by caregivers in the home.

Cylinder Oxygen

Cylinder oxygen can be used with any mask, catheter, cannula, or nebulizer if the appropriate regulator and connector are chosen. Cylinder oxygen is most cost-effective for high-flow use or for intermittent use up to 12 hours per day.[3] A source of humidity must be added to the system. Portability can be achieved by use of a small cylinder on a rolling stand, or of small, lightweight aluminum cylinders, which can be refilled from larger tanks.

Humidification Devices

Adequate humidity is necessary to prevent drying of the airways. Humidity can be delivered by jet nebulizer, cascade, or bubbler. The jet nebulizer delivers an aerosol mist, which is actually particles of water suspended in air. As these particles enter the airways, they can stimulate hyperreactive airways. The humidity provided by a cascade or a bubbler, on the other hand, consists of molecular water in the air and generally does not stimulate hyperreactive airways.

Delivery Methods

Oxygen delivery methods include the following: hood, tent, tracheostomy mask, Venturi mask, nasal catheter, and nasal cannula. The choice of delivery method should involve consideration of the infant's age and corresponding developmental, visual, and mobility needs. Consideration should also be given to the capacity to meet the infant's oxygen needs.

If an *oxygen hood or tent* is used, all but the smallest infants may be most comfortable in a medium-size tent, which will allow some room for gross motor movement. In a nontracheostomized infant, the use of a tent may be preferable to a nasal cannula for sleep time because it ensures continuous oxygen delivery, whereas the nasal cannula may slip off. However, active infants and children can easily wiggle out of the tent. Another potential problem with use of a tent is build-up of excessive moisture inside; if this occurs, a respiratory therapist can be consulted about either changing the humidity setting or cutting a small vent hole in the tent.

A *tracheostomy mask* is generally the preferred oxygen delivery device for an infant with a tracheostomy, because it provides a directed flow into the airway. If the mask frequently becomes dislodged at night, as the infant turns, a tent or hood may be useful then. *Venturi masks* are used with infants only on rare occasions.

Nasal catheters stay in place fairly well and do not limit the infant's interaction with the environment. They do have several disadvantages, however. For instance, catheters must be replaced daily, and even if the placement site is alternated, catheters can cause inflammation, rhinorrhea, and crusting of the nares.

Nasal cannulas, although they can roll off easily during sleep, have distinct advantages for use during the infant's waking hours. Like a catheter, the nasal cannula provides for a less restrictive visual, auditory, and motor environment than the oxygen tent. If a nasal cannula is used, it can be held in place by a headband, Velcro straps, tape, or a clear surgical adhesive dressing (e.g., Opsite or Tegaderm). If the cannula prongs do not fit the nares, as in a small infant, they can be clipped off.[4] In addition, as illustrated in Figure 9–1, other eyelet holes can be cut around the cannula to make oxygen available regardless of the cannula position under the nose. With the use of long tubing for the nasal cannula, caregivers can more easily take the infant from room to room. Long tubing is also useful for the toddler, who needs the opportunity to roam more freely.

Figure 9–1 Nasal Cannula for Oxygen Delivery

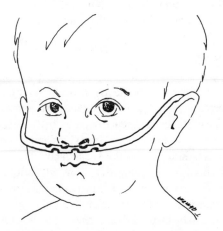

Source: Courtesy of Teresa Ahmann.

HOSPITAL DISCHARGE AND TRANSITION TO THE HOME

At the time of discharge from the hospital, coordination between the community health nurse and the hospital staff is important. The community health nurse should obtain complete information about the program of home oxygen therapy: the reason for oxygen use, the prescribed concentration and liter flow, hours per day to be used, and type of equipment recommended. The community health nurse may be asked to advise hospital staff on the most appropriate type of oxygen system for home use; factors to consider and information on the options are discussed earlier in this chapter. In this connection, a home care respiratory therapist can also contribute to making an appropriate choice. In *choosing an oxygen supplier,* a reliable company with 24-hour on-call service is important; other factors to consider are discussed in Chapter 2.

Prior to discharge, it is important for the home care nurse to ascertain what parents have been taught about the need for oxygen and its safe and appropriate use, as well as to ascertain parental confidence in providing care and concerns about home use of oxygen. Such information will enable the development of appropriate plans for follow-up teaching and support at home.

In addition, before discharge, the nurse should ensure that *emergency preparations* have been made, as discussed in Chapter 7. Similarly, plans for transporting the infant from hospital to home should be discussed with caregivers. If oxygen is required during transport, the supplier should be notified in advance to ensure that a portable cylinder or liquid oxygen system will be available. Safety measures for transportation include maintaining the oxygen source in an upright position at all times (to prevent leakage); securing the oxygen source with a belt or strap to prevent accidental falls; and maintaining adequate ventilation (a window should be slightly open). If public transportation is used, a ''no smoking'' sign should be displayed prominently to warn others of the safety hazard.

ROUTINE HOME VISITS

On every home visit, the nurse should *assess the infant's status,* beginning with the pulse and respiratory rate. The nurse should also assess the infant's color, noting particularly the presence or absence of pallor or cyanosis, particularly in the extremities. The infant should be observed for signs and symptoms of respiratory distress (including nasal flaring, retractions, and labored or rapid respirations). In addition, lung fields should be auscultated, and any adventitious sounds or areas of poor air exchange noted (see Chapter 7). Any deviations from the child's normal patterns should be discussed with parents and, if indicated, with the physician.

Equipment should also be inspected on every home visit. Oxygen and humidity settings should be checked against the recommended settings, and the oxygen source should be inspected for proper functioning and supply level. Of course,

Exhibit 9–1 Oxygen Safety Precautions

1. Post "no smoking" signs.
2. Avoid smoking, fire, or sparks in the patient's room.
3. Keep oxygen tank and patient's bed at least 5 feet from radiator or heater.
4. Ensure that oxygen tank is secured upright at all times.
5. Avoid use of alcohol, petroleum jelly (Vaseline) or other petroleum-based products, and aerosols.
6. Keep oxygen in a well-ventilated area at all times.
7. If using an oxygen concentrator, do not use an extension cord, and do not plug into outlets being used for other appliances.

ongoing observation for adherence to oxygen safety precautions, as listed in Exhibit 9–1, is critical.

On each home visit the nurse should also determine the frequency and duration of oxygen use, by parent report. The question of weaning is discussed in the final section of this chapter.

THE FIRST HOME VISIT

All aspects of the routine home visit should be addressed on the first home visit. In addition, the nurse must inspect the equipment and supplies and also assess parental preparation for the provision of safe and appropriate care.

On the first visit, a careful inspection of *equipment and supplies* is important. The oxygen source should be examined for proper functioning and for supply level. The source of humidity should be the type recommended and should also be assessed for proper functioning. Whatever source of humidity is used, the vessel should be kept full of sterile, boiled, or distilled water. Extra nebulizer vessels or a cascade and extra tubing should be available in the home to allow regular cleaning and replacement, as discussed in Appendix B at the end of this book.

In addition, parents and other caregivers should be evaluated for understanding and appropriate use of the oxygen delivery system. Each caregiver should be able to state and demonstrate the prescribed oxygen concentration and liter flow, humidity settings, and the prescribed times for oxygen use. The nurse should advise parents never to change the oxygen settings without consulting the physician. Parents should also be able to assess the amount of oxygen remaining if either a cylinder or liquid oxygen is used and should know the time at which to contact the supplier for a new supply. Finally, the nurse should observe that tent, cannula, or mask is being used correctly.

Adherence to *oxygen safety precautions,* as listed in Exhibit 9–1, should also be assessed during the first home visit. Precautions should be reviewed with parents and other caregivers, and a written list provided for reference use. Although unwarranted fears and misconceptions about having oxygen in the home should be dispelled, a healthy respect for its potential dangers should be encouraged.[5]

Parents should be assisted, as necessary, in developing appropriate plans in the event of either equipment malfunction or depletion of the oxygen supply. Depending on the severity of the underlying lung condition, it may be possible to wait for the supply company to repair or replace equipment or to supply additional oxygen. In other cases, it may be necessary to transport the child immediately to the nearest emergency room for supplemental oxygen until the home situation can be remedied. Guidelines for each infant should be developed in conjunction with the physician prior to discharge.

On the first home visit, the nurse should also determine parental ability to evaluate the infant's *respiratory status*. Knowledge and skills should be augmented by the nurse as needed. Parents must be able to assess the infant's color and to observe for signs and symptoms of respiratory distress. Parents may also wish to be taught to count the respiratory rate and pulse, and even to auscultate lung fields. Parents should be familiar enough with the infant's baseline respiratory status that deviations can be noted. Of course, if deviations occur, they should contact the infant's physician for advisement.

On this visit the parents should also be asked to describe and demonstrate CPR (see Chapter 7). CPR guidelines should be posted near the infant's crib for easy reference in an emergency, and CPR techniques should be reviewed regularly. Of course, if the infant has a tracheostomy or is on an apnea monitor or a ventilator, the nurse should complete pertinent assessments and teaching on the first home visit (see Chapters 8, 10, and 11).

SUBSEQUENT HOME VISITS

On each home visit, the nurse should elicit and address any parental concerns. At the same time, the nurse should have a plan in mind for ongoing assessment and teaching. The plan should address those areas described for routine home visits; any teaching initiated or problems addressed on the first visit; and the following aspects of care.

The nurse should discuss the importance of *regular cleaning and maintenance of supplies and equipment* to prevent infection; the warm, moist cascade and tubing provide a perfect medium for bacterial growth. In this regard, on a regular basis throughout the day, any excess humidity in the oxygen tubing can be drained by gravity or removed (when disconnected from the infant) by a high flow of oxygen through the tubing. The accumulated moisture should not be emptied back into the cascade. If an oxygen tent is used, its interior surfaces should be wiped daily with a half-strength white vinegar solution.[6]

On subsequent visits, the nurse should encourage *stimulation and developmentally appropriate activities* for the infant on oxygen. If the infant is in an oxygen tent, small colorful toys can be put inside the tent and pictures hung outside the tent to provide visual and motor stimulation. Parents may need encouragement not to be overcautious in handling of and play with the infant. If the infant is stressed by prolonged or intense activity, rapid, labored breathing, nasal flaring, retractions, pallor, or cyanosis may be noted. If this occurs, the activity should be stopped until the infant returns to normal; playtimes can still be encouraged, but for shorter periods. In some cases, the physician may recommend higher oxygen concentrations during activity. (Development is discussed in more detail in Chapter 17.)

Similarly, feeding is an activity that can be stressful for the infant requiring oxygen. Small, frequent high-calorie feedings may be helpful if the infant tires easily or shows prolonged cyanosis, flaring, or retractions with feeding. In occasional cases, supplemental tube feeding may be recommended. Chapters 5 and 6 discuss nutrition and feeding in greater detail.

As another means of stimulation, parents may enjoy taking the infant with them during walks outdoors; the nurse should encourage this activity unless contraindicated because of severe hyperreactive airways disease. A stroller with a rack can be helpful for carrying a portable source of oxygen. If caregivers are uncomfortable about stares or questions related to the oxygen, a blanket over the tank will hide it from view. Of course, parents should avoid exposure to any outdoor sparks or flames, and such excursions should be planned according to the time allowed by amount of oxygen in the portable supply.

On home visits, the nurse may note that the affected child's siblings are both curious about and afraid of the oxygen. Play with stethoscopes and tiny cannulas for their dolls, made from nasogastric tubes and rubber bands, and active involvement during each home visit may help to reduce their anxieties. Chapter 19 addresses sibling issues in more detail.

Since the infant requiring oxygen should never be left with anyone unfamiliar with the necessary specialized care, the family may have difficulty in finding a babysitter. At the same time, occasional relief from the infant's care is very important. On subsequent visits the home care nurse can offer assistance in training a willing friend or relative to babysit. Home nursing and respite care are other options that are discussed in Chapters 2 and 20.

ONGOING CONCERNS

Some parents may wish to wean their child from oxygen either for their own convenience or because they have noted that the child "looks fine" and does not "turn blue" when off the oxygen. It is important to stress that even if the child does not become cyanotic, the oxygen level in the circulatory system may be decreased, with adverse effects on all organ systems, including the brain. The nurse should explain that only tests of the blood oxygen levels can determine the infant's need for oxygen.

Discussions with the managing physician should be encouraged if weaning is desired by parents. Appropriate weaning follows a series of tests that may include transcutaneous oxygen testing, oxygen saturation determinations, pulse oximetry, and blood gas studies on and off oxygen. Testing should also be done during sleep and feeding times to assess oxygen requirements fully during these higher-demand activities.

NOTES

1. French T, National Medical Home Care, Oxygen Therapy Services Inc, Washington, DC: personal communication, 1985.

2. *Ibid.*

3. *Ibid.*

4. Jennings C: An alternative: nasal cannula oxygen therapy for infants who are oxygen dependent, *MCN: The American Journal of Maternal/Child Nursing,* March/April 1982, pp 89, 92.

5. An excellent guide for safe home oxygen use can be found in Ellmeyer P, Thomas NJ: A guide to your patient's home use of oxygen, *Nursing '82,* January 1982, pp 56–57. Manufacturer and supplier materials may also contain helpful guidelines and safety checklists.

6. French T: personal communication, 1985.

REFERENCES

Brunner LS, Suddarth DS (eds): *The Lippincott Manual on Nursing Practice,* ed 3. Philadelphia, JB Lippincott Co, 1982, Chapter 7.

Ellmeyer P, Thomas NJ: A guide to your patient's safe use of oxygen. *Nursing '82,* January 1982, pp 55–57.

Glassanos MR: Infants who are oxygen dependent—sending them home. *MCN: The American Journal of Maternal/Child Nursing* 5: 42–45, 1980.

Jennings C: An alternative: nasal cannula oxygen therapy for infants who are oxygen dependent. *MCN: The American Journal of Maternal/Child Nursing* 7: 89–92, 1982.

Jolly C: Ambulatory oxygen systems. *Rx: Home Care,* April 1983, pp 91–97.

Kieffer J: Oxygen therapy, in Bell CW, Blodgett D, Goike CA, et al (eds): *Home Care and Rehabilitation in Respiratory Medicine,* Philadelphia, JB Lippincott Co, 1984, p 179.

Lampton LE: Home and outpatient oxygen therapy, in Brashear RE, Rhodes ML (eds): *Chronic Obstructive Lung Disease: Clinical Treatment and Management.* St. Louis, CV Mosby Co, 1978, p 122.

Peth TL, Neff TA, Creagh CE, Sutton FD, Nett LM, Bailey B, Fernandez E: Outpatient oxygen therapy in chronic obstructive pulmonary disease. *Archives of Internal Medicine* 139: 28–32, 1979.

Voyles JB: Bronchopulmonary dysplasia. *American Journal of Nursing* 81: 510–514, March 1981.

Whaley LF, Wong DF: *Nursing Care of Infants and Children.* St. Louis, CV Mosby Co, 1983, Chapter 32.

Children's Hospital
National Medical Center
Home Care Team

Plan of Treatment

Page _____

Date _____ Case Manager _____

Name _____ Hosp# _____ DOB _____

PROBLEM: **RESPIRATORY COMPROMISE: OXYGEN**

GOALS/OBJECTIVES	*METHODS*	*STAFF/REVIEW*
Child to be at minimal risk for inadequate oxygenation/ respiratory distress.	Assess AP, RR.	
	Auscultate lung fields.	
	Assess color, flaring, retractions, level of activity each visit.	
	Assess/teach chest therapy and suctioning if indicated.	
	Contact supplier prn re: concerns related to equipment.	
Caregivers will correctly verbalize oxygen %, flow rate, humidity settings and safety precautions.	Assess appropriate use of oxygen (flow rate, tubing and administration set-up, hours/day used) each visit.	
	Teach oxygen safety measures; review prn.	

GOALS/OBJECTIVES	METHODS	STAFF/REVIEW
Caregivers will describe signs/symptoms of respiratory distress and inadequate oxygenation.	Assess/teach signs/symptoms of respiratory distress, inadequate oxygenation. Teach auscultation if appropriate.	
Caregivers to verbalize appropriate plan for respiratory distress.	Assess/teach emergency plans. Encourage contacting managing physician. Assess/review CPR regularly.	
Caregivers to verbalize appropriate back-up for equipment malfunction or electric failure.	Assess/assist in information of back-up plans. Arrange for back-up oxygen source. Encourage caretakers to call oxygen supplier, prn. Ensure that phone and electric companies, rescue squad, and appropriate emergency departments are aware of child's status.	
Caregivers to have appropriate plans for travel with oxygen.	Assess/assist in developing plans and arranging for portable equipment prn.	
Child to be at minimal risk for respiratory infection.	Teach/assess appropriate plans for oxygen equipment cleaning and maintenance. Encourage avoidance of exposure to people with upper respiratory infections.	

GOALS/OBJECTIVES	METHODS	STAFF/REVIEW
Child to have regular and prn follow-up by managing physician.	Encourage regular and prn appointments. Communicate/coordinate with managing physician on regular and prn basis.	

Source: Reprinted with permission of Home Care Program (Ahmann, Lierman, and Peck), Children's Hospital National Medical Center, Washington, D.C.

Children's Hospital National Medical Center Home Care Program Initial Home Assessment for Child Using Oxygen

Name _____ Hosp# _____ DOB _____

Primary caretaker _____ Back-up caretaker _____

Address _____ Address _____

_____ _____

Telephone _____ Telephone _____

Date of hospital discharge _____ Start of service date _____

Diagnoses _____

_____

_____

Reason for oxygen: _____

Physician managing: _____

Telephone _____ Page _____

Oxygen concentration _____ liter flow _____

Oxygen hours/day _____

Equipment supply company _____

Telephone _____ 24-hour service telephone _____

Funding for equipment _____

Humidity source and setting _____

EVERY VISIT: Obtain pulse, respirations. Assess respiratory pattern, color; auscultate lung fields; and assess for signs/symptoms respiratory distress. Check oxygen and humidity settings.

I. Equipment

	Date observed	N/A	Comments
Oxygen source type			
Humidity source type			
Oxygen tent			
Nasal cannula			
Trach mask			
Other:			
Extra tubing			
Portable oxygen source type			

II. Emergency notifications

	Date sent	N/A	Comments
Letter to Telephone Co.			
Letter to Electric Co.			
Letter to Rescue Squad			
Personal contact with Squad (opt)			
Letter to nearest emergency room			
Family given ER card			

III. Emergency information posted

	Date observed	N/A	Comments
Rescue Squad number			
Physician's number day/evng/wknd (see Vent. Home Assmnt)			
Equipment Supply Co. number			
Power Co. emergency number			
CPR Guidelines			
Patient's name & address (opt)			

IV. Emergency care
Mandatory for Primary Caretaker and Recommended for Back-up Caretakers

	Primary Caretaker Date	Back-up Caretaker Date	Comments
Describes signs/ symptoms of respiratory distress			
Describes emergency plan for: a. Respiratory failure			
b. Power failure			
Demonstrates CPR:			
Demonstrates use of ambu bag:			

V. Routine care

	Primary Caretaker Date	Back-up Caretaker Date	Comments
States reason for oxygen			
Demonstrates how to evaluate: a. Respiratory pattern			
b. Appropriate intervention for deviations from normal			
States oxygen concentration/liter flow			
States prescribed amount of time on oxygen/day			
Demonstrates & states correct settings for: a. Oxygen			
b. Humidity			
c. Other			
Demonstrates use of: a. Oxygen tent			
b. Nasal cannula			
c. Trach mask			
d. Blow by			
e. Other			

Describes how to
   assess amnt of
   oxygen remaining

Describes or
   demonstrates use
   of portable oxygen

Describes cleaning of
   supplies &
   equipment

VI. Safety precautions

	Date reviewed	N/A	Comments
Oxygen supports combustion			
No smoking sign posted			
Avoid flames, heat sources, sparks			
Ground all electrical equipment			
Avoid oil, grease, and aerosol sprays			
Keep oxygen in well ventilated areas			
Secure tanks or portable liquid systems			
Fire extinguisher in the home			

Comments: _____

VII. **Describe caretaker/child interaction (overall interaction and with respect to oxygen use)**

_____

_____

_____

_____

_____

_____

_____

VIII. **Describe caretakers' overall confidence and concerns about use of oxygen**

_____

_____

_____

_____

IX. **Assessment of problems identified**

_____

_____

_____

_____

X. **Plan to address problems identified**

_____

_____

_____

_____

_____

_____   _____
Signature   Date completed

Source: Reprinted with permission of The Home Care Program (Ahmann, Lierman, and Peck), Children's Hospital National Medical Center, Washington, D.C.

Chapter 10

Home Care of the Infant with a Tracheostomy

The high risk neonate, with a small airway and a history of multiple intubations for resuscitation, may develop subglottic stenosis, or narrowing of the tracheal airway. If this occurs, surgical creation of a tracheostomy, through which a tube is inserted, may be necessary to ensure an adequate airway until the trachea widens with the infant's growth. Use of a tracheostomy tube may also be indicated in some infants if long-term ventilation is required. In addition, tracheostomies may be used to manage other airway disorders or for optimal pulmonary toilet, as in some children with cystic fibrosis.

HOSPITAL DISCHARGE AND TRANSITION TO THE HOME

At the time of hospital discharge for any infant with a tracheostomy, coordination between the community health nurse and the hospital staff is important. Information about both the infant's diagnosis and the reason for the tracheostomy form the basis of the plan of care. The size and make of the tracheostomy tube are also important data for the community health nurse to gather prior to discharge since, in some infants, the incorrect tube can mean a compromised airway.

Before discharge, the home care nurse should also learn what parents have been taught about both the reason for the tracheostomy and routine and emergency care of the infant. Information about parental experience and confidence in providing tracheostomy care assists in the development of appropriate plans for follow-up teaching and support at home. (A predischarge teaching checklist for the child with a tracheostomy is provided in Appendix 2–A.)

Note: Appendix 10–A contains a standard home care plan for the infant with a tracheostomy. Appendix 10–B contains a home assessment form that may be useful in data collection and record keeping.

A predischarge home visit may be indicated in cases when the safety of the home environment may be in question or the family is uncertain about how to arrange the necessary equipment and supplies. Such a home visit is an opportune time to discuss predischarge emergency preparations, as detailed in Chapter 7.

Similarly, plans for *transportation from hospital to home* should be discussed with parents. Two adults should always be in the car so that one can safely drive while the other attends to the infant; suctioning of the tracheostomy tube and other respiratory care may be needed. Of course, a battery-operated suction machine or a mouth suction (DeLee trap) will be necessary in the car. Additionally, the supplies listed in Exhibit 10–1 should be carried with the infant at all times.

ROUTINE HOME VISITS

On each home visit, the nurse should note the infant's pulse and respiratory rate, auscultate the lung fields, observe the infant's respiratory pattern, and assess the quantity and quality of secretions.

Exhibit 10–1 Traveling with the Infant with a Tracheostomy: Instructions to Parents and Travel Supplies

GETTING OUT OF THE HOUSE!—SHORT AND LONG TRIPS

You and your family will want to go places and do things outside of your home. You should *not* feel you must keep your child with a tracheostomy at home. He will need to go out and do things just like every child. *You will need to make a Travel Kit* that you must always keep with your child when he is away from home, even if you are out for a very short time.

This kit will include:

1. Tracheostomy tube with ties in place in case you need to change the trach tube.
2. Trach tube one size smaller than one in place.
3. Bandage scissors to cut the trach ties if necessary.
4. DeLee mucus suction trap to suction when away from the machine.
5. Baby food jar with saline.
6. Addapak saline vials.
7. Handiwipes or tissues.
8. Ambu bag (this should be included if your child needs it when you suction him).

Source: Reprinted from *Home Care of Your Child with a Tracheostomy: A Parent Handbook* by P. Hennessy (Ed.), p. 32, with permission of Children's Hospital National Medical Center, Washington, D.C., © 1983.

A *source of humidity* is an essential component of routine tracheostomy care since the tube bypasses the nose and mouth, which normally humidify inspired air. For this reason the provision of adequate humidity should be determined on each home visit. Most frequently a compressor and nebulizer or cascade will be used for humidity, as discussed in Chapter 9; long tubing can be used to allow the infant or young child freedom to move.

If the child is to be off the regular source of humidity for a prolonged period of time, the nurse should instruct parents in several optional approaches. First, vaporizers or room humidifiers can assist in maintaining airway humidity. As a second alternative, if the infant begins to sound dry or raspy with breathing, a small amount of saline solution (several milliliters) can be instilled into the tracheostomy tube to prevent drying of secretions. Third, a tracheostomy humidifying filter, a small cover for the tube, can assist in keeping secretions moist (see Figure 10–1). It is also useful in preventing aspiration of dust and other particles when the child is outside or plays on the floor.

Assessment of *tracheal secretions* is another important aspect of routine nursing visits. The quality, color, viscosity, and odor (if any) of secretions should be observed and documented. Very thick secretions may indicate either insufficient humidity or an infection. Yellow, green, or odiferous secretions may signal an infection. If blood-tinged secretions are noted on a single suctioning, the technique may be too vigorous, or the humidity may be inadequate. If copious or recurrent bleeding from the tracheostomy is noted, the physician should be notified.

Figure 10–1 Tracheostomy Humidifying Filter

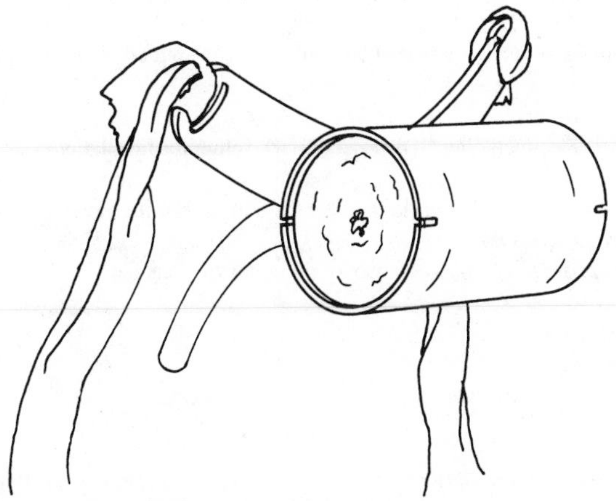

Source: Courtesy of Teresa Ahmann.

In addition to regular assessment of tracheal secretions, the nurse should regularly assess for *irritation and inflammation* at the tracheostomy site, which can be signs of bacterial or yeast infections. In this regard, the nurse should ask parents to demonstrate both routine care of the tracheostomy site, including the neck and stoma, and changing the ties. The neck and stoma site can be cleaned daily with a cotton swab and either hydrogen peroxide or soap and water, followed by a saline rinse. Tracheostomy ties should also be changed daily to prevent irritation to the neck; when changing the ties, caregivers should demonstrate holding the tracheostomy tube carefully in place to prevent it from falling out. Methods for holding the child still and securing the ties are presented later in this chapter.

THE FIRST HOME VISIT

The first home visit should incorporate all aspects of routine home visits. In addition, the nurse must determine that the needed supplies and equipment are in the home, that equipment is functioning properly, and that parents are prepared to provide safe and appropriate care for the infant.

An evaluation of the *equipment and supplies* in the home is important on the first visit. All supplies listed in Exhibit 10–2 should be in the home, and the nurse

---

Exhibit 10–2 Equipment and Supplies for Tracheostomy Home Care

The following equipment and supplies should be kept at the child's bedside at all times:

1. a *tracheostomy tube with ties on* it and the obturator in place
2. the *obturator* to the tube that is in the child (tape it to the wall near the bed)
3. a *tracheostomy tube one size smaller* than the one in your child to use in an emergency if needed
4. *blunt-end scissors*
5. *saline solution,* including "Dispose-a-Vial" saline for instillation
6. *paper cups*
7. *hydrogen peroxide solution* (kept in brown bottle) or *white vinegar solution*
8. *cotton swabs* (Q-tips)
9. *gauze pads* or *Handiwipes* or other *small cloths* to clean neck opening
10. *suction catheters*
11. *tracheostomy ties*
12. *shoulder roll*
13. *suction machine and tubing*
14. *Ambu bag.*

Source: Adapted from *Home Care of Your Child with a Tracheostomy: A Parent Handbook* by P. Hennessy (Ed.), p. 26, with permission of Children's Hospital National Medical Center, Washington, D.C., © 1983.

should check to assure that both the correctly sized tracheostomy tubes and appropriately sized suction catheters are available. (Table 10–1 indicates the recommended catheter sizes.) The suction machine and source of humidity, usually a compressor with a jet nebulizer or cascade, should be assessed for proper functioning.

The nurse should also assess the arrangement of equipment and supplies in the home. The source of humidity, the suction machine, and the apnea monitor, if used, should be arranged at the child's bedside on a set of shelves or a small table. Suction catheters, as well as a tracheostomy tube of the prescribed size and a tube with a lumen one size smaller, both with ties attached, should also be at the bedside. Access to these supplies will facilitate suctioning and an emergency tube change, if needed.

Families living in a large house may wish to have these emergency supplies available in several rooms of the house. If a battery-operated, portable suction machine is not available, mouth suction traps (DeLee traps) can be placed in other rooms for easy access. Mouth suction traps should always be available for use in case of either suction machine or power failure. (See Fig 7–1 for an illustration of the mouth suction trap.)

Table 10–1 Choice of Catheter for Tracheostomy Suctioning

Size of Tracheostomy Tube (Shiley)	Size of Catheter* (French)	Length to Insert (cm)
Neonatal		
00	6.5	5
0	6.5	5
1	6.5	5
Pediatric		
00	6.5	5.5–6
0	6.5	6
1	6.5	6
2	6.5	6–6.5
3	8	6.5
4	10	6.5–7 (8 for inner cannula)
6	12	9 (11 for inner cannula)

*For metal tracheostomy tubes, catheter size must be no greater than half the lumen size of tube or inner cannula.

Source: Adapted with permission from *Home Care Procedures Manual, IV,* "Suctioning the Tracheostomy Tube," Home Care Program, Children's Hospital National Medical Center, Washington, D.C.

On the first home visit, the nurse should assess each parent's competence in all aspects of tracheostomy care including suctioning; removing and inserting the tube; the procedure to follow if the tube is difficult to insert; and the procedure to follow if the infant has difficulty breathing. Anyone who will care for the infant even briefly should be knowledgeable in these procedures and proficient in CPR techniques.

Suctioning on a regular basis is important to maintain an open airway free of secretions and mucus. Hennessy suggests that suctioning is indicated whenever the following signs occur:[1]

1. Secretions can be heard bubbling in the airway.
2. Breath sounds are dry and wheezing.
3. Child complains of difficult breathing.
4. Child has fast breathing *not* caused by activity.
5. Child shows signs of low oxygen such as restlessness, fast heart rate, flaring of the nostrils, blue or dusky color around the mouth or nose.

Several approaches to home suctioning have been recommended: *clean* (non-gloved, washed hands), *clean-gloved*, and *sterile-gloved*. As long as the infant is not extremely young and is not prone to frequent infections, the caregiver may prefer to use the simplest and least expensive method, which is nongloved. Of course, if the child has any respiratory infection, clean-gloved or sterile-gloved techniques should be instituted during that time.

The basic techniques for *catheter suctioning* are discussed in Chapter 7. Chest therapy may be helpful prior to suctioning, and saline instillation may assist in loosening secretions. In suctioning, the catheter should be inserted into the tracheostomy without suction applied; then suction is applied, and the catheter is twirled only during its withdrawal from the tube. Withdrawal of the catheter should take no more than 5 seconds, and the infant should be allowed to breathe for 30 seconds before the catheter is reinserted. During this time, three or four breaths can be given with the Ambu bag.

On the first home visit, the nurse should also assess parental skill in the procedures for *removing and inserting the tracheostomy tube*. Supplies for this procedure should always be available at the bedside, in case of the need for an emergency tracheostomy tube change. The tube should be changed regularly, at least once a week, and more often if the infant is prone to tracheitis.[2] Of course, if the tube has an inner cannula, it should be removed and cleaned daily, as described in Appendix B at the end of this book.

When removing and inserting a tracheostomy tube, parents should use a shoulder roll to put the infant's neck in the optimal alignment; an active infant should be held by another adult or wrapped snugly in a sheet or blanket. Thorough handwashing and careful handling of the tube, by the flanges only, is important to reduce the risk of contamination. Parents should demonstrate removal of the tracheostomy tube by pulling out and down, along the curve of the tube. The new tube is then placed into the stoma and pushed gently in and down, also along the curve of the tube. The obturator must be removed immediately, and the ties secured snugly. Two methods for securing the tracheostomy tube are illustrated in Figure 10–2.

Parents should also be able to describe the procedure to follow if the tracheostomy tube is difficult to insert—a rare but life-threatening occurrence. In this situation, the infant's head should be repositioned, tipped slightly back; the skin of the stoma spread carefully with the fingers; and the tube inserted as the infant breathes in. If the tube is still difficult to insert, parents should be prepared to use a tube one size smaller. If even this tube cannot be inserted, a suction catheter can be

Figure 10–2 Methods for Securing the Tracheostomy Tube

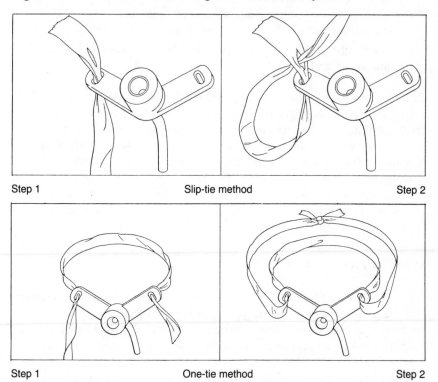

Step 1   Slip-tie method   Step 2

Step 1   One-tie method   Step 2

Source: Reprinted from *Home Care of Your Child with a Tracheostomy: A Parent Handbook* by P. Hennessy (Ed.), p. 12, with permission of Children's Hospital National Medical Center, Washington, D.C., © 1983.

placed in the stoma, secretions removed, and breaths given through the catheter. When the infant relaxes, another attempt should be made to insert the tracheostomy tube. If difficulty persists, the rescue squad should be contacted immediately, and the infant transported to the hospital.

An additional emergency plan that the nurse should review with parents involves the appropriate intervention if the infant either is having *difficulty in breathing* or *ceases to breathe*. In either case, the tracheostomy tube should be suctioned immediately. If respiratory difficulty continues, the tube may be plugged with secretions and should be removed and replaced immediately. If the infant ceases breathing or the heart stops beating, CPR is necessary. The following *modifications in the basic CPR procedure* should be noted:

- The head should be tilted back so that the chin does not cover the tracheostomy tube.
- In listening for breaths, the ear should be placed at the tube.
- When breaths are given, the infant's nose and mouth should be held closed, and breaths given into the tracheostomy tube.
- If no breaths go in, the tube should be changed immediately, and CPR continued as necessary.

Of course, the rescue squad should be contacted immediately.

CPR techniques should be reviewed with parents and other caregivers on the first home visit, as well as on a regular basis on subsequent visits. Each caregiver should describe and demonstrate the correct procedure and timing for CPR, as well as modifications in CPR procedure for a tracheostomy, as just outlined.

In regard to emergency situations, the nurse should warn parents that not all rescue squad personnel will have experience with tracheostomy care. In an emergency, parents may have to continue the procedures they have learned until the hospital staff takes over.

SUBSEQUENT HOME VISITS

On each home visit, the nurse should elicit and address any parental concerns. At the same time, the nurse should have a plan in mind for ongoing assessment and teaching. The plan should address those areas described for routine visits; any teaching initiated or problems addressed on the first visit; and the following aspects of care.

Preventing infection is an important aspect of tracheostomy care, and the nurse should review three relevant principles with parents. First, thorough handwashing prior to tracheostomy care, suctioning, and tube changes is key. Second, proper suctioning technique and regular, thorough cleaning of equipment and supplies are essential. Suction catheters must be rinsed with saline after each use; they then can be stored in a clean towel or plastic bag and reused for up to 6 hours unless the infant either has or is prone to frequent infections. Further instructions for cleaning equipment and supplies can be found in Appendix B at the end of this book. Third, because the child with a tracheostomy maybe especially susceptible, protection from exposure to others with upper respiratory infections is important.

The effect of the tracheostomy on the infant's *activities of daily living* is also important for the nurse to assess. In regard to feeding, most infants with a tracheostomy tube are able to eat and drink without difficulty. However, vomiting may occur when the infant attempts to cough up secretions during or after feedings; suctioning during or after feedings can also stimulate vomiting. To limit the risk of vomiting, the nurse should encourage parents to suction just before feedings, and not again until two hours afterward. If it is necessary to suction sooner, only gentle, brief suctioning should be used. (Nutrition and feeding are discussed in greater detail in Chapters 5 and 6.)

Bathing is another aspect of daily care that may concern parents. Although the infant should be carefully attended in the bathtub to avoid getting water into the tracheostomy, there is no reason not to bathe the infant or to wash the infant's hair. Swimming, however, is clearly contraindicated.

The nurse should also discuss with the parents the infant's sleeping arrangements. Because of the potential for respiratory emergencies at night, some parents choose to keep the infant in their room. Actually, most infants with a tracheostomy are likely to have an apnea monitor that can alert caregivers of difficulty. In addition, small bells can be sewn into the infant's clothes so that they will ring if the infant moves restlessly as an initial sign of distress. As an alternative, some parents purchase inexpensive intercoms so that they can hear the infant at all times. The nurse should assist parents as necessary in determining the arrangements that best meet their own needs for both security and privacy.

ONGOING CONCERNS

Communication development is a long-term concern for children with tracheostomies. The ability to vocalize with a tracheostomy in place may be limited, and parents may be concerned about the likelihood of resultant long-term communication disorders. In a study of 77 tracheostomized children, Simon and colleagues noted that extensive cooing and babbling was not necessary for later speech development.[3] Children decannulated prelinguistically mastered communication skills appropriate for their developmental level. Children decannulated during linguistic stages did exhibit some speech delays, although with speech or language therapy nearly all of the decannulated children showed eventual compensation for these delays. Chapter 15 offers a detailed discussion of speech and language development in the child with a tracheostomy; suggestions for intervention to minimize potential problems are included.

Sibling adjustment is a potential ongoing concern; anxiety, anger, and jealousy about the child with a tracheostomy are common. Chapter 19 provides a guide to assessment and intervention related to sibling adjustment.

In addition, home care of a child with a tracheostomy can shift all family member roles and responsibilities and can strain the family's daily schedule. Some families may appreciate the nurse's assistance in evaluating and reorganizing responsibilities and daily schedules. Assisting families to arrange respite care by training babysitters, or by arranging for home nursing or a respite program, can also be a key factor in making home care more manageable for the family of an infant with a tracheostomy. Family adjustment and useful community resources are discussed in detail in Chapters 18 and 20, respectively.

NOTES

1. Hennessy P: *Home Care of Your Child with a Tracheostomy: A Parent Handbook*, Washington, DC, Children's Hospital National Medical Center, 1983, p 6.
2. Foster S, Hoskins D: Home care of the child with a tracheostomy tube, *Pediatr Clin North Am* 28: 856, November 1981; Hennessy P: *Home care of your child*, p 13; Kennedy AH, Johnson W, Sturdevant EW: An educational program for families of children with tracheostomies, *MCN: The American Journal of Maternal/Child Nursing*, January/February 1982, p 46.
3. Simon BM, Fowler SM, Handler SD: Communication development in young children with long-term tracheostomies: preliminary report, *Int J Pediatr Otorhinolaryngol* 6: 37, 1983.

REFERENCES

Adamo P: *A Guide to Pediatric Tracheostomy Care*. Springfield, Ill, Charles C Thomas, 1981.

Albanese AJ, Toblitz AD: A hassle free guide to suctioning a tracheostomy. *RN*, April 1982, pp 24–29.

Aradine C: Home care for young children with long-term tracheostomies. *MCN: The American Journal of Maternal/Child Nursing* 5: 121–125, March/April 1980.

Aradine C, Ulman H, Shapiro V: The infant with a long term tracheostomy and the parents: a collaborative treatment. *Iss Compr Pediatr Nurs* 3: 29–41, July 1978.

Douglas GS: Tracheostomy in pediatric airway management. *Ear Nose Throat J* 57: 55–69, 1978.

Fearon B, Ellis D: The management of long term airway problems in infants and children. *Ann Otol Rhinol Laryngol* 80: 669–667, October 1970.

Foster S, Hoskins D: Home care of the child with a tracheostomy tube. *Pediatr Clin North Am* 28: 855–857, November 1981.

Gerson CG, Tucker GF: Infant tracheostomy. *Ann Otol Rhinol Laryngol* 91: 413–416, 1982.

Hennessy P: *Home Care of Your Child with a Tracheostomy: A Parent Handbook*. Washington, DC, Children's Hospital National Medical Center, 1983.

Kennedy AH, Johnson WG, Sturdevant EW: An educational program for families of children with tracheostomies. *MCN: The American Journal of Maternal/Child Nursing* 7: 42–49, January/February 1982.

Ruben RJ: Home care of the pediatric patient with a tracheostomy. *Ann Otol Rhinol Laryngol* 91: 633–640, 1982.

Simon BM, Fowler SM, Handler SD: Communication development in young children with long-term tracheostomies: preliminary report. *Int J Pediatr Otorhinolaryngol* 6: 37–50, 1983.

Talbere LR: The child with a tracheostomy: a holistic approach to home care. *Top Clin Nurs* 2: 27–44, October 1980.

Wetmore RF, Handler SD, Potsik WP: Pediatric tracheostomy: experience during the past decade. *Ann Otol Rhinol Laryngol* 91: 628–632, 1982.

Children's Hospital National Medical Center Home Care Team

Plan of Treatment

Page _____

Date _____ Case Manager _____

Name _____ Host # _____ DOB _____

PROBLEM: RESPIRATORY COMPROMISE: TRACHEOSTOMY

GOALS/OBJECTIVES	METHODS	STAFF/REVIEW
Child to be at minimal risk of occluded airway.	Assess AP, RR; auscultate lungs; observe for flaring, and retractions.	
	Assess secretions for viscosity, color, odor each visit.	
	Assess/teach appropriate use of humidity, suctioning.	
	Assess/teach correct procedures for trach change.	
	Assess supplies and equipment in the home for appropriateness and safe, easy access.	

GOALS/OBJECTIVES	METHODS	STAFF/REVIEW
Caregivers to have appropriate plans for emergency intervention.	Assess/teach appropriate plans for emergency intervention.	
	Assess/teach CPR for trach; review as necessary.	
	Assess plans/assist in planning when to call rescue squad/doctor.	
	Ensure that phone company, power company, appropriate rescue squads and ERs notified of child's status.	
Child will be at minimal risk for irritation at trach site.	Assess trach site each visit for redness, granuloma.	
	Assess/teach caregivers appropriate method and schedule for cleaning trach site, changing trach ties.	
Child will be at minimal risk for respiratory/ tracheal infection.	Assess/teach clean technique for suctioning/trach change.	
	Assess/teach appropriate method and schedule for cleaning equipment and supplies.	
	Teach family to keep child away from persons with URI.	
Caregivers to describe appropriate intervention for signs/symptoms of tracheal/respiratory infection.	Assess/teach caretakers plans for intervention.	

	If tracheal infection:
	    Contact doctor at early signs
	    More frequent change of suction catheters
	    More thorough cleansing of equipment	

GOALS/OBJECTIVES	METHODS	STAFF/REVIEW
	If respiratory infection: Contact doctor at early signs More frequent change of suction catheters Increase chest therapy	
Caregivers to describe/ demonstrate appropriate travel plans.	Review/assist in planning for safe travel prn. Assist to obtain needed travel supplies.	
Child to have regular and prn follow-up by managing physician.	Encourage regular and prn appointments. Communicate/coordinate with managing physician on regular and prn basis.	

Source: Reprinted with permission of Home Care Program (Ahmann, Lierman, and Peck), Children's Hospital National Medical Center, Washington, D.C.

Children's Hospital
National Medical Center
Home Care Program
Initial Home Assessment
for Child with a Tracheostomy

Name _____ Hosp# _____ DOB _____

Primary caretaker _____ Back-up caretaker _____

Address _____ Address _____

_____ _____

Telephone _____ Telephone _____

Date of hospital discharge _____ Start of service date _____

Diagnoses _____

_____

_____

Reason for tracheostomy: _____

Physician managing trach: _____
Telephone _____ Page _____

Type of trach _____ Size of trach _____

Equipment supply company _____
Telephone _____ 24-hour service telephone _____

Funding for equipment _____

EVERY VISIT: Assess vital signs, quantity and quality of secretions. Observe respiratory pattern, neck, and stoma site. Auscultate breath sounds, and assess for s/sx respiratory distress.

I. Equipment

	Date Observed	N/A	Comments
Humidification System			
Vaporizer (opt.)			
Apnea monitor (If yes, refer to Apnea Monitor Assessment in Appendix 8–B)			
Oxygen Source (prn) (If yes, refer to Oxygen Assessment in Appendix 9–B)			
Suction Machine			
Suction Catheters size #			
Portable Suction Catheter (DeLee) size #			
Tracheostomy Tubes: type & size			
prescribed size (min. of 4)			
1 size smaller			
Tracheostomy Ties (twill tape)			
Tracheostomy Humidifying filter			
Blunt End Scissors			
Dispose-A-Vial Saline			
Ambu Bag (size)			
Shoulder Roll			

White Vinegar	
Hydrogen Peroxide	
Q-Tips	
Paper Cups	
Wipes (kleenex, handiwipes, etc.)	
Phone (near patient)	
Travel Bag: prescribed trach tube (with ties)	
tube one size smaller (with ties)	
obturator	
addapak saline vials	
bandage scissors	
handiwipes or tissues	
portable suction catheter	
jar-sterile saline	

II. Emergency notifications

	Date sent	N/A	Comments
Letter to Telephone Co.			
Letter to Electric Co.			
Letter to Rescue Squad			
Personal contact with Squad (opt)			
Letter to nearest emergency room			
Family given E.R. card			

III. Emergency information posted

	Date observed	N/A	Comments
Rescue squad number			
Physician's number			
Equipment supply co. number			
Power co. emergency number			
CPR guidelines			
Patient's name & address (opt)			

IV. Emergency care

Mandatory for Primary Caretaker and Recommended for Back-up Caretakers

	Primary Caretaker Date	Back-up Caretaker Date	Comments
Demonstrates one-person trach change (pt. or doll)			
Describes procedures when trach tube insertion is difficult			
Describes signs and symptoms of respiratory distress			
Describes emergency plan for: a. Respiratory failure			
b. Respiratory distress			
c. Power failure			
Demonstrates CPR:			

V. Routine care

	Primary Caretaker Date	Back-up Caretaker Date	Comments
States reason for tracheostomy			
Describes pulmonary anatomy			
Describes how to evaluate:			
a. Quality & quantity			
b. Respiratory pattern			
c. Appropriate interventions for deviations from normal			
Demonstrates tracheostomy change			
Demonstrates cleaning of neck and stoma			
Demonstrates changing trach ties			
Demonstrates chest therapy			
Demonstrates use of Ambu bag:			
Demonstrates operation of apnea monitor, prn			
Demonstrates operation of humidification system			
Demonstrates operation of suction equipment			
Demonstrates safe use of oxygen, prn			
Describes cleaning of supplies & equipment			
Describes appropriate arrangement of supplies			

VI. Safety precautions

	Date reviewed	N/A	Comments
Trach tube, prescribed size, with ties on at bedside			
Trach tube, one size smaller, with ties on, at bedside			
Scissors & extra trach ties at bedside			
Suction catheters available at bedside			
Travel bag on all trips out of house			
No swimming			
No clothing obstructing trach			
No small beads as toys			
Comments: _____			

VII. Describe caretaker/child interaction (overall interaction and with respect to trach case)

_____

_____

_____

_____

_____

_____

_____

_____

VIII. **Describe caretakers' overall confidence and concerns about tracheostomy care**

IX. **Assessment of problems identified**

X. **Plan to address problems identified**

Signature _____ Date completed _____

Source: Reprinted with permission of Home Care Program (Ahmann, Lierman, and Peck), Children's Hospital National Medical Center, Washington, D.C.

Chapter 11

Home Care of the Infant Requiring Mechanical Ventilation

The use of mechanical ventilation at home has been increasing over the past 10 years. Although the majority of experience has been with adults, some experience has been gained with young children having either spinal cord injuries, congenital hypoventilation, or bronchopulmonary dysplasia.

DECIDING ON HOME CARE

In considering the feasibility of home ventilation, several factors are important. The first factor relates to the relative *stability of the underlying disease process* and the inability to wean from mechanical ventilation. The *attitude of the parents* toward home mechanical ventilation and their motivation and ability to learn the necessary care are other important factors. In this connection, parents must be thoroughly informed that home ventilation involves a commitment of 24 hours each day. Likewise, they must be advised of its risks and its benefits, as well as other options for the child's ongoing care. A third factor in considering home ventilation is the *home environment*. Electrical capability of the home can be assessed by a supplier of home ventilators. Space for needed equipment and for supply storage must also be assessed. A telephone should be available in the home. Finally, a *community support system* must be considered in planning for home ventilator care. This should include availability of 24-hour servicing for equipment and supplies, reasonable accessibility to both rescue squads and an emergency facility, availability of appropriately trained nurses or other support personnel to provide back-up care, and adequate financial resources, private or public, to support the costs of home care.

Note: Appendix 11–A contains a standard home care plan for the infant requiring mechanical ventilation. Appendix 11–B contains a home assessment form that may be useful in data collection and record keeping.

195

PREDISCHARGE PLANNING

If home care is determined to be feasible, the parents and other caregivers must be thoroughly educated (see Exhibit 11–1). Each must be involved in discussion, demonstration, and repeat demonstration of all components of the child's care.

Exhibit 11–1 Predischarge Teaching for Home Ventilator Care

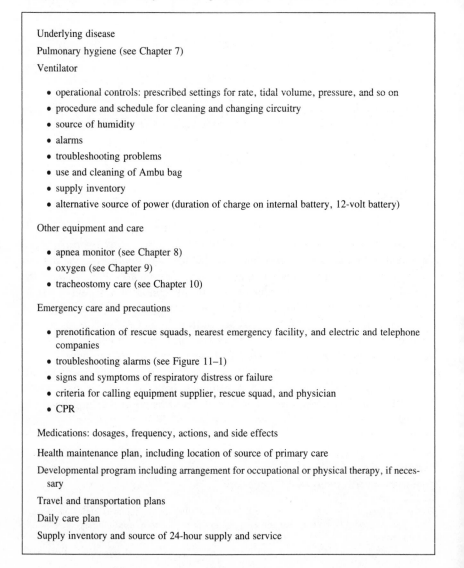

Underlying disease

Pulmonary hygiene (see Chapter 7)

Ventilator

- operational controls: prescribed settings for rate, tidal volume, pressure, and so on
- procedure and schedule for cleaning and changing circuitry
- source of humidity
- alarms
- troubleshooting problems
- use and cleaning of Ambu bag
- supply inventory
- alternative source of power (duration of charge on internal battery, 12-volt battery)

Other equipment and care

- apnea monitor (see Chapter 8)
- oxygen (see Chapter 9)
- tracheostomy care (see Chapter 10)

Emergency care and precautions

- prenotification of rescue squads, nearest emergency facility, and electric and telephone companies
- troubleshooting alarms (see Figure 11–1)
- signs and symptoms of respiratory distress or failure
- criteria for calling equipment supplier, rescue squad, and physician
- CPR

Medications: dosages, frequency, actions, and side effects

Health maintenance plan, including location of source of primary care

Developmental program including arrangement for occupational or physical therapy, if necessary

Travel and transportation plans

Daily care plan

Supply inventory and source of 24-hour supply and service

The teaching should be followed by a 24- to 48-hour period during which home caregivers provide the child's complete care in the hospital, with nurses, respiratory therapists, and physicians available only as consultants. Even with such practice, written instructions for all aspects of routine and emergency care, including equipment inventory and daily schedules or checklists, can be helpful to the family at home.

The *financial support* for home care must also be thoroughly investigated before a decision to discharge can be made. Private insurers and Medicaid vary in the amount and extent of coverage provided for home care.[1] Creative approaches to financing home care may be necessary (see Chapters 2 and 20).

If funding is available to cover the cost of home nursing for from one to three shifts a day, the transition from hospital to home may be eased. If the family and the health care team agree that home nursing would be helpful, nurses can be located through nursing agencies, or through newspaper advertisements. Of course, nurses with ventilator experience are preferable, and any nurses recruited should be trained in the specifics of the infant's care prior to discharge.

CHOICE OF A VENTILATOR

Choice of a home ventilator depends on several factors:

- the child's underlying disease process
- the mode of ventilation required
- the need for positive end-expiratory pressure (PEEP)
- the need for oxygen
- ventilator capabilities, including ease of operation, portability, and reliability
- space in the home
- power source in the home.

The LP-4, the Thompson Mini-lung, and the Emerson volume ventilator are frequent choices for home use with children. The family, and any nurses providing care for the child at home, should be thoroughly familiar with the operation of the chosen ventilator.[2] It is important to have an authorized dealer and 24-hour servicing available in case of malfunction. It is also advisable to have a back-up ventilator, either in the home or readily available, in case of malfunction.

HOSPITAL DISCHARGE AND TRANSITION TO THE HOME

As discharge approaches, the community health nurse should obtain a thorough history of the child's hospital course and information about the underlying disease process leading to the need for continued mechanical ventilation. The nurse should

Exhibit 11–2 Ventilator Settings*

Mode (Control, IMV, or CPAP)

Pressure limit

PEEP (positive end-expiratory pressure)

Rate

Inspiratory time

Expiratory time

IMV (intermittent mandatory ventilation)

Volume (where applicable)

   *These settings may apply to some, but not all ventilators, and some but not all modes of ventilation. The settings may vary drastically depending on the child's underlying condition.

---

also obtain, in writing, the physician's instructions for ventilator settings (see Exhibit 11–2). By gaining familiarity in the hospital with the ventilator to be used at home and with the daily care of the child, the nurse will be better able to address issues and problems arising in home care. An awareness of the parents' skill with the infant's special care, their understanding of the infant's condition, and their general level of acceptance will form the basis for initial support and teaching at home.

It may be useful to make a home visit prior to discharge from the hospital, as mentioned earlier, to assess the adequacy of space in the home for the necessary equipment and supplies. During the visit, the nurse can also assist parents, as needed, to determine optimal locations for equipment and supplies in the home. In this regard, ease of care and ready access in case of emergencies are primary considerations.

Prior to discharge, it is important to ensure that *emergency preparations*, as discussed in Chapter 7, have been addressed. The nurse should also discuss with parents plans for safe transportation of the child. Arrangements should be made either for use of a portable ventilator, run on a 12-volt battery, or for transport in an ambulance in which the ventilator can be connected. If no other alternative is available, an Ambu bag may be used during transport. Two adults should always be in the vehicle when the child is transported; this permits at least one adult to respond to emergencies.

ROUTINE HOME VISITS

On all home visits, vital signs should be assessed, and the observed respiratory rate should be checked against the rate of the ventilator. In addition, when an infant is being mechanically ventilated, it is important to assess regularly both the infant and the ventilator to identify actual or potential problems. For *assessment of the infant*, skin color and respiratory pattern should be noted, and the chest observed for regular rise and fall with each breath. Lung fields should be auscultated for the presence of adventitious sounds, and the infant should be assessed for signs and symptoms of respiratory distress or failure. Deviations from the child's normal condition should be brought to the attention of both the parents and the infant's physician.

For *assessment of the ventilator*, all settings should be checked against those recommended. The ventilator should also routinely be observed for the following:

- alarm lights on
- bellows rising
- humidifier filled
- tubing without kinks or water accumulation
- connections secure.

Any problems should be brought to the attention of the parents and, as appropriate, the physician, the supply company representative, or respiratory therapist.

The care plan for a mechanically ventilated child should also address the risks of *barotrauma* (e.g., pneumothorax or pneumomediastinum), *decreased cardiac output*, and *fluid imbalance*. Although these particular risks are low when a child has stabilized on mechanical ventilation, it is nevertheless important to assess for these problems on each home visit. Presumably, parents have already been informed of these risks. They should also be taught to observe their child for the *signs and symptoms of cardiorespiratory problems*: dyspnea, restlessness, pallor, fatigue, and periorbital edema. If such changes are noted, the physician should be contacted promptly.

Atelectasis is also a potential problem for the mechanically ventilated child, particularly if mobility is limited. The nurse should review instructions for frequent position changes, regular and vigorous chest therapy, and periodic hyperinflation as preventive measures. Suctioning as needed can assist in the removal of copious secretions, which may otherwise contribute to the risk of atelectasis as well as inadequate ventilation. (Suctioning is discussed in more detail in Chapters 7 and 9). Hyperinflation and hyperoxygenation before and after suctioning are sometimes recommended, particularly in infants because of their small lung volumes. It is also important to ventilate the infant, mechanically or manually, between each pass of the catheter.

THE FIRST HOME VISIT

All aspects of routine home visits should be addressed on the first home visit. In addition, the nurse must determine that needed supplies and equipment are available in the home, that equipment is functioning perfectly, and that parents are prepared to provide safe and appropriate care.

Essential *supplies and equipment* for respiratory care should be available in the home, both at the infant's bedside and at any other location at which care may be provided. (A list of supplies is part of Appendix 12–B). Some families find shelved carts with wheels very useful.

Essential bedside supplies include the following: an extra tracheostomy tube with ties attached, a tube one size smaller, and an Ambu bag with tracheostomy adapter attached. All tracheostomy supplies, cardiorespiratory (apnea) monitor supplies, and oxygen equipment, if needed, should be arranged for safety and ready access. A back-up power source for the ventilator should also be available for use in an electrical "brown-out" or "black-out"; 12-volt batteries are often used for this purpose. Some families may need an electrical generator for the house to ensure adequate power. If a back-up power source is an impractical expense, parents must be instructed in ventilation using an oxygen cylinder and a manual resuscitator, in case of power loss.

In regard to the ventilator, on the first home visit the nurse should assess parental knowledge of the prescribed *ventilator settings*. It can be helpful to post prescribed settings on or near the ventilator for quick reference (see Exhibit 11–2). The settings should be checked every 3 to 4 hours if the infant is on the ventilator continuously, and before use if mechanical ventilator is needed only at night. Parents should also have an understanding both of the meaning of each setting and of the ventilator functioning. In this regard, they should be asked to describe the ventilator circuitry, including the source of humidification. If there are curious siblings in the family, or if the ventilated child is ambulatory, it is important to child-proof the ventilator dials and switches. Putting the ventilator out of reach and using child-proof plastic panels to cover control knobs will help ensure that the settings are not mistakenly changed by curious hands. Such panels can be obtained from the manufacturer or supplier.

On the initial visit the nurse should also assess parental knowledge of signs and symptoms of *respiratory distress, inadequate ventilation,* and *respiratory failure* and appropriate interventions. Respiratory distress (described in Chapter 7) may result from partial or complete occlusion of the tracheostomy tube, from hyper-reactive airways disease, from a pulmonary infection, or from other cardiopulmonary disorders. Basic *guidelines for intervention* in the event of respiratory distress, which must take into consideration the child's underlying lung condition, should be developed in conjunction with the physician prior to discharge. Parental familiarity with these guidelines is essential, and parents should be encouraged to contact the physician as necessary.

Both inadequate ventilation and respiratory failure may have various causes. Of primary importance is the ability to differentiate between ventilator problems and problems originating in the infant, as indicated in Figure 11–1. Caregivers should

Figure 11–1 Troubleshooting Mechanical Ventilation Alarms

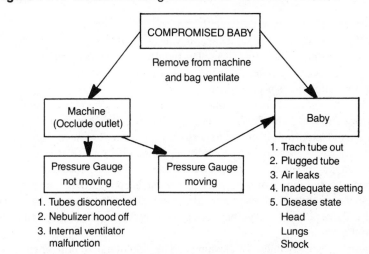

Source: Adapted from "Basic Concepts in Positive Pressure Ventilation of the Newborn" by S.K. Gottschalk, B. King, and C.R. Schuth, *Perinatology/Neonatology*, Vol. 4, with permission of Brentwood Publishing Corporation, © March-April, 1980.

be familiar with methods of *troubleshooting ventilator alarms*. In this regard, they should know that the first step upon hearing an alarm sound is to assess the infant. If the alarm is not merely signaling a disconnection of circuitry, the infant should be removed from the ventilator and manually ventilated with the Ambu bag until the reason for the alarm is identified and corrected. A manual or set of written instructions detailing troubleshooting methods, generally supplied by the manufacturer, should always be kept near the ventilator. Additionally, the 24-hour number for the equipment supplier should be posted near the telephone (see Exhibit 7–1). Guidelines for when to contact the equipment supplier, the physician, and the rescue squad are an important element of planning for potential emergencies. They should be developed in conjunction with the physician prior to discharge and reviewed with caregivers at home both initially and again at intervals as necessary.

In regard to ventilatory insufficiency and possible respiratory failure, it is essential that caregivers be able to clear an obstructed airway and to provide CPR, if indicated. These crucial skills should be reviewed on the first home visit and subsequently at regular intervals. (Chapters 7 and 10 are useful resources in this regard.) If a cardiorespiratory monitor or oxygen is being used, the essential knowledge and skills for their safe and appropriate use should likewise be reviewed (apnea monitoring and home oxygen therapy are discussed in Chapters 8 and 9, respectively).

SUBSEQUENT HOME VISITS

Home visits should generally begin by addressing any problems or concerns identified by caregivers. At the same time, the nurse should have a plan in mind for ongoing assessment and teaching. The plan should address those areas described for routine home visits; any teaching initiated or problems addressed on the first visit; and the following aspects of care.

The *prevention of infection* is one important aspect of the care plan for a child on a ventilator. The nurse should stress thorough handwashing and should caution parents to avoid exposing the infant to persons with upper respiratory infections. Although surgical masks are not generally recommended for use at home, they may appropriately be used by a parent during care of the tracheostomy.

Another potential source of infection is water that accumulates in the ventilator tubing. As it accumulates, the water should be emptied from the circuit. It can be disposed of into a plastic-lined garbage can placed nearby; it should not be emptied back into the cascade.

The methods and schedules for cleaning and disinfection of ventilator circuitry are also important. Although there is debate over how often, if ever, tubing and connections can reasonably be reused, financial constraints will sometimes necessitate the reuse of at least some of the equipment. The tracheostomy tube adapter should not be reused because this is the most frequent source of accidental disconnections from the ventilator.[3] If portions of the ventilator circuitry are to be reused, regular cleaning is essential (see Appendix B). If problems occur with frequent tracheitis, unusually frequent upper respiratory infections, or pneumonia, a more stringent cleaning and disinfection schedule as well as sterile technique for tracheostomy care are recommended.

Health maintenance needs must also be addressed (see Chapter 4); in the midst of the many demands of caring for a ventilated child, they can be easily neglected. The family may need assistance in locating a pediatrician or nurse practitioner who will make home visits. Alternatively, the nurse can assist in arranging health maintenance visits at the medical center in conjunction with any visits with other specialists. Visits should be coordinated in order to limit the number of trips the family must make to the medical center. Examination rooms must, of course, be arranged to accommodate the ventilator and suction machine. In addition, transportation to and from visits to the doctor or clinic will need careful planning. Some families may be able to purchase a van or may already have a station wagon; others may need to use ambulance services. Families using their own vehicles should be advised to obtain handicapped license plates to facilitate parking.

ONGOING CONCERNS

Care of an infant requiring mechanical ventilation at home can be very time-consuming and complex. Caregivers may benefit from assistance in organizing their daily or weekly care plans or checklists (see Exhibit 11–3). Furthermore, although parents will often be reluctant to leave the infant with anyone else, over the long term some form of respite from the demands of care will be important. (Chapters 2 and 20 address this issue.)

A major strain of home care for most families is *financial pressure*. Supplies and equipment are costly, utility bills increase, and both doctor visits and occasional rehospitalization are costly. At the same time, some insurance plans and health maintenance organizations offer limited home care benefits.[4] Piecing funds together from programs such as Supplemental Security Income (SSI) and Medic-

---

Exhibit 11–3 Sample Weekly Schedule for Care of a Mechanically Ventilated Child

To Do	Sun	Mon	Tues	Wed	Thurs	Fri	Sat
Tracheostomy care, change ties	X	X	X	X	X	X	X
Tube change	X						
Check ventilator settings	X	X	X	X	X	X	X
Chest therapy	X	X	X	X	X	X	X
Rinse and wash suction container	X	X	X	X	X	X	X
Make fresh saline		X		X		X	
Soak parts of suction machine		X		X		X	
Clean Ambu bag and valve	X	X	X	X	X	X	X
Empty and refill cascade on ventilator	X			X	X		X
Change ventilator tubing and soak all parts		X		X		X	
Check oxygen level in all tanks		X			X		
Check contents of emergency boxes		X			X		
Inventory all supplies		X					

aid, as well as various community organizations, may be necessary to assure financial stability for the family of a ventilator-dependent child. Consultation with a nurse or social worker who is aware of available community resources, coupled with a creative and assertive approach, may be helpful. (See Chapters 2 and 20). Additional concerns related to family adjustment are addressed in Chapters 18 and 19.

NOTES

1. Medicaid coverage of the pediatric population, *Caring*, May 1985, p 52; Private health care coverage for children, *Caring*, May 1985, p 53. The cost effectiveness of home care for ventilator-dependent individuals has been documented by many programs. A review of the topic can be found in Cabin B: Cost effectiveness of pediatric home care, *Caring*, May 1985, pp 48–52.

2. An excellent set of questions that can help familiarize parents or nurses with any ventilator can be found in Brunner LS, Suddarth DS (eds): *The Lippincott Manual of Nursing Practice*, ed 3, Philadelphia, JB Lippincott Co, 1981, p 1200.

3. Janowski MJ: Accidental disconnections from breathing systems, *Am J Nurs*, February 1984, p 243.

4. Private health care coverage for children, p 53.

REFERENCES

Banaszak EG, Travers H, Frazier M, et al: Home ventilator care. *Resp Care* 26: 1262–1268, 1981.

Brunner LS, Suddarth DS (eds): *The Lippincott Manual of Nursing Practice*, ed 3. Philadelphia; JB Lippincott Co, 1982, Chapter 7.

Burr BH, Guyer B, Todres ID, et al: Home care for children on respirators. *N Engl J Med* 309: 1319–1323, 1983.

Cabin B: Cost effectiveness of pediatric home care. *Caring*, May 1985, pp 48–51.

Feldman J, Tuteur PB: Mechanical ventilation: from hospital intensive care to home. *Heart Lung* 11: 162–165, 1982.

Gilmartin M, Make B: Home care of the ventilator dependent person. *Resp Care* 28: 1490–1497, 1983.

Gottschalk SK, King B, Schuth CR: Basic concepts in positive pressure ventilation of the newborn. *Perinatol Neonatol* 4: 15–19, 1980.

Janowsky MJ: Accidental disconnections from breathing systems. *Am J Nurs*, February 1984, pp 241–243.

Lawrence PA: Home care for ventilator dependent children: providing a chance to live a normal life. *Dimens Crit Care Nurs* 3: 42–52, 1984.

Maguire M, Miller TV, Young P: Teaching patients' families to provide ventilator care at home *Dimens Crit Care Nurs* 1: 244–255, 1982.

Medicaid coverage of the pediatric population. *Caring*, May 1985, p 52.

Nielson L: Mechanical ventilation: patient assessment and nursing care. *Am J Nurs*, December 1984, pp 2191–2217.

Private health care coverage for children. *Caring*, May 1985, p 53.

Schraeder BD: A creative approach to caring for the ventilator dependent child. *MCN: The American Journal of Maternal/Child Nursing* 4: 168–170, 1979.

Worthington de Toledo L: Caring for the patient—instead of the ventilator. *RN*, December 1980, pp 22–23ff.

Children's Hospital National Medical Center Home Care Team

Plan of Treatment

Page _____

Date _____ Case Manager _____

Name _____ Hosp# _____ DOB _____

PROBLEM: **VENTILATOR**

GOALS/OBJECTIVES	METHODS	STAFF/REVIEW
Child will be at minimal risk of respiratory failure.	Obtain AP and RR each visit; check vent settings each visit; assess for spontaneous respirations; assess color, respiratory pattern; auscultate lung fields for signs/symptoms of respiratory distress or failure each visit.	
Caregivers will state correct settings for vent and will demonstrate correct/safe operation of ventilator and humidifier.	Assess knowledge and observe use of equipment; teach/reinforce as necessary. Observe arrangement of equipment and supplies for safety and accessibility.	
Caregivers will describe signs/symptoms of respiratory distress and inadequate ventilation.	Assess knowledge; teach/reinforce as necessary.	

GOALS/OBJECTIVES	METHODS	STAFF/REVIEW
Caregivers will develop appropriate plans for emergency intervention.	Ensure that phone and electric companies, rescue squads, and emergency departments are aware of child's status.	
	Assess knowledge of when intervention is necessary. Teach/review as needed.	
	Assess knowledge of how to troubleshoot ventilator alarms. Teach/review as needed.	
	Assess plans for emergency intervention and assist in developing as needed.	
	Assess caregivers' ability to provide CPR competently; teach/review regularly.	
	Review with caregivers the indications for calling doctor/equipment supplier/rescue squad.	
The child will be at minimal risk of infection or atelectasis.	Assess for signs of infection or atelectasis.	
	Review preventive measures each visit.	
Infant to have age and condition appropriate developmental stimulation and motor activity.	Assess appropriateness of developmental stim and motor activity; offer recommendations prn.	
	Consult with OT/PT as necessary in planning.	
Caregivers to adjust to activities of daily living to allow for hearing vent alarms at all times.	Assess effect of home ventilation on caregivers' daily schedules. Assist in developing new patterns	

GOALS/OBJECTIVES	METHODS	STAFF/REVIEW
	of family member responsibilities and/or developing clear daily schedules for the child's care if needed.	
	Assist in developing safe travel plans if needed.	
Caregivers to have all needed supplies and to clean reusable supplies appropriately.	Assess regularly for adequate stock of needed supplies.	
	Assist caregivers in developing inventory list, schedule for ordering supplies.	
	Communicate with supplier(s) prn re: concerns.	
	Assess caregivers' schedule, and techniques for cleaning reusable supplies and equipment; teach prn.	
Child to have regular and prn follow-up by managing physician.	Encourage regular and prn visits with managing physician.	
	Assist in arranging plans for safe visits to physician or home visits by physician.	
	Communicate/coordinate with managing physician(s) on a regular basis and as needed for problems.	

Source: Reprinted with permission of Home Care Program (Ahmann, Lierman, and Peck), Children's Hospital National Medical Center, Washington, D.C.

Appendix 11–B

Children's Hospital National Medical Center Home Care Program Initial Home Assessment for Child with a Ventilator

Name _____ Hosp# _____ DOB _____

Primary caretaker _____ Back-up caretaker _____

Address _____ Address _____
_____ _____

Telephone _____ Telephone _____
Date of hospital discharge _____ Start of service date _____
Diagnoses _____
_____
_____

Reason for ventilator: _____
Physician managing ventilator: _____
Telephone _____ Page _____
Type of ventilator _____ Humidity source _____
Prescribed settings _____
Prescribed time on ventilator _____
Equipment supply company _____
Telephone _____ 24-hour service telephone _____
Funding for equipment _____

EVERY VISIT: Assess vital signs, observe respiratory pattern and color. Auscultate breath sounds, assess for signs/symptoms of respiratory distress. Check ventilator settings for accuracy.

I. Equipment

	Date observed	N/A	Comments
Ventilator (type)			
Portability			
Humidity (source)			
Compressor			
Ventilator tubing			
Extra peep valve			
Ambu bag			
Ambu bag trach adaptors			
Sterile water			
Suction machine & catheters (refer also to Trach Assmnt, Appendix 10–B)			
Apnea monitor ___ (If yes, refer to Apnea Monitor Assmnt, Appendix 8–B)			
Oxygen source ___ (If yes, refer to Oxygen Assmnt, Appendix 9–B)			

II. Emergency notifications

	Date sent	N/A	Comments
Letter to Telephone Co.			
Letter to Electric Co.			
Letter to Rescue Squad			
Personal contact with Squad (opt)			
Letter to nearest emergency room			
Family given ER card			

III. Emergency information posted

	Date observed	N/A	Comments
Rescue squad number			
Physician's number (day,evng,wknd)			
Equipment Supply Co. number			
Power Co. emergency number			
CPR guidelines			
Patient's name & address (opt)			

IV. Emergency care

Mandatory for Primary Caretaker and Recommended for Back-up Caretakers (See also Tracheostomy Assessment)

	Primary Caretaker Date	Back-up Caretaker Date	Comments
Describes signs and symptoms of respiratory distress:			
Describes signs and symptoms of inadequate ventilation:			
Describes emergency plan for:			
a. Respiratory distress			
b. Respiratory failure			
c. Ventilator alarm			
d. Power failure			
Demonstrates CPR:			
Demonstrates use of Ambu bag:			

V. Routine care (see also Tracheostomy assessment, Appendix 10–B)

	Primary Caretaker Date	Back-up Caretaker Date	Comments
States reason for ventilator			
Describes pulmonary anatomy			
Describes how to evaluate respiratory pattern			
Describes appropriate interventions for deviations from normal			
States ventilator settings			
Demonstrates operation of ventilator & humidification			
Demonstrates operation of apnea monitor			
Demonstrates operation of suction equipment			
Demonstrates safe use of oxygen			
Demonstrates cleaning of supplies & equipment			
Demonstrates appropriate arrangement of supplies			
Demonstrates vent. circuit change			
Describes travel plan			

VI. Safety precautions (see also Trach Assessment, Appendix 10–B)

Date reviewed   N/A   Comments

Can hear ventilator alarms at
    all times

Transport with two adults

Check ventilator settings
    regularly/post near vent.

Check ventilator circuit
    connections regularly

Shake excess water out of
    tubing regularly

Child proofing equipment
    settings prn

Car battery for power back-
    up

Phone near child's bedroom

Ventilator manual in home

Comments: _____

_____

_____

_____

Caretaker description of planning daily tasks to enable hearing ventilator
(e.g., vacuuming)

Primary caretaker: _____

_____

_____

_____

_____

Back-up caretaker: _____

_____

_____

_____

_____

VII. Describe caretaker/child interaction (overall interaction and with respect to ventilator)

_____

_____

_____

_____

_____

_____

_____

VIII. Describe caretakers' overall confidence and concerns about ventilator

_____

_____

_____

_____

IX. Assessment of problems identified

_____

_____

_____

_____

_____

X. Plan to address problems identified

_____

_____

_____

_____

_____

_____   _____

Signature   Date completed

Source: Reprinted with permission of Home Care Program (Ahmann, Lierman, and Peck), Children's Hospital National Medical Center, Washington, D.C.

Chapter 12

Home Care of the Infant with Hydrocephalus

Connie Jo Lierman, RN, MSN
Jeanne O'Connor Egan, RN, MSN

Hydrocephalus means "water head" and is defined as a condition of accumulating fluid within the ventricles of the brain. It results from a congenital or an acquired alteration in the normal absorption or production of cerebrospinal fluid. In some cases the specific cause may be unknown; in other cases the causative factor may be any of the following:

- congenital problems
- infections
- trauma (including intraventricular hemorrhage)
- tumors.

This chapter discusses the pathophysiology of hydrocephalus, new treatment approaches, and issues relevant to home care of the infant with hydrocephalus.

PATHOPHYSIOLOGY OF HYDROCEPHALUS

Cerebrospinal fluid (CSF) is formed continuously by both the lining of the ventricles and the brain parenchyma. The function of the CSF is thought to be essentially mechanical: it protects the CNS by acting as a shock absorber, thereby reducing the force of impact on the brain. CSF also carries nutrients into and waste products away from the brain.

CSF circulates from the two lateral ventricles through the foramina of Monro to the third ventricle, which communicates posteriorly through the aqueduct of Sylvius, to the fourth ventricle (see Figure 12–1). The CSF then passes into the

Note: A standard home care plan for the infant with hydrocephalus is provided in Appendix 12–A.

Figure 12–1 Ventricles of the Brain

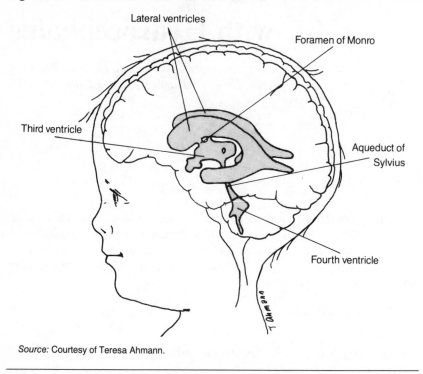

Source: Courtesy of Teresa Ahmann.

---

subarachnoid space to eventually be reabsorbed into the venous system of the brain.

Two major types of hydrocephalus are defined by the point of obstruction of the CSF. *Noncommunicating hydrocephalus* is the result of obstruction of the normal flow at some point within the ventricular system. *Communicating hydrocephalus* results from obstruction distal to the outlets of the fourth ventricle in the subarachnoid space (see Figure 12–1). In this case, there is no obstruction of the normal flow between ventricles.

Intraventricular hemorrhage (IVH) is a potential cause of hydrocephalus in premature infants, particularly those less than 32 weeks gestation. The immature brain of the premature infant contains richly vascular areas that are poorly supported by tissue mass; it is in these areas that hemorrhage occurs. The amount of hemorrhage can vary and is graded, by findings on CT (computerized tomography) scans, as follows:[1]

Grade 1—subependymal hemorrhage (bleeding in lining over ventricles)
Grade 2—IVH without ventricular dilatation (blood in the ventricles)

Grade 3—IVH with ventricular dilatation (blood in enlarged ventricles)
Grade 4—IVH with parenchymal hemorrhage (bleeding in the tissues of the brain.

As Pape has noted, "either acute obstructive hydrocephalus or secondary communicating hydrocephalus" can result from IVH.[2]

TREATMENT

The goal of neurosurgical care for the infant with hydrocephalus is removal of the obstruction or, if this is not possible, diversion of the CSF produced into another body cavity. Control sometimes can be achieved with medication to reduce the amount of CSF produced. More commonly, surgical placement of a *shunt device* is used. Shunts divert the CSF from the ventricles either to the peritoneal cavity (ventriculoperitoneal shunt) or to the atrial cavity of the heart (ventriculoatrial). In infants, placement of a ventriculoperitoneal shunt, a relatively simple procedure, is the method of choice (see Figure 12–2). An extra length of catheter is generally coiled in the peritoneum to extend as the infant grows.

A wide variety of shunts is manufactured. Each type consists of three basic components: (1) the ventricular catheter (proximal end), (2) the reservoir (a pump with or without a valve), and (3) the peritoneal or atrial drainage end (distal catheter). Shunts are designed to permit only unidirectional flow of CSF, away from the ventricles.

HOSPITAL DISCHARGE AND TRANSITION TO THE HOME

In preparing parents for home care of an infant with hydrocephalus, instructions should be given regarding shunt function, signs and symptoms of shunt failure and infection, how and when to contact the physician, and the infant's general care. Any parental concerns should also be addressed.

The community health nurse should obtain information from the hospital staff regarding the infant's particular history, including the following:

- previous symptoms of increased intracranial pressure (ICP)
- the location of the shunt
- a record of serial measurements of the infant's head circumference
- a history of the infant's overall neurologic status
- prognosis as explained to the parents
- parental understanding of the infant's problem.

Figure 12–2 Ventriculoperitoneal Shunt

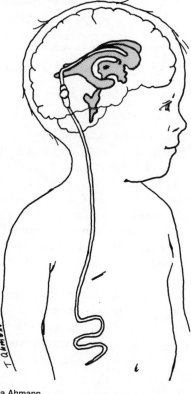

Source: Courtesy of Teresa Ahmann.

This information will assist the nurse in developing an appropriate home care plan.

ROUTINE HOME VISITS

On each home visit, the nurse should assess the infant's status relative to the hydrocephalus. Important elements of the history and physical examination include the following:

- level of orientation
- alertness
- behavior
- sleep patterns
- neck range of motion

- head circumference
- fontanels
- suture lines
- shunt insertion site
- eye movements

Examination of the head is critical and begins with measurement of the *head circumference*. If the infant's head circumference is increasing more rapidly than is normal, as indicated by the normal curve on a growth chart, the caregiver should plan to see the physician within a few days. The character of the *anterior fontanel* should also be noted: on a quiet infant in the sitting position, the site should be soft and flat. On palpation, *suture lines* (coronal, sagittal, lambdoidal) should not be appreciably split or overlapping. The *shunt insertion site,* usually located above and slightly behind the ear, should be gently palpated and checked for redness, edema, or drainage. Ability to pump the reservoir does not indicate functioning; this maneuver can, in fact, lead to problems and should not be done unless the parent has special instructions from the neurosurgeon.

To determine that there is full *range of motion* (ROM) in the neck without guarding, the nurse should gently turn the infant's head from side to side. (*Guarding* results from residual tenderness following insertion of the shunt.) If guarding or decreased ROM is noted, the parents should be encouraged to begin gently moving the infant's head from side to side several times a day.

As part of the physical examination, the nurse should observe the infant's *eye movements*:

- Does the infant follow an object in all visual fields?
- Is there nystagmus (rapid involuntary eye movement)?
- Can the infant look above midline without tilting his head?
- Can the infant visually converge on an object?

On each routine home visit, the nurse should also both question parents about and observe the infant for symptoms of the two major potential complications related to shunts: shunt obstruction and infection. The shunt can become blocked, for various reasons; this obstruction will lead to increased ICP. *Symptoms of shunt obstruction* in infants include the following:

- a tense, bulging fontanel
- increased head circumference
- vomiting
- change in appetite
- irritability
- increased sleepiness
- ''sunset'' eyes (intermittent or continuous downward deviation of the pupils).

Although parents need not regularly measure the head circumference, they should be instructed to regularly check the infant's fontanel. The nurse can demonstrate this procedure with the infant in a quiet sitting position, and parents should be asked to provide a return demonstration.

Infection of the shunt, another potential complication, can lead to ventriculitis or meningitis. If this occurs, the infant may exhibit the signs of shunt obstruction. In addition, fever, redness, and tenderness or puffiness along the shunt tract may be noted. Abdominal distension and tenderness may also be indicative of a shunt infection.

Other less frequent complications related to the use of a shunt are the following:

- subdural hematoma (bleeding over the brain): signs include increasing head circumference, full anterior fontanel, sunset eyes, and other signs of hydrocephalus.
- paralytic ileus (abnormal bowel blockage): signs include enlarged abdomen, vomiting, and absence of bowel sounds.
- cranial stenosis (early closure of cranial sutures): signs include a change in head contour, particularly overlapping or ridges along the suture lines.

THE FIRST HOME VISIT

On the initial home visit, the nurse should complete a thorough history, including a prenatal and natal history, and a detailed physical examination of the infant, for the purpose of establishing a baseline assessment. (See Chapter 3.) Assessment should also include all the elements of a routine visit, discussed in the previous section.

On the first home visit, it is generally helpful to review with parents the pattern of CSF flow and the specific cause of the hydrocephalus, if known, in their infant. Pictures such as those in Figures 12–1 and 12–2 can be used to help the parents understand the problem. The functioning of the shunt should also be reviewed, and the nurse should assess parental knowledge of the signs and symptoms of potential shunt complications, particularly obstruction and infection.

In regard to the shunt, the nurse should review with parents *guidelines for contacting the physician.* These guidelines should be developed for each infant prior to hospital discharge for each infant. In general, the doctor is contacted not for one episode of vomiting but rather for an overall pattern indicative of increasing ICP, including several of the symptoms described earlier. However, some infants may have no symptoms of problems with the shunt except for a rapidly increasing head circumference. Therefore, if this is noted, it is a sufficient reason to contact the physician. The parents should know how to contact the physician at all times, including nights and weekends.

Related to the question of when to contact the physician is the issue of distinguishing shunt failure from a viral infection. Since the presenting symptoms may be similar, parental anxiety may be considerable. If parents have any concern, an appointment should be made for assessment. They should be aware, however, that if the infant experiences a change in level of consciousness accompanied by decreased alertness, immediate medical attention is critical.

SUBSEQUENT HOME VISITS

On subsequent home visits, parental concerns and questions should be elicited and addressed. At the same time, the nurse should have a plan in mind for ongoing assessment and intervention. This plan should address all elements of routine home visits and of the first home visit previously discussed in this chapter. In addition, the following areas should be addressed.

A *developmental screening evaluation,* such as the Denver Developmental Screening Test, should be completed by the nurse to determine the infant's baseline development status (see also Chapter 17). If the tool indicates a delay, the nurse should contact the physician to request a formal evaluation. If deficits are confirmed, the nurse can then assist the parents to obtain physical or occupational therapy or to enroll the infant in a developmental program. The nurse can also provide guidance to families regarding normal developmental activities (see also Chapter 17).

Some parents will be concerned about the *physical appearance* of the infant with a shunt. In an infant, the shunt site and the tubing will be noticeable. The nurse can reassure parents, however, that as the child grows and develops more subcutaneous fat and thicker hair, the shunt will no longer be visible (although it can usually still be felt under the skin). In addition to the physical appearance of the shunt, parents are often concerned about the *safety* of play and other daily activities with respect to the shunt. The nurse should reassure them that it is very difficult to injure the shunt and that the shunt will not become dislodged during normal activities. The only contraindicated activity in infancy is prolonged use of a head-down position, since the shunt (although it has a one-way valve to prevent backward flow) functions by gravity. As children get older, some practitioners discourage direct-contact sports such as football. Other activities, however, should be encouraged; and parents should be assisted, as necessary, to allow their child to become independent.

On subsequent home visits, it is also important for the nurse to assess the infant's *nutritional intake and growth pattern.* Some neurologically involved infants feed poorly and have erratic growth patterns. The nurse can provide guidance regarding recommended intake, feeding patterns, and methods to supplement the infant's caloric intake as necessary. Chapter 5 provides an in-depth discussion of assessment and intervention related to both nutrition and feeding.

ONGOING CONCERNS

A major concern for most parents is the possibility of *brain damage.* In general, the long-range prognosis for infants with hydrocephalus is uncertain and depends on both the cause and severity of the hydrocephalus and the effectiveness of treatment. If the physician has given the parents a specific prognosis, the nurse should support it. At the same time, parents should be encouraged to express any concerns and to ask any questions they might have.

As the infant grows older, the sutures become more tightly closed (generally around 18 months of age), and the *symptoms of increased ICP may worsen*. At that age, the cranial vault will not expand as easily to accommodate increased amounts of CSF. Therefore, pressure on brain tissue may develop more rapidly and can cause acute symptoms such as vomiting, headache, lethargy, and abnormal eye movements. Parents should be given anticipatory guidance regarding these changes and should be advised that, should such acute symptoms occur, prompt medical attention is essential.

SUMMARY

Technical advances and ethical dilemmas dominate the care of neurologically impaired infants with hydrocephalus. The shunt may be required for a lifetime. The prognosis depends on the individual child, the specific cause of the hydrocephalus, and other factors such as the frequency of necessary surgical revisions and episodes of ventriculitis. In recent years, with technical advances, care has improved; this correlates with an improved prognosis for children with hydrocephalus. Nursing care is directed toward supporting an improved prognosis both by assessment of the infant, to promote early intervention if problems arise, and by family education.

NOTES

1. Pape K: Intraventricular hemorrhage: diagnosis and outcome, *Birth Defects* 17: 145, 1981.
2. Papile LA, Bernstein J, Bernstein R, et al: Incidence and evolution of subependymal and intraventricular hemorrhage. *J Pediatr* 92: 530, 1978.

REFERENCES

Carini E, Owens G: *Neurological and Neurosurgical Nursing*. St Louis, CV Mosby Co, 1982.

Hammock MK: *CCT in Infancy and Childhood*. Baltimore, Williams & Wilkins Co, 1981.

Hausmann K: Nursing care of the patient with hydrocephalus. *J Neurosurg Nurs* 13: 326–332, 1981.

Jackson P: Ventricular-peritoneal shunts. *Am J Nurs* 80: 1104–1109, June 1980.

McElroy D: Hydrocephalus in children. *Nurs Clin North Am* 15: 23–35, March 1980.

Milhorat TH: *Hydrocephalus and cerebrospinal fluid*. Baltimore, Williams & Wilkins Co, 1972.

Milhorat T: *Pediatric Neurosurgery*. Philadelphia, FA Davis Co, 1978.

Pape K: Intraventricular hemorrhage: Diagnosis and outcome. *Birth Defects* 17: 143–147, 1981.

Papile LA, Bernstein J, Bernstein R, et al: Incidence and evolution of subependymal and intraventricular hemorrhage. *J Pediatr* 92: 529–531, 1978.

Children's Hospital National Medical Center Home Care Team

Plan of Treatment

Page_____

Date_____ Case Manager_____

Name_____ Hosp#_____ DOB_____

PROBLEM: **HYDROCEPHALUS**

GOALS/OBJECTIVES	METHODS	STAFF/REVIEW
Child will maintain adequate drainage of CSF.	Measure head circumference at each home visit.	
	Assess for symptoms of increased ICP: bulging fontanel, sunset eyes, vomiting, lethargy, irritability, headache, change in level of consciousness, failure to thrive.	
Child will receive prompt treatment for signs and symptoms of increased ICP or infection.	Assess caregivers' knowledge of signs and symptoms of increased ICP or infection; teach/ review as needed.	
	Assist caregivers in planning how to contact physician when problems are noted (including nights, weekends).	

GOALS/OBJECTIVES	METHODS	STAFF/REVIEW
Child will be at low risk of infection.	Assess for swelling or redness along shunt track.	
	Review signs and symptoms of infection with caregivers.	
Child will receive well-coordinated care.	Communicate with primary physician or neurosurgeon as indicated.	
Child will be able to function with minimal restrictions.	Discuss with family the effects of hydrocephalus on life style of child and family: babysitters, vacations, activity.	
	Provide information as needed.	

Source: Reprinted with permission of Home Care Program (Ahmann, Lierman, and Peck), Children's Hospital National Medical Center, Washington, D.C.

Chapter 13

Home Care of the Infant with Seizures

Jeanne O'Connor Egan, RN, MSN
Connie Jo Lierman, RN, MSN

Seizures are defined by Volpe as "clinical manifestations of hypersynchronous firing of cerebral cortical neurons."[1] The disturbed pattern of nerve cell activity represents a problem with the normal activity of the brain. A seizure is not a disease in itself but a symptom, the cause of which must be sought and corrected if possible. Somewhat above 4 percent of all children experience one or more seizures between infancy and childhood.[2] Roughly 1 percent of all neonates will have a seizure; and the incidence among premature infants in the modern neonatal intensive care unit is approximately 25 percent.[3]

This chapter reviews the signs and symptoms of seizures and both the etiology and treatments for infants. The nursing role with respect to home care of the infant with seizures, including family support and education, is also addressed.

IDENTIFICATION OF SEIZURES

The immaturity of the infant's central nervous system (CNS) may lead to random or abnormal movements that can be insignificant in an otherwise healthy infant. For this reason, correct identification of a seizure in a neonate is difficult. The difference between seizure activity and jitteriness is indicated in Exhibit 13–1. Movement that is repetitive and stereotypic is probably a seizure. Neonatal seizures are manifested differently from those occurring later because of the immaturity of the brain structures during this period. Seizure activity in the neonate may be mainly confined to the brainstem and spinal cord reflexive responses.[4]

Seizures in neonates rarely present as classic tonic-clonic (grand mal) seizures; more often, seizure activity is subtle, with repetitious, nonspecific movements. Manifestations of subtle seizures may include any of the following:

Note: A standard home care plan for the infant with seizures is provided in Appendix 13–A.

225

Exhibit 13–1 Differentiating Seizure Activity and Jitteriness

Seizure Activity	Jitteriness
Usually accompanied by abnormalities of gaze or extraocular movements	Not accompanied by abnormalities of gaze or extraocular movements
Dominant movements with a fast component or a clonic rhythmic jerk	Dominant movements slow and of equal rate and amplitude
Not usually stimulus-sensitive	Very stimulus-sensitive
"Rowing" movements of upper limbs, pedaling movements of lower limbs, or rigid posturing of a limb	Subsides when limb is restrained
Increased body tone, usually generalized, with limbs held in extension and/or resting flexion	
May be accompanied by apnea or cyanosis	

- fluttering or blinking of eyelids
- tonic deviation of the eyes (nystagmus)
- drooling
- mouth movements (e.g., sucking, tongue thrusting, lip smacking)
- tonic posturing of a limb
- "bicycling" movements of lower extremities
- apnea.

Apneic spells, especially in the premature infant, are usually related to pathologic mechanisms other than seizures. The nurse should note that if apnea occurs, one or more of the other subtle manifestations must be present for the episode to be considered a seizure.[5]

The electroencephalogram (EEG) may be particularly helpful in differentiating subtle seizures from the random movements of jitteriness. Confirmation of seizures comes not only from observation of the activity but from electrical recordings obtained by placing electrodes on the infant's scalp.

Although subtle seizures occur most frequently in the neonate, myoclonic seizures tend to occur more frequently in children over 1 month of age; tonic and clonic seizures may also be seen. For reference, the International Classification of seizures is listed in Exhibit 13–2;* in this classification, the infant's patterns are

---

*The terms epilepsy and seizure disorder are used synonymously for the condition in which the child has recurrent seizures.

Exhibit 13–2 International Classification of Epileptic Seizures

Generalized seizures

- Tonic-clonic (grand mal)
- Absence (petit mal)
- Infantile spasms
- Other (e.g., myoclonic seizures, akinetic seizures, undetermined)

Partial seizures

- Simple partial seizures (e.g, disturbances in movement only)
- Complex partial seizures (psychomotor, other)
- Secondarily generalized seizures

This listing is a condensed form of the new internationally accepted descriptive terms and classifications of epileptic seizures.

Source: Reprinted from "Epilepsy: Hope through Research," p. 4, NIH Publication No. 81–156, U.S. Government Printing Office, July 1981.

often classified as "other" because of the immature brain functioning and resulting atypical physical reactions.

The terminology relating to seizure types is currently in flux; therefore, the nurse may most accurately document the infant's seizure activity by describing observed behaviors rather than applying a label. Examples of such descriptions can be found in Exhibit 13–3.

Exhibit 13–3 Sample Descriptions of Seizures

Type of Seizure	*Description*
Tonic-clonic	Flexion of upper limbs and extension of lower limbs, or tonic extension of all limbs
Complex partial	Jerking movements of one limb that migrate to another area
Focal clonic	Characterized by well-localized clonic jerking
Partial	Flexion spasms of all four limbs, or of only the upper or the lower extremities, which can be single or repetitive; should not be confused with the Moro reflex, which is stimulus-induced; a cry may accompany the spasm.

ETIOLOGY AND TREATMENT OF SEIZURE DISORDERS

Seizures may have many different causes, including the following:

- metabolic disturbance
- intracranial infection[6]
- trauma to the head
- intraventricular hemorrhage (IVH)
- anoxia
- developmental anomalies
- drug withdrawal.

IVH (discussed in Chapter 12) has been noted as a major cause of seizures in infants weighing less than 2500 g.[7] Metabolic disturbances leading to seizures can result from birth trauma or apnea, both of which are also potential problems for the high risk premature infant.

Prompt identification and treatment of seizures are essential since prolonged seizure activity can lead to brain injury. If the cause of seizures is unknown, the infant may require diagnostic testing to determine laboratory values related to metabolic imbalances or infections; electroencephalography to define seizure activity; and head ultrasonography and computerized tomography (CT) to assess for developmental anomalies, trauma, or bleeding. Determination of the specific cause of the seizures will assist in planning the most appropriate treatment.

Most commonly, anticonvulsant therapy will be instituted; phenobarbital and phenytoin (Dilantin) are the drugs most commonly used to treat infants with seizures of nonmetabolic origin. Other drugs are also used, depending upon the type of seizure and the physician's clinical judgment; Appendix 13–B provides a table describing medications. If the underlying disorder is a metabolic disturbance (e.g., hypoglycemia, hypomagnesemia, hyponatremia, or hypernatremia), these imbalances can be corrected medically. In regard to these metabolic disturbances, the nurse should monitor the infant's nutritional status (including weight gain and amount, frequency, and type of feeding). Some formulas may prove to be inadequate for certain infants' metabolic needs; dietary consultation may be useful.

HOSPITAL DISCHARGE AND TRANSITION TO THE HOME

Prior to the infant's discharge from the hospital, the community health nurse should obtain complete information on the infant's condition:

- the type of seizures
- how they manifest
- the infant's behavior after seizures
- prescribed medications
- history of reactions to the prescribed anticonvulsant drugs.

In addition, the nurse should obtain information regarding the parents' understanding of and their reactions to the infant's seizure disorder.

As part of the planning for discharge, the nurse should determine that parents have been instructed in *care of the child during a seizure*. The aim of care during a seizure is both to ensure the safety of the infant and to observe activity during and after the seizure carefully. Depending on the seizure type, no intervention at all may be necessary. However, should the infant lose consciousness, placement in a comfortable position with the head protected and the clothing loosened is important. It has previously been common practice during a grand mal seizure to place a firm, soft object, such as a padded tongue blade or a leather belt, between the teeth. However, because of the risk of injury to the child this is no longer recommended. An infant should, however, be turned to the side if coughing or vomiting occurs during the seizure, to avoid aspiration. Observation after the seizure, until the infant returns to the preictal state (i.e., the condition prior to the seizure), is important in order to evaluate the effect of the seizure on the infant and to observe for the occurrence of other seizures.

Prior to hospital discharge, the nurse should also see that parents are given *guidelines on when to seek medical attention*. Such guidelines generally include the following parameters:

- if a seizure is prolonged (of more than 10 to 15 minutes' duration)
- if the frequency or duration of the seizures changes significantly
- if a new type of seizure occurs
- if the infant is not retaining the medication because of vomiting.

Provision of specific guidelines can help prevent unnecessary telephone calls and hospital visits.

Plans for medical follow-up should also be determined prior to discharge; and both parents and the home care nurse should know who will be managing the infant's seizure disorder. In some cases, ongoing care is managed by the pediatric primary care provider, with referral back to the neurologist on a routine basis (e.g., every 6 months or 1 year) or for specific problems. In other situations, the neurologist oversees all care relative to the seizure disorder. The initial follow-up visit is frequently scheduled prior to discharge.

ROUTINE HOME VISITS

Each home visit should include an assessment of the infant's status, including vital signs, character of respirations, level of alertness, and both ocular and motor responses to stimuli.

In addition, the nurse should question parents about any seizures the infant may have had. For an *accurate record* regarding the infant's seizure activity, parents may be asked to note in writing the following information:

1. date and time of seizure
2. the infant's activities immediately prior to the seizure (e.g., changes in behavior, muscle tone)
3. description of the seizure activity (e.g., changes in color, respirations, muscle tone; duration of the seizure; types of movements involved)
4. the behavior, appearance, and level of alertness of the infant after the seizure (e.g., sleepy, difficult to arouse, or normal).

At each home visit, the nurse should review the seizure record with parents. This is important in order to see whether the seizures are under adequate control. If there has been a significant change in frequency or type of seizures, the physician should be contacted. A change in the medication may be necessary in order to obtain improved seizure control.

In regard to seizure control, if the infant is on *anticonvulsant medications,* the nurse should also review with parents the medication dosage and administration. In addition, the nurse should observe the infant for any medication side effects (see Appendix 13–B).

THE FIRST HOME VISIT

The first home visit should incorporate all aspects of the routine visit. In addition, the nurse should obtain a health history, assess the infant's status and safety, and determine that parents are prepared to provide appropriate care. While taking the health history, the nurse can question parents about their understanding of the seizure disorder and its cause if known. Misconceptions about seizures are common, and families often need to be provided with accurate information. This process of education will begin in the first visit but will probably continue over several visits as the parents develop increasing rapport with the nurse.

The initial evaluation of the infant should also include a physical examination, with particular attention to vital signs, character of respirations, level of alertness, and ocular and motor responses to stimuli.

If the infant is on *anticonvulsant medications*, the dosage, administration, and possible side effects should be reviewed with the parents. The nurse can ask to see the bottles of medication and also the spoons or syringes with which parents measure the medication. The nurse should check the label on the medication bottle against the prescription and should observe while each parent measures the prescribed dose. Accurate dosage of medications is essential to avoid hazardous toxic doses. If a medication is a suspension, parents should be reminded to shake the bottle vigorously before each use since the medication settles to the bottom of the bottle. As a final point, the nurse can also review with parents the medication schedule; the times may be adjusted to best fit with the family and infant's schedule. For example, it may be a family's preference to give the medication at feeding times.

Common *side effects of medications* should also be reviewed with parents (see Appendix 13–B). A rare but potentially fatal disorder known as Stevens-Johnson syndrome can occur with use of almost all anticonvulsants. The initial sign of this syndrome is development of a rash. For this reason, parents should be advised to contact the neurologist immediately if a rash develops. An additional caution related to anticonvulsant therapy regards regularity of administration, requiring timely renewal of prescriptions. Abrupt cessation of medication can, in itself, precipitate seizures, including status epilepticus, a condition in which the infant passes from one seizure into another without regaining consciousness.

Safety factors should also be reviewed with parents on the first visit. Infants and young children should never be left alone in situations where loss of consciousness could cause an injury (e.g., the bathtub or pool). When in an infant seat or highchair, they should be strapped securely to prevent falls. Additional precautions recommended by the physician will depend on the type and frequency of seizures; these precautions should also be reviewed with parents.

Finally, on the first home visit the nurse should review with parents *indications for contacting the physician*; these instructions should be based on the guidelines the nurse has received from the hospital. The nurse should also determine that parents know which physician to call regarding any seizures and how to reach a physician at all times (most physicians will have some sort of on-call system). If the physician cannot be reached, however, parents may need to call a local emergency facility. In addition, the nurse should instruct parents regarding when to take their infant immediately to the emergency facility: if an infant has repeated grand mal seizures without regaining consciousness, prompt ambulance transport to the nearest medical center is critical.

SUBSEQUENT HOME VISITS

On each subsequent home visit, the nurse should elicit and address any concerns or questions parents may have. At the same time, the nurse should have in mind a plan for overall assessment and teaching. This plan should incorporate those aspects of care described for both routine visits and the first visit. In addition, it should address the following areas.

With respect to *anticonvulsant medication*, the nurse should inform parents that, since the dosage is based on weight, it will probably need to be increased as the infant grows. The nurse can also discuss with parents where the medications can be obtained and can assist the family to plan ahead so they do not run out of medication. Many pharmacies will supply the anticonvulsants. In addition, the Epilepsy Foundation of America (EFA) provides a discount pharmacy service for its members. Information on membership and prices can be obtained by contacting EFA Pharmacy Service, 6 North Michigan Avenue, Chicago, Illinois 60602, (312) 332–6888.

Additional follow-up frequently includes *blood tests* scheduled on a routine basis. Blood tests are used to monitor whether the serum level of anticonvulsant is staying within a therapeutic range (see Appendix 13–B). Blood tests are also used to check for possible metabolic side effects of the medication. The nurse should assist parents, as necessary, in arranging for follow-up laboratory work, as recommended by the physician.

The nurse should also provide parents with anticipatory guidance about circumstances likely to precipitate seizures. Such *precipitating factors* include intercurrent infections or illnesses, elevated temperature, emotional stress or fatigue, and irregular or inadequate doses of medication. Parents should be counseled to avoid such circumstances when possible (e.g., by keeping the infant on regular medication and by promptly treating elevated temperatures) and otherwise to closely observe the infant during these times.

Since infants with seizures are frequently at risk for a range of developmental problems, a *developmental screening examination*, including vision and hearing assessment, should be completed by the nurse. (See Chapters 14 through 17.) Infants with a seizure disorder should be reevaluated on a regular basis. If concerns arise, referral for a more in-depth developmental evaluation should be discussed with the physician. In some cases, infants may already be receiving therapy or educational services, and the nurse should work closely with these specialists to educate the family regarding the child's special needs.

ONGOING CONCERNS

Since seizures are symptoms of an underlying problem, the long-term prognosis is related both to the nature and severity of the causative disorder and to the promptness of appropriate intervention. A high percentage of infants who have had a seizure during the neonatal period are normal. In some cases in which the infant has experienced problems that may cause brain damage such as asphyxia, apnea, or CNS infections, the prognosis may be more guarded. In these situations, unless obvious damage such as weakness or spasticity is present, parents will not generally be given a long-term prognosis early on. Rather, the infant's development will be monitored over time, frequently for several years, before an accurate future picture can be suggested. In such cases, parents will need continued reassurance and support as they deal with the uncertain prognosis.

Home visits also provide the opportunity for the nurse to elicit any parental concerns or misconceptions. Questions should be answered in honest, simple terms. In educating parents, it may be helpful to provide written material. Some pamphlets regarding seizure disorders are available through local and national organizations, including the following:

- Epilepsy Foundation of America
  1828 L Street, N.W.
  Washington, D.C. 20036
- National Epilepsy League
  203 North Wabash Avenue
  Chicago, Illinois 60604.

If there are other children in the family, it is important to clarify what the affected child's siblings understand about seizures (see Chapter 19 for a detailed discussion of sibling adjustment). As necessary, the nurse may provide assistance to parents as they decide how to explain the seizure disorder to other family members or friends.

Another important and challenging issue for families is finding and educating a babysitter to care for the infant with a seizure disorder. Moreover, many parents are very reluctant to leave their infant for fear that a seizure may occur. The nurse can provide support to parents for planning activities for themselves. The nurse can also review important instructions for a sitter and assist in training the sitter as necessary or appropriate. Finding a babysitter willing to care for a health-impaired child and also respite care options are discussed in Chapters 2 and 20.

Finally, it is important that parents be encouraged to take their infant for health maintenance care and to discuss the infant's seizure disorder with the pediatric primary care provider. The *pertussis immunization* may be withheld because it is known to have potentially serious side effects in infants with neurologic problems.

As the infant grows, all aspects of care may need to be reviewed periodically with parents. Parental understanding may change over time; the infant's needs also change. The overall goals of home care for infants with seizures include optimal control of the seizures, promotion of growth and development, and support of parental coping abilities.

NOTES

1. Volpe J: *Neurology of the Newborn*, Philadelphia, WB Saunders Co, 1981, p 111.
2. Brill CB, Mitchel MH: Seizures and other paroxysmal disorders, *Adv Pediatr* 28: 441, 1981.
3. Painter MJ, Pippenger C, MacDonald H, et al: Phenobarbital and diphenylhydantoin levels in neonates with seizures, *J Pediatr* 92: 315, 1978.
4. Volpe J: *Neurology of the Newborn*, p 112.
5. Schulte FJ: Neonatal convulsions and their relation to epilepsy in early childhood, *Dev Med Child Neurol* 8: 381, 1966.
6. Volpe J: *Neurology of the Newborn*, p. 123.
7. *Ibid.*, p 120.

REFERENCES

Brill CB, Mitchel MH: Seizures and other paroxysmal disorders. *Adv Pediatr* 28: 441–89, 1981.

Bocchese J, Merker A: Seizure disorders in the neonate. *Crit Care Nurse*, November/December 1983, pp 42–46.

Conway BL: *Pediatric Neurological Nursing*. St Louis, CV Mosby Co, 1977.

Epilepsy: Hope Through Research (pamphlet). NIH publication 81–156, July 1981.

Lombroso CT: Prognosis in neonatal seizures. *Adv Neurol* 34: 101–113, 1983.

Mitchell W, O'Tuama L: Cerebral intraventricular hemorrhages in infants: a widening age spectrum. *Pediatrics* 65: 35–39, 1980.

Nursing '85 Drug Handbook. Springfield, Pa, Intermed Communications Inc, 1985.

Painter MJ, Pippenger C, MacDonald H, et al: Phenobarbital and diphenylhydantoin levels in neonates with seizures. *J Pediatr* 92: 315, 1978.

Parrish MA: A comparison of behavioral side effects related to commonly used anticonvulsants. *Pediatr Nurs* 10: 149–152, March/April 1984.

Schulte FJ: Neonatal convulsions and their relation to epilepsy in early childhood. *Dev Med Child Neurol* 8: 381, 1966.

Volpe J: *Neurology of the Newborn*. Philadelphia, WB Saunders Co, 1981.

Children's Hospital
National Medical Center
Home Care Team

Plan of Treatment

Page _____

Date _____   Case Manager _____

Name _____ Hosp# _____ DOB _____

PROBLEM: **SEIZURE DISORDER**

GOALS/OBJECTIVES	*METHODS*	*STAFF/REVIEW*
Child will have minimal number of seizures (____ per week or month) with minimal medication side effects.	Assess number and type of seizures on each home visit. Assess for medication side effects on each home visit. Communicate with physician as needed.	
Caregivers will describe seizure disorder and describe and demonstrate appropriate care.	Assess caregivers' knowledge about seizure disorders and care of the child during a seizure; teach/review as necessary. Teach factors that may increase the frequency of seizures (e.g., fever, illness, stress).	

GOALS/OBJECTIVES	METHODS	STAFF/REVIEW
	Assess caregivers' knowledge of appropriate administration of medications, including doses and frequency; teach/review as needed.	
	Assess caregivers' knowledge of medication side effects; teach/review as needed.	
Caregivers will state when to contact physician.	Assess caregivers' knowledge of when to contact physician: after what type of seizure; medication reaction; questions or concerns.	
Child will be able to function with minimal restrictions.	Discuss with family the effects of seizure disorder on life style of child and family: babysitters, vacations, seizures in public, peer relationships, safety considerations.	
	Provide information as needed.	
Child will receive well-coordinated care.	Communicate with primary physician and neurologist as necessary.	
	Educate family concerning risks of pertussis vaccine.	
	Discuss with family necessary follow-up evaluations including blood tests for serum	

GOALS/OBJECTIVES	METHODS	STAFF/REVIEW
	levels of anticonvulsants, EEG, and other tests as ordered.	
	Assist family to prepare child for examinations as required.	

Source: Reprinted with permission of Home Care Program (Ahmann, Lierman, and Peck), Children's Hospital National Medical Center, Washington, D.C.

Appendix 13–B

Medications Used in the Management of Seizures

Medication	Common Indications	Dosage	Optimal Serum Level (therapeutic range)	Side Effects and Nursing Considerations*
Phenytoin (Dilantin)	Major motor, psychomotor, and focal seizures	5–8 mg/kg/day	10–20 µg/ml	Nystagmus, ataxia, slurred speech, mental confusion, dizziness, insomnia, transient nervousness, motor twitching, hirsutism

Nausea, vomiting, constipation; may decrease if given after meals

Rashes: scarletiniform, bulbous, exfoliative purpura, dermatitis, lupus; also Stevens-Johnson syndrome, which *can be fatal* (first signs usually appear 7–10 days after beginning medication): if rash develops, contact physician immediately |

238

				Gingival hyperplasia; encourage gum brushing, gum massage and good dental care
				Available as suspension, but must be shaken well
				Contraindicated in hepatic damage
Phenobarbital	Major motor seizures	4–6 mg/kg/day	15–40 µg/ml	Sedation (frequently decreases after the first few days); excitability with increased motor activity, short attention span, distractibility and hyperactivity; sleep disturbances (especially in toddlers); depression; potentiation of existing behavior problems
				Dizziness, headache, "hangover," exacerbation of preexisting pain
				Diplopia, nystagmus, nausea and vomiting, epigastric pain
				Hypotension

Medication	Common Indications	Dosage	Optimal Serum Level (therapeutic range)	Side Effects and Nursing Considerations*
				Hypotension, facial edema, skin rash, purpura, erythema multiforme, exfoliative dermatitis (severe rash may indicate degenerative changes in liver)
				Megaloblastic anemia, agranulocytosis, thrombocytopenia
				Abrupt cessation (missed dose) may cause tremulousness, weakness, insomnia, convulsions, delirium
				Contraindicated in severe renal or hepatic dysfunction or in patients with hypersensitivity to barbiturates
Clonazepam (Clonapin)	Petit mal, minor motor, akinetic, and myoclonic seizures	0.1–0.2 mg/kg/day	20–60 ng/ml	Changes may be dosage-related and can be exaggerated.
				Drowsiness, tremor, ataxia, nausea, bradycardia, hypotonicity, rash, personality

				changes (such as hyperactivity, irritability, depression, sedation, aggression)
				May cause increase in nasopharyngeal secretions
				Diplopia, nystagmus, constipation, gastritis, nausea, dysuria, enuresis, urinary retention
				Contraindicated in hepatic disease with benzodiazepine sensitivity; use with caution in chronic respiratory disease; never withdraw drug suddenly
Valproic acid (Depekane)	Major motor, minor motor, petit mal, and focal seizures	10–40 mg/kg/day	50–100 µg/ml	Nausea, vomiting, and indigestion (may be transient); diarrhea, abdominal cramps and constipation
				Sedative effects (mostly if combined with other drugs), ataxia, headache, nystagmus, diplopia, "spots before eyes," tremor, dysarthria, dizziness, incoordination

Medication	Common Indications	Dosage	Optimal Serum Level (therapeutic range)	Side Effects and Nursing Considerations*
				Transient hair loss, emotional upset, depression, psychosis, aggression, hyperactivity, behavioral deterioration
				Altered bleeding time, thrombocytopenia
				Advise patients to take with meals
				Obtain liver function studies, platelet count, and prothrombin time initially and on regular basis
				Contraindicated in patients who have any hepatic condition; may cause acute hepatic necrosis
Carbamazepine (Tegretol)	Psychomotor and temporal lobe or generalized tonic-clonic (grand mal) seizures Mixed seizures of above or partial general seizures	7–20 mg/kg//day	8–12 µg/ml	Dizziness, vertigo, drowsiness, fatigue, ataxia, congestive heart failure, hypotension, conjunctivitis, dry mouth and pharynx, blurred vision, diplopia, nystagmus, nausea, vomiting, diarrhea, anorexia,

urinary frequency, glycosuria, water intoxication, skin rash

Diplopia may be first sign that dose is too high; potentially serious side effects include aplastic anemia; get pretreatment blood counts to rule out abnormalities and repeat frequently; stop drug with bone marrow depression: monitor status with CBC, platelet and reticulocyte counts, serum iron determinations, liver function studies

NOTIFY DOCTOR if symptoms of fever, sore throat, ulcers in mouth, easy bruising petechiae, purpura (early toxic signs) appear

Eye changes; baseline and periodic eye examinations are essential

Renal dysfunction; baseline and periodic determinations of urine and BUN are essential

Medication	Common Indications	Dosage	Optimal Serum Level (therapeutic range)	Side Effects and Nursing Considerations*
				Contraindicated in patients with bone marrow depression
Ethosuximide (Zarontin)	Petit mal, akinetic, and myoclonic seizures	20–30 mg/kg/day	40–100 µg/ml	Nausea, vomiting, leukopenia, eosinophilia, agranulocytosis, pancytopenia, aplastic anemia, drowsiness, headache, dizziness, ataxia, irritability, hiccups, euphoria, lethargy, myopia
				Diarrhea, weight loss, cramps, anorexia, epigastric and abdominal pain, vaginal bleeding, urticaria, pruritic erythematous rashes
				Use with caution in hepatic or renal disease
				Obtain regular CBC
Adrenocorto-tropic hormone (ACTH)	Infantile spasms	Dosage varies; must be given by injection; often given on a daily basis		Edema with weight gain, sodium and potassium retention, muscle weakness and loss of muscle mass, irritability,

petechiae, acne, hirsutism, hypertension, headache, thrush, vertigo, negative nitrogen balance, allergic response to proteins, dizziness, nausea, vomiting, diarrhea

Will need to monitor blood pressure

Abbreviations: µg = micrograms; ng = nanograms; CBC = complete blood count; BUN = blood urea nitrogen.

*For additional information, consult Parrish's article and the *Nursing '82 Drug Handbook*, listed in References for this chapter.

Chapter 14

Hearing Impairment in the High Risk Infant

B. Patrick Cox, PhD
Elizabeth Ahmann, RN, MS, FNP

Hearing is integrally related to a child's communication, speech and language, intellectual, and psychosocial development. Although each of these areas will develop to some degree without hearing-related stimulation and interaction, optimal development is achieved when any hearing impairment is detected early and the appropriate intervention initiated. Failure to identify the hearing-impaired child early enough may lead to delayed expressive and receptive language, speech problems, and even social and emotional problems such as manipulative behavior, confusion, anger, and poor self-image.[1]

RISK FACTORS FOR HEARING IMPAIRMENT

Many factors may place the newborn infant at risk for hearing impairment. There is currently no ideal register of risk factors that is sufficiently specific to clearly identify a hearing-impaired child. The risk register now in widest use was developed by the Joint Committee on Infant Hearing.[2] This risk register includes a wide range of factors; some of the most important are included in Exhibit 14–1.

The exact percentage of infants predisposed to hearing impairment by each risk factor is difficult to predict. Abramovitch suggests that 8 to 9 percent of very low birth weight (VLBW) infants may have significant hearing impairment.[3] Gerkin and Downs suggest that 30 percent of babies with symptomatic congenital cytomegalovirus (CMV) infection may also have some degree of impairment.[4] Many infants have more than one risk factor, and the risk factors tend to be interactive.

Note: Appendix 14–A contains a sample hearing assessment form that provides guidelines for assessment.

Exhibit 14–1 Some Risk Factors for Hearing Impairment in Infants

---

- Birth weight less than 1500 grams
- Bilirubin level high enough to necessitate intervention
- Family history of childhood-onset hearing impairment
- Congenital or perinatal infection (e.g., toxoplasmosis, rubella, cytomegalovirus infection, herpes virus infection, syphilis)
- Anatomic malformations of the head or neck
- Bacterial meningitis, especially that caused by *Hemophilus influenzae*
- Severe asphyxia (Apgar score 0–3)
- No spontaneous respirations by 10 minutes after birth
- Hypotonia present at 2 hours of age
- Use of ototoxic drugs (including Kanamycin, streptomycin, neomycin, gentamicin)
- Exposure to high levels of environmental noise

CHARACTERISTICS OF HEARING IMPAIRMENT

Regardless of its cause or origin, hearing impairment varies substantially in nature. It may be *unilateral* (one ear affected) or *bilateral.* The degree of impairment may be *mild* (in which audible sound begins at a range of 25 to 40 decibels [dB], as determined on the audiogram), *moderate,* or *profound* (audible sounds of 90 to 120 dB). The *configuration* of the hearing impairment may be symmetric, with equal impairment over the entire range of human hearing frequencies, or the loss may be more pronounced at particular frequencies (e.g., high-frequency hearing loss). Finally, the impairment can be classified, according to the ear structures involved, as conductive, sensorineural, or mixed.

Conductive hearing impairment involves the outer (external) ear or the middle ear (the spaces beyond the tympanic membrane with the three tiny bones or ossicles), or both. The causes of conductive hearing loss include wax accumulation, perforated tympanic membrane, middle ear infection (otitis media), otosclerosis, and more serious disorders associated with conditions such as Treacher-Collins or Pierre Robin syndrome. Conductive impairment is characterized by a decrease in perceived loudness of sound that ranges in degree from mild to moderately severe. Any conductive disorders that cannot be remedied by medical or surgical intervention require vigorous nonmedical intervention such as hearing amplification and aural habilitation (auditory training, parent teaching and counseling, and other activities as the infant ages).

Sensorineural hearing impairment involves the inner ear (the delicate structures of the cochlea and the auditory nerve fibers leading to the brain). These losses occur when the inner ear structures fail to develop, develop only partially, or are damaged after they have formed. Sensorineural hearing impairment results in a decrease in clarity of sound as well as in loudness. This disorder is often referred to as either a speech or word discrimination disorder. At the present time, there are no medical or surgical treatments that reverse sensorineural hearing impairment.

The third type of hearing impairment is mixed, and involves a combination of conductive and sensorineural impairments. A mixed hearing impairment results from a problem in the outer or middle ear and the inner ear and may occur at all or some of the frequencies of human hearing.

IDENTIFICATION OF INFANTS WITH HEARING IMPAIRMENT

Regardless of the infant's type of hearing impairment, early detection is important. Early detection is dependent on cooperation between the infant's family and the health care professionals who have contact with the infant. Parents should be encouraged to share any suspicions they have concerning a hearing problem as soon as possible; any delay only places the infant at further risk for hearing difficulties.

Early detection of hearing impairment is the joint responsibility of parents and professionals. Professional responsibility is often shared, depending on the locale and service availability. Identification of infants with hearing impairment involves screening and diagnostic evaluation; appropriate intervention is then instituted.

Hearing Screening

The purpose of screening is to identify infants who are suspected of having a hearing loss. As recommended by the Joint Committee on Infant Hearing[5] and as suggested by clinical studies, screening should include a thorough case history and review of risk factors. In addition, behavioral observation or electrophysiologic testing (or both) is recommended. All infants who are at risk for hearing impairment should be screened at birth, if possible, but certainly no later than at 6 months of age.

Nurses are in a particularly advantageous position to identify infants at risk for hearing impairment. The intensive care nurse is well aware of the infant's problems and can ensure that a risk register for hearing impairment is used to evaluate the infant. If this is not possible, the nurse can make an appropriate referral through the infant's family and physician. Other nurse specialists are also intimately involved with the follow-up care of infants: the nurse practitioner who takes a developmental history; the nurse in a physician's office; and the community health nurse. They, too, play a role in identification and referral.

History

A complete history should address the risk factors identified in Exhibit 14–1. If the family does not have all the necessary information, hospital or physicians' records should be reviewed.

History taking should also address any parental concerns and include careful questioning regarding their observations. A list of questions appropriate to the age of the infant is provided in Exhibit 14–2. A note of caution is in order here: parents may not suspect a hearing loss because the child is vocalizing, which many parents believe to be a sign of normal hearing. In fact, however, children with the most profound hearing loss often engage in automatic, reflexive babbling. In many cases, it is not until later, when babbling fails to lead to speech, that parents become concerned.

Informal Auditory Behavioral Screening

After a complete case history has been taken, the nurse's assessment continues with an informal auditory behavioral screening of the infant. Casual observation of the infant's apparent responses to sound, however, may be misleading to the parents as well as to the nurse. At birth and in the early months of life, infants attend best to sounds that contain multiple frequencies, such as speech, noise-maker sounds, and environmental sounds. On the basis of reactions to these sounds alone, it is impossible to state unequivocally that the baby hears. For example, a baby may have hearing only in the lower frequency range yet may still appear to startle to a hand clap, especially if it is near the ear.

In the informal behavioral screening procedure, the nurse may use a group of noisemakers with known intensity and frequency characteristics such as those provided in the HEAR Kit.[6] This Kit includes five noisemakers with sounds that collectively span the human hearing range. These noisemakers have specified peak intensity (loudness) levels. At the same time, each noisemaker sound contains a number of frequencies (pitches). Therefore, the nurse must be cautious in interpreting reactions to each noisemaker; the child may respond to only some of the represented frequencies and may have significant losses in others. If the HEAR kit is not available, a variety of noisemakers can be obtained for use. An audiologist can ascertain the appropriateness of the chosen noisemakers as well as the frequency and intensity characteristics of each.

To conduct the screening, the infant is held in the parent's lap, and the nurse kneels alongside, just behind the infant's line of sight. While attracting the infant's visual attention straight ahead with an interesting toy (included in the HEAR Kit), the nurse activates one of the noisemakers at a specified distance from the infant's ear and out of the visual field (at a 45-degree angle from the plane of the infant's forward orientation). At the same time, the nurse closely observes the infant's response to the sound stimuli. Each stimulus is presented two or three times, and

Exhibit 14–2 Questions to Elicit Parental Observations

2 MONTHS

1. Have you had any worry about your child's hearing?
2. When he's sleeping in a quiet room, does he move and begin to wake up when there's a loud sound?

4 MONTHS

1. Have you had any worry about your child's hearing?
2. When he's sleeping in a quiet room, does he move and begin to wake up when there's a loud sound?
3. Does he try to turn his head toward an interesting sound, or when his name is called?

6 MONTHS

1. Have you had any worry about your child's hearing?
2. When he's sleeping in a quiet room, does he move and begin to wake up when there's a loud sound?
3. Does he turn his head toward an interesting sound or when his name is called?

8 MONTHS

1. Have you had any worry about your child's hearing?
2. When he's sleeping in a quiet room, does he move and begin to wake up when there's a loud sound?
3. Does he turn his head directly toward an interesting sound or when his name is called?
4. Does [he] enjoy ringing a bell or shaking a rattle?

10 MONTHS

1. Have you had any worry about your child's hearing?
2. When he's sleeping in a quiet room, does he move and begin to wake up when there's a loud sound?
3. Does he turn his head directly toward an interesting sound or when his name is called?
4. Does he try to imitate you if you make his own sounds?

12 MONTHS

1. Have you had any worry about your child's hearing?
2. When he's sleeping in a quiet room, does he move and begin to wake up when there's a loud sound?
3. Does he try to turn his head toward an interesting sound or when his name is called?
4. Is he beginning to repeat some of the sounds that you make?

Source: Excerpted from "Questions to Ask Mother at the Well Baby Examination" in *Hearing in Children*, 2d ed., by J.L. Northern and M.P. Downs, pp. 215–217, with permission of The Williams & Wilkins Company, © 1978.

the procedure is then repeated at the other ear. Typical age-appropriate orienting responses are described in Exhibit 14–3.

Judging whether an infant is responding to a noisemaker is not easy, even for the most seasoned observer. The observer must depend on reflexive behaviors in infants under 4 months of age, owing to the immaturity of integrative processes and auditory-motor coordination.[7] In these very young infants, responses generally include startle, eye blink, body jerk and movement, crying or cessation of crying, and changes in respiratory rate.[8] After 4 months of age, however, the infant's ability to listen and to attempt to locate sound is developing. In infants between 4 months and 2 years of age, behavioral screening is dependent on the orienting responses, as indicated in Exhibit 14–3.[9]

Informal behavioral screening as described is valuable. It must, however, be done with great care. The reliability of the screening procedure can be increased in the following ways:

Exhibit 14–3 Development of Infant's Orienting Responses to Noisemakers

Age (months)	Responses
0 to 4 months.	Eye widening, eye blink (in a very quiet environment), or arousal from sleep as in newborn testing.
4 to 7 months.	By 4 months, a "rudimentary" head turn is seen: a "wobble" of the head even slightly toward the sound.

This response gradually matures until at 6 months the head turn is definite, toward the side of the sound, but only on a plane level with the eyes. He does not fixate the sound source in the lower level where it comes from.

By 7 months there is an inclination to find the sound source on the lower level; the child will look first to the side and then down. He may even be mature enough to find the source directly. |
7 to 9 months.	At the beginning of this period he should soon find the sound source on the lower level directly, but if the sound is presented on a level above his head, he will only look toward the side. At the end of this period he may begin to look toward the side and then up, to fixate the higher sound source.
9 to 13 months.	At 9 months, the beginning indirect localization of the higher level will be seen which soon turns to direct localization. We thus see shortly after 1 year of age a direct localization of sounds in any plane.
13 to 24 months.	The same type of orientation prevails for the older child as was seen for the 13-month-old. In other words, the full maturation of the auditory behavior of the child occurs at about 13 months and does not change significantly after that.

Source: From *Hearing in Children,* 2d ed., by J.L. Northern and M.P. Downs, pp. 213–214, with permission of The Williams & Wilkins Company, © 1978.

1. Test in a quiet room that is free of visual distractions.
2. Test when the infant is reasonably quiet or has just fallen asleep.
3. Test between feedings.
4. Use familiar and interesting sounds (as provided in the HEAR kit).
5. Change back and forth between the noisemakers, as necessary, to limit the effect of the infant's adaptation to the sound.
6. Be sure that the airflow from the squeeze toy does not stimulate a false positive response in the infant.
7. Take care not to touch the infant's ear immediately before or during the activation of a noisemaker.
8. If possible, have a parent or other helper conduct the visual distraction so that the tester is fully out of view of the infant.

Informal behavioral screening should also be interpreted with caution. Emphasis should be placed on the maturing auditory response in relationship to the overall development of the infant. In this regard, the factor of prematurity should be considered. As a safeguard, it is best to assume that the premature infant will respond to sound at the expected intensity level without age correction but may not show the age-appropriate motor response to the sound.

In addition, the nurse is cautioned that the informal hearing screening procedures described here indicate only whether an infant or child appears not to be deaf or appears to have a hearing impairment. The screening cannot accurately yield any finer interpretation. For this reason, if any of the risk factors are present, or if an impairment is suspected according to results of informal behavioral screening, the infant should be promptly referred to a certified audiologist and an otologist. The infant's primary pediatric care provider should also be notified.

When referrals are made, the nurse should continue to be an advocate for the infant or child and to ensure that the family follows through with the recommendations for audiologic and medical evaluation. If intervention is warranted, the nurse can also facilitate its implementation.

Audiologic Evaluation

When an infant or child is referred by the nurse for suspected hearing impairment, the infant should receive a complete audiologic and medical evaluation. (The medical evaluation is discussed in the following section.)

The audiologic evaluation includes a complete history, which amplifies the nursing history; diagnostic testing designed to determine the type and extent of hearing loss; and family counseling regarding the results of the evaluation. If the child is found to have a hearing loss, further work with the audiologist may include selection of appropriate hearing aids, additional counseling regarding both the audiologic findings and the family's feelings about having a hearing-impaired child, and referral for appropriate educational and communication development intervention.

The diagnostic tests used by an audiologist may be behavioral or electrophysiologic. Behavioral tests rely on the overall developmental level of the infant or child, as is the case for informal auditory behavioral screening. For the child up to the age of 2 years, these procedures include the following:

- *behavior observation audiometry* (BOA), which is similar to the informal screening described earlier but uses more carefully specified signals and is conducted by an audiologist or team of audiologists
- *animated visually reinforced audiometry* (AVRA), in which a child is rewarded with an animated toy when correctly localizing
- *conditioned-play audiometry* (CPA), in which the child is taught to perform a motor act (e.g., to put a peg in a pegboard) upon hearing the sound
- *tangible-reinforced operant-conditioned audiometry* (TROCA), in which the child pushes a button when the sound is heard and is rewarded with an edible or nonedible reinforcer.

When the audiologist achieves consistent results with any one of these techniques and finds the results to be supported by the parents' report, the findings are considered reliable. In the event that the results of behavioral audiometry are equivocal, the audiologist may conduct an *auditory brainstem response (ABR) test,* an electrophysiologic test that has gained popularity in the past several years (this test is also referred to as evoked response audiometry or auditory evoked potential audiometry).

ABR tests are frequently administered by neurologists as well as audiologists. Some hospitals have ABR screening programs that are staffed by volunteers and supported by philanthropic groups; typically, these programs screen the hearing of any newborns who meet the high risk criteria. However, owing to the cost of equipment and the time needed both to conduct the actual screening and to interpret the results, ABR screening is often available only in regional centers.

Threshold testing with the ABR procedure is very helpful when performed appropriately and interpreted in conjunction with behavioral data. Not all infants or children need to have ABR testing; it should be reserved for those cases in which behavioral results are equivocal.

Medical Evaluation

Any child found to have a hearing impairment should be referred for a complete otologic evaluation. This includes a review of the audiologic, developmental, and medical histories, as well as a thorough physical examination of the ears, head, and neck to identify any observable abnormalities. The otologist may also order laboratory tests that help to detect the cause of the hearing impairment and that determine both its progression and the prognosis. The otologist will also refer the family to other medical specialists (e.g., geneticists or birth defects specialists) when appropriate. In addition, the otologist certifies that the infant or child with a hearing loss has no physical problems that preclude use of a hearing aid if this is indicated.

INTERVENTION

As noted previously, early intervention is paramount to optimizing the growth and development of the infant with a hearing impairment. The nurse, the physicians, the audiologist, the speech and language pathologist, the teacher of the hearing-impaired, and the parents must collaborate in developing an appropriate program for the infant.

An example of the need for collaboration relates to the use of *hearing aids*. Hearing aids may be difficult to keep on an infant, and parents may feel reluctant to use them because they provide such visible evidence of a problem. The nurse and the audiologist can easily cooperate in this area. If the nurse sees the family more often than the audiologist, the nurse can both help parents deal with their feelings and offer practical suggestions concerning how to keep the hearing aids in place.

A *home stimulation program* is an important component of intervention for the infant with hearing impairment. Such programs are often directed by trained teachers of the hearing-impaired, speech and language pathologists, or audiologists. The programs are reinforced by stimulation programs conducted by nurses or child development specialists. Home-based (parent-infant) programs teach parents both how to optimize the auditory environment and how to talk with their infant. Since speech and language intervention is almost always needed by the child with hearing impairment, home programs should also offer instruction in the sequence of language development to guide parental stimulation efforts.[10] Alternative methods of communication, including sign language and cued speech (lip reading), may also be appropriate. Many parents of children with hearing impairments will also benefit from learning behavior management strategies.[11] Personal counseling for the parents or other family members may also be indicated.

The long-term picture for the infant with hearing impairment is optimized with early and routine screening for risk factors, parental concerns, and hearing status. Early intervention, preferably before 9 to 12 months of age, will optimize developmental opportunities.

NOTES

1. Boothroyd A: *Hearing Impairments in Young Children*, Englewood Cliffs, NJ: Prentice-Hall Inc, 1982), pp 3–5.

2. American Academy of Pediatrics Joint Committee on Infant Hearing, Position statement 1982, *Pediatrics* 70: 496–497, September 1982, Joint Committee on Infant Hearing, 1982 statement, *Asha* 24: 1017–1018, 1982.

3. Abramovitch SJ, Gregory S, Slemick M, et al: Hearing loss in the very low birthweight infants treated with neonatal intensive care, *Arch Dis Child* 54: 421, 1979.

4. Gerkin KP, Downs MP: The high risk register for newborn hearing programs, *Semin Hear* 5: 1, 1984.

5. Joint Committee on Infant Screening: 1982 statement, pp 1017–1018.

6. The HEAR Kit is available from BAM World Markets, Inc., P.O. Box 10701, University Park Station, Denver, Colorado 80210.

7. Northern JL, Downs MP: *Hearing in Children*, ed 2, Baltimore, Williams & Wilkins Co, 1978, p 122.

8. Weiss CE, Lillywhite HS: *Communication Disorders: Prevention and Early Intervention*, ed 2, St Louis, CV Mosby Co, 1981, p 106.

9. Northern JL, Downs MP: *Hearing in Children*, p 106.

10. *Ibid.*, p 13.

11. Horton KB: Early intervention through parent training, *Otolaryngol Clin North Am* 8: 152, 1975.

REFERENCES

Abramovitch SJ, Gregory S, Slemick M, et al: Hearing loss in the very low birthweight infants treated with neonatal intensive care. *Arch Dis Child* 54: 421, 1979.

American Academy of Pediatrics Joint Committee on Infant Hearing: Position statement 1982. *Pediatrics* 70: 496–497, September 1982.

Bergstrom L, Stewart J: New concepts in congenital deafness. *Otolaryngol Clin North Am* 4: 431–443, 1971.

Bergstrom L, Hemenway WG, Downs MP: A high risk registry to find congenital deafness. *Otolaryngol Clin North Am* 4: 369–399, 1971.

Boothroyd A: *Hearing Impairments in Young Children*. Englewood Cliffs, NJ, Prentice-Hall Inc, 1982.

Chow MP, Durand BA, Feldman MN, et al: *Handbook of Pediatric Primary Care*, ed 2. New York, John Wiley and Sons, 1984, Chapter 25.

Downs MP: Guidelines for hearing screening of the infant, preschool and school-age child, in Krajicek MJ, Tearny AI (eds): *Detection of Developmental Problems in Children*. Baltimore, University Park Press, 1977, p 111.

Downs MP, Silver HK: The A.B.C.D.'s to H.E.A.R. *Clin Pediatr* 11: 563–566, 1972.

Fitzhardinge PM, Pape KE: Follow-up studies of the high-risk newborn, in Avery GB (ed): *Neonatology: Pathophysiology and Management of the Newborn*. Philadelphia, JB Lippincott Co, 1981, p 350.

Fry DB: The development of the phonological system in the normal and deaf child, in Smith FS, Miller GA (eds): *The Genesis of Language*. Cambridge, Mass, MIT Press, 1966, p 187.

Gerkin KP, Downs MP: The high risk register for newborn hearing programs. *Semin Hear* 5: 1, 1984.

Horton KB: Early intervention through parent training. *Otolaryngol Clin North Am* 8: 143–57, 1975.

Joint Committee on Infant Hearing: 1982 statement. *Asha* 24: 1017–1018, 1982.

Lillywhite HS, Young NG, Olmstead PW: *Pediatrician's Handbook of Communication Disorders.* Philadelphia, Lea & Febiger, 1970.

Northern JL, Downs MP: *Hearing in Children,* ed 2. Baltimore, Williams & Wilkins Co, 1978.

Weiss CE, Lillywhite HS: *Communication Disorders: Prevention and Early Intervention,* ed 2. St Louis, CV Mosby Co, 1981.

Children's Hospital
Home Care Program
National Medical Center
Hearing Assessment of the Infant

Name_____ Hosp#_____ DOB_____

HISTORY

1. Family member with hearing defects. Explain_____ ____yes ____no
   _____

2. Congenital rubella or other non-bacterial uterine ____yes ____no
   infection (CMV, herpes, syphilis)_____
   _____

3. Birthweight—less than 1500 grams_____ ____yes ____no
4. Severe asphyxia including Apgar score of 3 or less_ ____yes ____no
5. History of serum bilirubin level greater than ____yes ____no
   15 mg/100 (premie)
   20 mg/100 (full term) ____yes ____no
6. Defects of ear, nose or throat. Describe_____ ____yes ____no
   _____

7. Ototoxic drugs (Kanamycin, streptomycin, neo- ____yes ____no
   mycin, gentamycin)
   Duration_____
8. Meningitis, hemophilus influenza, scarlet fever, ____yes ____no
   mumps (circle)
9. Ingestion of arsenic or lead (circle) ____yes ____no
10. Six or more ear infections within one year or fluid in ____yes ____no
    middle ear which does not clear over two months.
11. Trauma to skull. Describe_____ ____yes ____no
    _____

PARENT REPORT

Parental concerns_____

_____

Awakens to sound (voice)_____

Previous hearing tests   *Date*   *Type and result*

____   _____

____   _____

____   _____

*Hearing screening**   *Rattle*   *Bell*   *Squeak*

Response on RIGHT_____

Response on LEFT_____

*Procedure based on "Testing with One Observer—A Simplified Procedure" from "Guidelines for Hearing Screening of the Infant, Pre-school, and School-age Child" (Chapter VII), in: *Detection of Developmental Problems in Children,* by M.J. Krajicek and A.I. Tearney (Eds.), University Park Press, © 1977.

General developmental screening (Denver 0–3 years)

_____

_____

_____

_____

_____

Assessment

_____

_____

_____

_____

_____

Plan

_____

_____

_____

_____

_____

_____   _____

Signature of person completing assessment   Date

Source: Reprinted with permission of Home Care Program (Ahmann, Lierman, and Peck), Children's Hospital National Medical Center, Washington, D.C.

Chapter 15

Speech and Language Development in the High Risk Infant

Bonnie M. Simon, MA, CCC-SP

Initial development in speech and language may be affected by acute or chronic illness in the infant and by lengthy hospitalization. Careful screening of the high-risk infant and timely intervention, if indicated, are important in the prevention of long-term communication impairment. This chapter introduces the community health nurse to the following pertinent issues:

1. the communication process and its development
2. factors contributing to speech and language problems in the high risk infant
3. identification of specific problems
4. methods for language stimulation
5. the special needs of the tracheostomized and ventilator-dependent child, including postdecannulation follow-up.

Guidelines for referral to a speech-language pathologist or otolaryngologist, or both, are also offered.

COMMUNICATION DEVELOPMENT

The communication process should be analyzed in terms of two systems: expression and reception. Both of these systems begin to develop immediately after birth. *Expression* involves any form of communicating needs or ideas, whether verbally or nonverbally. *Reception* involves the ability to comprehend the language and symbols of one's environment. A child may develop normal recep-tive skills but demonstrate a specific expressive speech disorder. Conversely, a

The author wishes to thank Rhona Mondelblatt for her help in preparation of this chapter.

child with an auditory deficit may have normal speech potential, which cannot develop until receptive skills begin to emerge.

Receptive Functioning

Receptive functioning develops as a child begins to respond to auditory stimuli in the environment (see Chapter 14). During the first few months of life, an infant refines this ability to respond to relevant auditory stimuli and learns to block out what is not needed. With continued maturation of auditory skills, a child begins to symbolize, and the ability to comprehend language develops. By 12 to 15 months of age, a child should recognize familiar environmental elements and respond to simple directions. Receptive vocabulary and cognitive skills continue to develop.

Expressive Functioning

The infant's first cry begins expressive communication with the environment. The development of early prespeech communication is an important foundation for later speech and language skills. Parents can learn to differentiate the reasons for their infant's cries, which can be due to hunger, discomfort, or boredom.[1] Later emergence of *cooing* is followed by *babbling* at 4 months of age. Mature babbling involves some intentional communication.[2] It can persist to as late as 12 months of age, gradually becoming interspersed with meaningful words. The next stage of prespeech communication is labeled *jargon*, which can be defined as meaningless, unintelligible sound sequences. This early form of purposeful communication has been described by parents as sounding like a foreign language. It occurs simultaneously with the development of meaningful words and can continue throughout the child's second year of life. By 18 months of age, *echolalia* is seen. This is described as the imitative production of words, phrases, or sentences. It can be present both with and without comprehension of the utterances. Echolalia normally continues until the age of 3 years. However, by this time, the young child should be primarily communicating in simple sentences, with a gradual decrease in echolalic responses.

By age 3, the young child should be generally intelligible to the family and usually is understood by peers. At this age, it is important to differentiate between speech and language. *Speech* involves the oral-motor coordination of the jaw, tongue, lips, and palate with respiration and phonation. A child's speech development is analyzed in terms of the ability to be understood and the specific ability to produce phonologic sequences (consonant and vowel combinations). *Language* involves word order and the ability to combine meaningful words into comprehensible sentences. A child's language development is judged in terms of vocabulary, syntax (grammatical structures), word order, and sentence length. Language development is also described in terms of pragmatic skills or the appropriateness of language use.

Reasons for Speech and Language Delay

Any child who has had a difficult neonatal course may be at risk for speech or language difficulties. Severe medical problems can affect the infant's overall development, and the acutely ill infant may also experience periods of inactivity that lead to less than optimal environmental experiences. Additionally, respiratory disorders can impair the development of vocalization.

The hospital environment itself also affects development. For example, many high risk infants spend lengthy periods in intensive care units, which may have high ambient noise levels and excessive visual stimulation. Difficulties in learning to attend to relevant auditory and visual stimuli may develop if the young child cannot learn to differentiate important from unimportant stimuli. Some infants respond by overreacting to the excessive environmental stimulation, whereas others become unresponsive and listless.

The high risk infant may also be at risk for becoming a passive communicator.[3] *Communicative passivity* arises not only because of the young child's inability to communicate, or because of immaturity, but also as a result of inexperience and the absence of an environmental need for expression. Chronically ill infants who are in need of extensive medical attention often do not have the need to communicate because they already have constant adult attention; they may express themselves only when asked questions.

IDENTIFICATION OF SPEECH AND LANGUAGE PROBLEMS

The pediatric home health nurse should be aware that early feeding difficulties may be a warning sign of later speech difficulties. The high risk infant's ability to respond to the environment, both through auditory responsiveness and through prespeech communication, must also be monitored throughout early childhood. Indeed, early identification must be based on a thorough assessment of the infant's auditory awareness. Any infant who does not appear to respond consistently to noises or to the human voice should be referred for further diagnostic assessment by an audiologist, with coordinated otolaryngologic consultation (see Chapter 14).

If specific hearing problems are not obvious, but the child does not appear to symbolize or comprehend language by 12 to 15 months of age, a full diagnostic developmental assessment should be considered to determine why the child's development of comprehension and cognitive functioning is delayed. Certainly by 18 months of age all children should be able to follow simple directions without gestural and situational cues. They should also recognize family members and favorite toys.

Expressive speech and language disorders are more difficult to identify at an early age because of the variability of developmental patterns among children. Most children should be using a few meaningful words by 12 to 15 months of age and may have a vocabulary of more than 10 words by 18 months. Other children, however, do not begin talking until 15 to 18 months or later. These late talkers may demonstrate normal speech and language development at a more rapid pace once speech begins to emerge. It is important to become aware of several elements in determining the need for speech and language evaluation, as indicated in Exhibit 15–1. If communication delay is expected, referral to a speech-language pathologist should be initiated to aid in identifying possible contributing factors and to determine the appropriate time for speech and language therapy, if necessary.

LANGUAGE STIMULATION SUGGESTIONS

To maximize the need for communication, caregivers should use appropriate techniques of speech and language stimulation. All vocal attempts by an infant should be imitated by an adult to encourage their recurrence. Verbalization of a young child's activities and the activities of others in the immediate environment helps the child to learn appropriate words and to expand language concepts. In this regard, language stimulation activities should be coordinated with daily care (i.e., eating, bathing, and dressing). The repetition involved in these activities enables more effective language learning.

Even the chronically ill child who is unable to vocalize requires continuous language stimulation both for the development of receptive skills and as prepara-

---

Exhibit 15–1 Tool for Identifying Potential for Speech and Language
            Disorders

1. Does the child seem to comprehend much more than suggested by the ability to speak? Is there a gap between expressive and receptive skills?
2. Does the child appear to respond by demonstrating awareness of sound?
3. Does the child seem to be frustrated by an inability to communicate his or her needs?
4. Does the family or caregiver appear to be frustrated by the child's limited capacity for self-expression?
5. Is the child difficult to understand although able to speak?
6. Do the child's communication skills seem disproportionate to (or below) developmental levels?
7. Are there feeding problems?

tion for later verbal development. Normal language stimulation should merely provide an accepting environment for facilitating any communicative attempts. It is important, however, to stress that no child should be forced to communicate. If forcing persists, verbal withdrawal may occur.

COMMUNICATION PROBLEMS IN CHILDREN WITH A TRACHEOSTOMY

The child with a tracheostomy is at high risk for communication problems. Often the tracheostomized child requires excessive attention from medical and nursing personnel; as a result, the need for communication is minimal. Furthermore, the presence of the tracheostomy tube in the upper airway can create *aphonia*, or the inability to produce voice.[4] Other factors causing the lack of vocalization include weakened respiratory muscles, poor diaphragmatic movement, and use of a ventilator.

Since the tracheostomy tube is placed above the vocal cords, a leak of air around the cannula and past the vocal cords is necessary in order to obtain vocalization. If there is no space around the tracheostomy tube because of a tight-fitting cannula, or if the upper airway is narrowed as a result of subglottic stenosis, the air will not pass through the glottis, and aphonia occurs.[5]

If some air can leak around the cannula, if the child's respiratory muscles are strong, and if the upper airway is patent with good vocal cord movement, voice can sometimes be obtained. *Vocal intensity* (loudness), however, may be weak unless the stoma is covered. Thus, to vocalize effectively, many children with tracheostomies who are not totally ventilator-dependent must learn to cover the stoma and coordinate exhalation with blockage of the air at the stoma site. Some children learn to lower the chin in order to cover the stoma and thus develop a more intense vocal production. As the size of the tracheostomy tube is changed to accommodate normal growth, the ability to vocalize also changes, and the child must accommodate these alterations.

Vocal quality in a tracheostomized child can be hoarse; this also affects the intensity levels. A hoarseness and raspy vocal quality may be temporary or permanent, depending on the child's underlying respiratory condition and on the frequency and length of intubation. *Pitch* can vary, but inappropriate pitch does not appear to be as significant a problem as hoarseness or weak intensity. *Resonance* problems (hyponasality, hypernasality) do not occur more frequently in the tracheostomized population than in the normal population. For this reason, any child with questionable resonance problems should be referred to an otolaryngologist for further assessment of palatal functioning and upper airway status.

Weakened breath support is commonly found in the tracheostomized population. It affects not only the initiation of vocalizations but also intensity levels, duration of phonation, and verbal intelligibility. Specific exercises to improve breath support can be recommended by a physical therapist or a speech-language pathologist.

The child who is ventilator-dependent must use a complex method of communication. For the child who is totally ventilator-dependent, ventilator pressure changes can be used to support vocalizations. Vocalizations aided by the ventilator are produced on inhalation; those produced independent of the ventilator require exhalation. For the young infant or child being weaned from the ventilator, or requiring only intermittent ventilation, vocalization mechanisms become difficult to coordinate. Breaths provided by the ventilator must be coordinated with self-initiated breaths.

The confusing vocal experience that results can contribute to delayed vocalization in a young ventilator-dependent child, long after the ability to produce voice has developed. It is important that a speech-language pathologist become involved as early as possible in order to alleviate some of these complex vocal problems and attempt to obtain more consistent vocalizations. Such children must be taught to utilize a functional communication system appropriate for both inconsistent verbal attempts and changing respiratory needs.

New techniques for obtaining vocalization in the tracheostomized individual are being developed by surgeons and otolaryngologists throughout the country. Although most of the recent advances have been developed for older children or adults, parents should be encouraged to discuss the child's vocal capabilities with a speech-language pathologist or an otolaryngologist. These professionals should be aware of the appropriateness of new techniques for children and can determine the optimal approach for obtaining vocalization.

ALTERNATIVE AND AUGMENTATIVE COMMUNICATION SYSTEMS

The child with a tracheostomy is at high risk for an expressive communication delay. As the young child matures and develops a need for communication, frustration with aphonia or inconsistent vocal productions may become apparent.

In an attempt to decrease communicative passivity and related frustration in the child with a tracheostomy, any form of nonvocal communication should be accepted, and the child should be encouraged to initiate communication.

Nonvocal, gestural systems are often developed by the child in an attempt to have needs met. In infants, common nonverbal communication attempts include smiling, reaching, pointing, and showing excitement with arm and leg movements in recognition of familiar people or favorite toys. Parents and caregivers can learn to interpret many gestures generated by the child if they are frequently used. However, as the child matures, these primitive gestures may not be sufficient for effective communication.

Once the child shows a need for more complex communication and appears to demonstrate a comprehension of the environment, a more formal mode of communication (even if temporary) may be required during the period of cannulation. Alternative or augmentative communication systems may be helpful for the child who is aphonic, inconsistent in vocal attempts, or ineffective in spoken communication. Four alternative or augmentative communication systems can be considered:[6]

1. Signed English
2. spoken language through artificial voice (electrolaryngeal speech)
3. esophageal speech
4. manual or electronic communication systems.

Signed English is the most successful system for young children.[7] It utilizes the young child's natural self-generating gestures and expands them into more standard signs.It is one of the least restrictive systems of communication for the young child because it allows the child total physical control. Sign language can be an enjoyable system for siblings and young peers as well as for the child with a tracheostomy. It must be emphasized to parents and other professionals that sign language does not inhibit verbal communication. Rather, it aids verbal communication when vocalizations begin to occur.[8] Once the child begins to develop spoken communication and can be understood by a listener, sign language rapidly disappears from the communicative repertoire.

Artificial voice through an electrolarynx can be used for children with long-term or permanent tracheostomies.[9] It is helpful in aiding children with early prespeech imitation, especially those who later will be able to produce vocalizations. It is also useful for children who have not been able to learn esophageal speech because of structural problems or poor motor coordination. In some children, the electrolarynx can augment an alternative form of communication (such as Signed English) and prepare the child for eventual speech production following decannulation. A variety of electrolarynges are available for use with adults. Specific considerations for children, including unit size, loudness level, and the ability to hold and initiate the artificial vocal sound, must be assessed in the choice of an appropriate instrument. Consultation with a speech-language pathologist is important when the use of an electrolarynx is considered.

Esophageal speech is one of the least restrictive systems of communication for an older child,[10] but it also is the most difficult to initiate for very young children. In an occasional young child with severe subglottic stenosis, however, it has been seen to emerge spontaneously. Esophageal speech also is difficult for the ventilator-dependent child because of the need to coordinate the air injection into the esophagus with the coordination of the breaths from the ventilator.[11] The continued involvement of a speech-language pathologist is crucial to maintain and expand esophageal utterances.

The fourth alternative mode of communication is the *manual or electronic communication system* that synthesizes speech, thus improving the child's ability to be understood.[12] Use of these systems is appropriate only for children who are physically disabled or for those who are unable to produce intelligible or consistent verbalizations. Such systems are expensive and cumbersome and require complex programming in conjunction with the assistance of a specially trained speech-language pathologist.

POSTDECANNULATION FOLLOW-UP

Parents and professionals may be encouraged to know that follow-up assessment in a large population of tracheostomized children revealed that those who were decannulated *before* the establishment of symbolic communication were able to master communication skills commensurate with developmental level.[13] The maturational process occurred without the need for intensive speech and language therapy. The communication skills of those children who were decannulated *after* the initiation of comprehension and the use of language were more severely impaired. This more mature population of children exhibited a greater need for speech and language intervention for longer periods of time. Voice problems were present in both groups of children, although these difficulties were not consistent in all children who previously had tracheostomies. Breath support was weakened in all ventilator-dependent children; this decreased intensity levels of the decannulated child's voice.

The need for speech-language therapy does not cease once the tracheostomized child is decannulated. Speech and language therapy may actually be even more important after decannulation, since the child must learn to transfer skills learned in alternative modes of communication to the spoken language system. Assessment for speech, language, and voice quality is recommended. Full developmental testing may also be necessary for the child who appears to demonstrate specific difficulties in gross or fine motor skills as well as communication delays.

NOTES

1. Caplan F: *The First Twelve Months of Life*, New York, Grosset & Dunlap, 1972, p 30.
2. Oller DK, et al: Infant babbling and speech, *J Child Lang* 63: 1–11, 1976.
3. Simon BM, Fowler SM, Handler SD: Communication development in young children with long-term tracheostomies: preliminary report, *Int J Pediatr Otorhinolaryngol* 6: 37, 1983.
4. Simon B, Handler SD: The speech pathologist and management of children with tracheostomies, *J Otolaryngol* 19: 440, 1981.

5. Fowler SM, Simon BM, Handler SD, Communication development in children, in Meyers EN, Stool SE, and Johnson JT (eds) *Tracheostomy*, New York, Churchill Livingstone, 1985.

6. Simon BM, Fowler SM, Handler SD: Communication development in young children, p 37.

7. *Ibid*. See also English ST, Prutting CA: Teaching American sign language to a normally hearing infant with tracheostenosis, *Clin Pediatr* 14: 1141, 1975.

8. Simon B, Handler SD: The speech pathologist, p 440.

9. Fowler SM, Simon BM, Handler SD: Communication development.

10. Kaslon KW, Grabo DE, Ruben R: Voice, speech and language habilitation in young children without laryngeal function, *Arch Otolaryngol* 104: 737, 1978.

11. Simon BM, Fowler SM, Handler SD: Communication development in young children, p 37.

12. Fowler SM, Simon BM, Handler SD: Communication development in children.

13. Simon BM, Fowler SM, Handler SD: Communication development in young children, p 37.

REFERENCES

Bernbaum JC, Pereira G, Watkins JB, et al: Non-nutritive sucking during gavage feeding enhances growth and maturation in premature infants. *Pediatrics* 71: 41, 1983.

Bowman SA, Shanks JC, Manion MW: Effect of prolonged nasotracheal intubation on communication. *J Speech Hear Disord* 33: 403, 1972.

Caplan F: *The First Twelve Months of Life*. New York, Grosset & Dunlap, 1972.

Connor FP, Williamson GG, Siepp JM (eds): *Program Guide for Infants and Toddlers with Neuromotor and Other Developmental Disabilities*. New York, Teacher's College Press, 1978.

English ST, Prutting CA: Teaching American sign language to a normally hearing infant with tracheostenosis. *Clin Pediatr* 14: 1141, 1979.

Fowler SM, Simon BM, Handler SD: Communication development in children, in Meyers EN, Stool SE, Johnson JT, (eds): *Tracheostomy*, New York, Churchill Livingstone, 1985.

Handler SD, Simon BM, Fowler SM: Speech and the child with a long-term tracheostomy: the problem and the otolaryngologist's role. *Trans Pa Acad Ophthalmol Otolaryngol* 36: 67, 1983.

Harlor M: Communication strategies for a child having total laryngeal stenosis: a case report. *J Pa Speech Lang Hear Assoc* 16: 2, 1983.

Kaslon KW, Grabo DE, Ruben R: Voice, speech and language habilitation in young children without laryngeal function. *Arch Otolaryngol* 104: 737, 1978.

Morris SE: Normal acquisition of oral feeding skills: implications for assessment and treatment. New York, Therapeutic Media Inc, 1981.

Northern JL, Downs MP: Development of auditory behavior, in Northern JL, Downs MP (eds): *Hearing in Children*, ed 2. Baltimore, Williams & Wilkins Co, 1974.

Oller DK, Weiman LA, Doyle WJ, et al: Infant babbling and speech. *J Child Lang* 3: 1–11, 1976.

Peterson HA: A case report of speech and language training for a two year old laryngectomized child. *J Speech Hear Disord* 38: 275, 1973.

Reilly AP (ed): *The Communication Game*. Pediatric Roundtable Series 4. 1980.

Ross GS: Language functioning and speech development of six children receiving tracheostomy in infancy. *J Commun Disord* 15: 95, 1982.

Schraeder BD, Donar ME: The child with chronic respiratory failure: a special challenge, in Stahler-Miller K (ed): *Neonatal and Pediatric Critical Care Nursing*. New York, Churchill Livingstone, 1983.

Simon B, Handler SD: The speech pathologist and management of children with tracheostomies. *J Otolaryngol* 19: 440, 1981.

Simon BM, Fowler SM, Handler SD: Communication development in young children with long-term tracheostomies: preliminary report. *Int J Pediatr Otorhinolaryngol* 6: 37, 1983.

Stark RE: Infant speech production and communication skills. *Allied Health Behav Sci* 1: 131–151, 1976.

Trykowski LE, Kirkpatrick BV, Leonard EL: Enhancement of nutritive sucking in premature infants. *Phys Occu Ther Pediatr* 1: 27, 1981.

Tucker HA, Rusnov M, Cohen L: Speech development in aphonic children. *Laryngoscope* 92: 566, 1982.

Chapter 16

Visual Impairment in the High Risk Infant

Premature and low birth weight (LBW) infants are at risk for visual impairments including refractive errors, ocular muscle imbalance, and even blindness. Vision screening, therefore, should be a routine part of follow-up evaluation in premature infants. Since visual stimulation is an integral component of normal development, visual deficits should be corrected or compensated for early in order to promote optimal development of the infant.

SOME COMMON VISION PROBLEMS

Retinopathy of prematurity is a potential problem for early premature and LBW infants. Ocular muscle imbalance and cortical deficits may also be noted.

Retinopathy of Prematurity

Retinopathy of prematurity (ROP), or retrolental fibroplasia (RLF) is the most frequent cause of blindness in children of the United States.[1] Its prevalence is highest in premature infants born at or before 30 weeks' gestational age and having a birth weight of less than 1250 to 1500 grams.[2] Although some infants without supplemental oxygen develop ROP, oxygen is known to have toxic effects on immature retinal vessels. Exposure to high levels of oxygen causes vessel vasoconstriction. Although this condition initially is reversible, continued vasoconstriction can lead to an irreversible destruction of the vessels. The degree of vessel destruction appears to be proportional to at least three factors: the degree of immaturity of the vessels, the duration of oxygen therapy, and the concentration of

---

Note: Appendix 16–A contains a sample vision screening assessment form.

271

oxygen administered. Thus, early premature or LBW infants with a history of oxygen use are at risk of developing ROP.[3]

ROP is graded, or staged, according to its severity as determined by findings on ophthalmologic examination. Grade I is the earliest stage, and Grade V, the latest and most severe. ROP may subside and, in mild cases, even regress over time, resulting in good visual acuity.[4] The extent of regression varies with the severity of the active phase, and many infants will be left with some degree of *myopia* in one or both eyes. *Strabismus* (an abnormality in which the visual axes of the eyes lack parallelism) is another frequent complication. In severe cases, ROP can also lead to *retinal detachment* and *blindness*; retinal detachment can occur at any age in infants or children with severe ROP.[5]

Various types of treatment have been attempted for ROP. Vitamin E has been shown to limit the severity of ROP in kittens raised in high-oxygen environments but has not been shown to reverse damage once incurred.[6] Cryotherapy and photocoagulation, used in the early stages of ROP, are currently under investigation as treatment modalities.[7] Vitreous surgery, for later retinal detachment, has been shown to have beneficial results, with some return of vision in 45 to 50 percent of cases.[8] With successful surgical results, parents can expect the child to recognize faces and objects, to maneuver without assistance, and to watch television; any finer visual ability is unlikely.[9]

Since any premature or LBW infant with a history of oxygen use is at risk for ROP, it is critical to ascertain whether an ophthalmologic screening examination was actually performed to rule out ROP. If neither the family nor the community health nurse has been given this information, a review of the infant's hospital records or a discussion with the hospital's ophthalmologist will be necessary. If a screening examination was performed, the child's age at the time of the examination is important to determine, since screening prior to 7 or 8 weeks of age may be too early to detect ROP in many cases.[9]

If an infant at risk for ROP either has not had a screening examination or was examined too early to ensure the absence of ROP, the family should be informed about this risk and encouraged to arrange for an ophthalmologic examination for the infant. An ophthalmologic examination is also indicated if any abnormalities are noted on routine vision screening (Appendix 16–A). Any infant determined to have ROP needs regular ophthalmologic follow-up.

Ocular Muscle Imbalance

Strabismus, also called squint, is seen in a number of LBW infants. It can be caused by ocular muscle imbalance and may be noted in association with visual acuity deficits. Routine vision screening should include observation for strabismus (as described later under Vision Screening).

Cortical Deficits

The visual and motor cortexes of the brain affect the coordination of the mechanisms involved in visual following. Several studies indicate that visual behavior in the neonate may be a significant predictor of central nervous system functioning.[10] If following is not noted on vision screening, an ophthalmologic and a neurologic work-up may be indicated.

VISION SCREENING

Prior to vision screening it is important to obtain information about oxygen use in the neonatal period (concentration and duration), and about any family history of visual deficits. Eliciting parental observations and any parental concerns related to the infant's visual abilities should also precede screening. An example of a documentation form for vision screening is provided in Appendix 16–A.

Vision screening should include a complete inspection of the external eye including the lids, pupils, conjunctiva, and sclera. Lesions or discharge should be noted, as well as ptosis, pallor of the conjunctiva, and unequal or absent pupillary reaction to light. For testing the pupillary reaction to light, the room must be darkened. The examiner shines a penlight into one pupil while observing for pupillary constriction in the same and the opposite eye. The procedure is repeated on the other pupil.

The eyes should also be inspected for nystagmus and strabismus. *Nystagmus* is a rhythmic oscillation of the eyes that can be intermittent or continuous; eye movements may be vertical, horizontal, rotatory, or mixed. *Strabismus* can be detected by shining a penlight into the infant's eyes, or above the nose. If the reflection does not come from corresponding parts of the cornea, strabismus is suspected. The cover-uncover test, described in other texts, may also be used in infants more than 12 months of age post term.

In addition, the eyes should be inspected for the *red reflex*. An ophthalmoscope is used if available; alternatively, a penlight may be used. The light beam is directed at the pupil from 15 degrees lateral and about 15 inches away while the pupils are focused straight ahead. A red-orange glow in the pupil is the expected finding.

A routine screening examination should also include observation for age-appropriate characteristics of visual development, as described in Table 16–1.

INTERVENTION

Intervention with visually impaired infants has two dimensions. First, the impact of visual impairment on the parent-infant relationship should be assessed.

Table 16–1 Chronology of Visual Development

Age	Level of Development
Birth	Awareness of light and dark. Infant closes eyelids in bright light.
Neonatal	Rudimentary fixation on near objects (3–30 inches)
2 weeks	Transitory fixation, usually monocular at a distance of roughly 3 feet.
4 weeks	Follows large, conspicuously moving objects.
6 weeks	Moving objects evoke binocular fixation briefly.
8 weeks	Follows moving objects with jerky eye movements. Convergence beginning to appear.
12 weeks	Visual following now a combination of head and eye movements. Convergence improving. Enjoys light objects and bright colors.
16 weeks	Inspects own hands. Fixates immediately on a 1-inch cube brought within 1–2 feet of eye. Vision 20/300–20/200 (6/100–6/70).
20 weeks	Accommodative convergence reflexes all organizing. Visually pursues lost rattle. Shows interest in stimuli more than 3 feet away.
24 weeks	Retrieves a dropped 1-inch cube. Can maintain voluntary fixation of stationary object even in the presence of competing moving stimulus. Hand-eye coordination appearing.
26 weeks	Will fixate on a string.
28 weeks	Binocular fixation clearly established.
36 weeks	Beginning of depth perception.
40 weeks	Marked interest in tiny objects. Tilts head backward to gaze up. Vision 20/200 (6/70).
52 weeks	Fusion beginning to appear. Discriminates simple geometric forms (squares and circles). Vision 20/180 (6/60).
12–18 months	Looks at pictures with interest.
18 months	Convergence well established. Localization in distance crude—runs into large objects.
2 years	Accommodation well developed. Vision 20/40 (6/12).
3 years	Convergence smooth. Fusion improving. Vision 20/30 (6/9).
4 years	Vision 20/20 (6/6).

Parents may need assistance both to notice the realms, other than visual, in which their infant does respond to them, and to optimize communication through sound and touch.

Second, attention to developmental intervention is important. For the visually impaired infant, stimulation should enhance tactile, proprioceptive (position, balance, and movement), auditory, and other sensory modes. To encourage appropriate gross motor development, which is closely tied to vision, programs of activities encouraging normal movement patterns are also important. Early intervention and parent instruction by trained therapists can optimize the developmental potential of the visually impaired infant.

NOTES

1. Charles S: *Retrolental Fibroplasia,* Memphis, University of Tennessee Medical Center, undated (unpublished).

2. Charles S: *Retrolental Fibroplasia;* Friendly DS: *Retrolental Fibroplasia,* Washington, DC, Children's Hospital National Medical Center, Department of Ophthalmology, undated (unpublished).

3. It is estimated that 10 percent of premature infants requiring oxygen will develop active proliferative ROP; over 25 percent of those developing ROP will have some permanent damage; and approximately 25 percent of those with permanent damage will have severe impairment or total blindness (as noted in Friendly DS: *Retrolental Fibroplasia*).

4. About 80 percent of mild cases of ROP will demonstrate complete spontaneous regression (as reported in Friendly DS: *Retrolental Fibroplasia*).

5. Fitzhardinge PM, Pape KE: Follow-up studies of the high risk newborn,'' in Avery GB (ed): *Neonatology: Pathophysiology and Management of the Newborn,* Philadelphia, JB Lippincott Co, 1981, pp 350–370.

6. Charles S: *Retrolental Fibroplasia*; Friendly DS: *Retrolental Fibroplasia.*

7. *Ibid.*

8. The optimal time for surgery is when Grade V develops, generally between 4 and 10 months of age (as noted in Charles S: *Retrolental Fibroplasia*).

9. The American Academy of Pediatrics has recommended an ophthalmologic screening examination for ROP at the time of nursery discharge and again at 3 to 6 months of age; James LS, Lanman JT (eds): Oxygen therapy and RLF, Report of Committee on Fetus and Newborn, American Academy of Pediatrics. *Pediatrics* 57 (suppl): 591–642, April 1976. Palmer, however, feels that these recommendations are too vague and may yield false positive results. On the basis of his study of 149 LBW infants, Palmer believes that the optimal time for ophthalmologic screening examinations for ROP is between 7 and 9 months of age. He recommends normal findings on two ophthalmologic examinations before ruling out ROP, optimally at 6 and 10 weeks, with follow-up at 4 to 6 months. (See Palmer EA: Optimal timing of examination for acute retrolental fibroplasia, *Ophthalmology* 88: 662–668, 1981).

10. Brazelton TB, Scholl ML, Robey JS: Visual responses in the newborn, *Pediatrics* 37: 284–290, 1966; and Sigman M, Kopp CB, Parmelee AH, et al: Visual attention and neurological organization in neonates, *Child Development* 44: 461–466, 1973.

REFERENCES

Brazelton TB, Scholl ML, Robey JS: Visual responses in the newborn. *Pediatrics* 37: 284–290, 1966.

Brazelton TB: Behavioral competence of the newborn infant, in Avery GB (ed): *Neonatology: Pathophysiology and Management of the Newborn.* Philadelphia, JB Lippincott Co, 1981, pp 322–349.

Charles S: *Retrolental Fibroplasia.* Memphis, University of Tennessee Medical Center, undated (unpublished).

Fitzhardinge PM, Pape KE: Follow-up studies of the high risk newborn, in Avery GB (ed): *Neonatology: Pathophysiology and Management of the Newborn.* Philadelphia, JB Lippincott Co, 1981, pp 350–367.

Friendly DS: Eye disorders in neonates. In Avery GB (ed): *Neonatology: Pathophysiology and Management of the Newborn.* Philadelphia, JB Lippincott Co, 1981, pp 1128–1143.

Friendly DS: *Retrolental Fibroplasia.* Washington, DC, Children's Hospital National Medical Center, Department of Ophthalmology, undated (unpublished).

James LS, Lanman JT (eds): Oxygen therapy and RLF. Report of Committee on Fetus and Newborn, American Academy of Pediatrics. *Pediatrics* 57 (suppl): 591–642, April 1976.

Palmer EA: Optimal timing of examination for acute retrolental fibroplasia. *Ophthalmology* 88: 662–668, 1981.

Sigman M, Kopp CB, Parmelee AH, et al: Visual attention and neurological organization in neonates. *Child Development* 44: 461–466, 1973.

Children's Hospital
Home Care Program
National Medical Center
Vision Assessment of the Infant

Name ———————— Hosp# ———————— DOB ————————

HISTORY

1. Family member with visual defects ————yes ————no
   Explain ————————————
2. History of trauma to the eye ————yes ————no
   Describe ————————————
3. History of infections in the eye ————yes ————no
   Describe ————————————
4. Oxygen use in infancy ————yes ————no
   Concentration and duration ————————

PARENT REPORT

Parental concerns ——————————————————————
————————————————————————————————————
————————————————————————————————————

Previous vision or eye exams   *Date*   *Type and result*

———   ————————————————————

———   ————————————————————

———   ————————————————————

————————————————————————————————————

Right	Left	*External exam*	*Indication for referral*	*Comment*
————	————	Pupil (PERLA)*	unequal	————
————	————	Conjunctiva (clear)	pallor, lesions	————
————	————	Sclera (clear)	lesions	————
————	————	Lids (ptosis)	if positive	————
————	————	Lesions (describe)	if positive	————

Right	Left	Nystagmus	If present	Comment
_____	_____	vertical: _____		
_____	_____	horizontal: _____		
_____	_____	rotary: _____		
_____	_____	mixed: _____		
_____	_____	intermittent: _____		
_____	_____	continuous: _____		
_____	_____	Light reflections from center of pupil	if off-center/absent	_____

Right	Left	Developmental Skills	Indication for referral	Comment
_____	_____	red reflex (birth–1 yr)	if not red/not centered	_____
_____	_____	responsive smile (4wks)	if behind chron/adju age	_____
_____	_____	follows 180° (4–12 wks)		_____
_____	_____	fixates easily (4–12 wks)		_____
_____	_____	inspects own hands (12–20 wks)		_____
_____	_____	fixates on objects up to 3 ft away (12–20 wks)		_____
_____	_____	hand-eye coordination developing (20–28 wks)		_____
_____	_____	rescues dropped blocks (20–28 wks)		_____
_____	_____	displays interest in tiny objects (28–44 wks)		_____
_____	_____	tilts head back to see up (28–44 wks)		_____
_____	_____	cover/uncover (toddler)	if objects to one eye being covered	_____
_____	_____	EOMs (toddler)	if not full in all directions	_____

Right	Left	*Developmental Skills*	*Indication for referral*	*Comment*
————	————	enjoys looking at picture books (toddler)	if no	————
————	————	vision 20/40 with E cards at 20 ft (3–5 yrs)	if less than 20/40	————

Assessment ————————————————————————————————
——
——
——

Plan ———————————————————————————————————————
——
——
——

——

Signature of nurse completing assessment   Date

*PERLA = pupils equal, reactive to light, and accommodation.

Source: Reprinted with permission of Home Care Program (Ahmann, Lierman, and Peck), Children's Hospital National Medical Center, Washington, D.C.

Chapter 17

Developmental Issues in Care of the High Risk Infant

Rebecca Ichord, MD

The community health nurse is in a unique position to address the developmental needs of the high risk premature infant. In this regard, the role of the nurse includes home-based developmental screening, parent counseling and education, collaboration with other professionals, and referral to appropriate therapeutic services when needed. This chapter presents a framework for understanding developmental issues in relation to home care of the high risk infant.

To assist the community health nurse in understanding and addressing the developmental needs of the high risk infant, this chapter provides the following:

- a conceptual framework for the understanding of normal developmental patterns
- an outline of the spectrum of developmental problems associated with prematurity
- a discussion of assessment strategies and common terminology
- an outline of the nurse's role in assessment and intervention (including suggested sources of referral for developmental intervention).

The reader is cautioned, however, that this chapter is only a starting point. Each practitioner's own interest and training determine the depth of knowledge and level of skill that are brought to bear with respect to the high risk infant's developmental problems.

BASIC CONCEPTS OF NORMAL DEVELOPMENT

The principles of normal child development were eloquently described and meticulously documented by Arnold Gessell and his colleagues beginning in the 1930s.[1] Their observations and ideas formed the basis for many subsequent works, including the widely used Denver Developmental Screening Test.[2] Gessell and colleagues found that, in normal, healthy children, development proceeds along a predictable sequence at a predictable rate. They described the typical age for attainment of specific behaviors (within specific testing situations). These behaviors, such as sitting alone, obtaining a pellet, or solving a formboard, represent a convergence of motor, perceptual, and cognitive abilities in response to the infant's physical and social environment.

In an effort to understand and explain the evolution of infant behavior, Gessell and colleagues subdivided it into several fields: gross motor, fine motor, language, personal-social, and adaptive abilities (see Table 17–1). In each field, development proceeds in a sequence beginning with simple, nonspecific, and sometimes reflex-mediated behaviors. As the infant matures and gathers experience, the behaviors in each field become more efficiently executed and more specific in effect. As the infant masters behaviors in each field, reflexive behavior becomes either inhibited or subservient to more consciously directed and purposeful behavior. Similarly, simple maneuvers are incorporated into more complex maneuvers.

The development of head control provides an example of this process. In the newborn, head position is determined, for the most part, by neck muscle tone, by reflexive responses to both gravity and the infant's arm position (TNR reflex), and by stereotypic survival behaviors such as the rooting reflex. With time, neck muscle tone and strength mature. The brain also matures, and as visual and auditory information is processed in higher cortical centers, these centers also begin to inhibit reflexive behavior. The infant soon develops adequate neuromuscular control to enable purposeful head turning in the direction of environmental stimuli. For example, the infant may turn toward the sound of the mother's footsteps, the sight of her smile, or the smell of her milk. In the mother who is a sensitive caregiver, the infant's behaviors (e.g., head turning) will elicit

---

Table 17–1 Developmental Fields in Infant Behavior

Developmental Field	Related Skills
Gross motor	Overall posture and mobility
Fine motor	Upper extremity and hand movements, including eye-hand coordination
Language	Receptive and expressive use of words
Personal-social	Interpersonal skills Social learning Formation of interpersonal relationships or attachments
Adaptive	Self-care Ability to solve novel problems

an appropriate response, which then provides reinforcement for the infant. The cycle continues in this manner, encouraging continuing development.

The cycle of development may, however, be broken at several points. First, abnormal motor development in an infant may delay the neuromuscular component of the cycle. Second, the infant's cognitive and perceptual development may be deficient, making it difficult for the baby to "understand" the connections between events. Third, the infant's ability to selectively attend to and respond to a specific sight or sound may be inadequately developed. Fourth, parental responsiveness may be inadequate to provide the necessary reinforcement.

In recent years Gessell's work has been augmented by new approaches that refocus the attention of developmentalists on infant behavioral organization. One such approach, described by Prechtl and by Brazelton,[3] involves detailed observations of (1) the infant's ability to regulate internal biological responses to environmental conditions and (2) the quality of the infant's social interactions. The observations can then be used to formulate specific suggestions for optimizing the infant's capacity to learn from experience. For example, the health care professional may observe that an infant becomes overexcited by unfamiliar inanimate sounds; accordingly, parents can be instructed in a specific routine of swaddling, cuddling, and quiet talking to improve the infant's readiness to look, listen, and learn from the external environment. Although its validity and clinical usefulness are not yet confirmed, this approach does provide another view of a very complex process and may help parents and professionals to individualize their caregiving strategies.

THE SPECTRUM OF DEVELOPMENTAL OUTCOME IN PREMATURITY

Nature equips term infants with the motor, perceptual, and cognitive skills and the behavioral organization needed to survive the physical dependence and learning requirements of that stage of life. Premature infants, however, are ill-equipped to meet these same requirements at birth.[4] Muscle strength and tone are insufficient. Movement is poorly coordinated. Regulation of sleep-wake cycles and level of awareness is inadequately developed. Even basic survival mechanisms such as breathing and feeding are not perfected. Gradually, however, the nervous system matures, and as the premature infant approaches the full gestational age, behavior generally more closely resembles that of a term infant.

Subsequent developmental outcomes will vary, however. Thus parents of at-risk infants ask new development-related questions at each stage of their child's life: "Will my child walk? talk? attend a regular school? be a happy independent adult?" Neonatologists ask these same questions from a slightly different perspective: "What is the incidence of major handicap in a particular birth weight category? Does prematurity affect IQ?'' Despite the availability of data from many research studies, there are no final answers to these questions.

In large part, this uncertainty arises from the intrinsic biologic variability of neonatal problems and variability in the developmental process. Uncertainty also stems from the rapidly changing nature of medical therapeutic technology: the conclusions drawn from results with therapies of a decade ago should be projected cautiously to results with therapies currently in use. Nonetheless, a number of trends have become apparent that shed some light on development-related questions.

With respect to developmental outcome, the premature infant who has suffered no serious brain insult will generally follow the same sequence of development as for a term infant. Frequently, however, the rate of development will be slow in proportion to the degree of prematurity. In the otherwise healthy premature infant, the resultant delay will be mild, and by the age of 2 years, in most cases, delay will no longer be readily apparent to the untrained observer. However, specialized detailed testing of motor and intellectual skills as late as age 5 years suggests that subtle differences do exist in the population of prematures when compared with nonprematures.[5]

On the other hand, the sick premature infant, particularly one who has had brain injury in the neonatal period, is more likely to show both a delayed rate and an abnormal pattern of development. There is a wide spectrum of type and degree of disability among survivors of prematurity.[6]

Table 17–2 summarizes the findings of selected outcome studies performed on infants born in the 1970s and later.[7] Several trends are apparent. First, as previously indicated, the vast majority of prematures who survive, even the smallest ones, do not have a major disability. Second, the incidence of all forms of

Table 17–2 Incidence of Developmental Disabilities in Premature Infants

	Percent of Infants Affected Prematures			
Disability	<1500 gm	<1000 gm	<750 gm	General Population
Cerebral palsy	2–16	4–25	6–24	0.5
Mental retardation	4–12	8–15	6–26	2.0
Hearing impairment	0.8–10	3–12	5–19	0.5–4
Visual impairment	1–5	4–5	1–8	0.5
Mild developmental dysfunction	35–55	?	?	14

Source: Abstracted from Bennett F: Growth and development of infants weighing less than 800 gm at birth, *Pediatrics* 71: 319–323, 1983; Drillien C: LBW children at early school-age: A longitudinal study, *Dev Med Child Neurol* 22: 26–47, 1980; Horwood S: Mortality and morbidity of 500 to 1479 gm birth weight infants live born to residents of a defined geographic region, *Pediatrics* 69: 613–620, 1982; and Kitchen W: Changing outcome over 13 years of VLBW Infants, *Semin Perinatol* 6: 373–389, 1982.

disability increases with decreasing birth weight (usually correlated with gestational age). Third, the incidence of mild forms of developmental dysfunction is not well understood but may be very much higher in the premature than in the general population.

Certain medical disorders are associated with an incidence of developmental dysfunction beyond the ranges outlined in Table 17–2. The presence of any of the following disorders indicates the need for increased vigilance in assessment of developmental problems and the need for possible early intervention:

- perinatal asphyxia
- bacterial meningitis
- chronic lung disease
- poor postnatal head growth
- severe intracranial hemorrhage
- posthemorrhagic hydrocephalus
- abnormal findings on neurodevelopmental examination in the neonatal period or during the first year of life.

The mechanisms by which these factors affect development in the premature are complex. A variety of processes may be involved, including the nature of the parent-infant interaction, the developmental stimulation and care provided by the parents, and the infant's degree of behavioral organization, as well as the extent of recovery and the maturation of the infant's central nervous system. A more in-depth discussion of these interrelated processes and related research approaches may be found in T. Field's *Infants Born at Risk*.[8]

The spectrum of developmental dysfunction[9] may be subdivided into several groups according to functional area affected and severity, as shown in Table 17–3. The term ''major dysfunction'' implies that there is lifelong impairment of the

Table 17–3 Spectrum of Developmental Dysfunction

| | Associated Dysfunctions | |
Functional Area	Minor	Major
Motor function	Clumsiness and motor immaturity	Cerebral palsy
Language, cognitive, and learning function	Learning disability, mild language disorders	Mental retardation, severe language disorders
Sensory function	Partial hearing impairment Nearsightedness	Deafness Blindness
Social function	Behavior disorders	Autism

basic functions that are necessary for full and independent existence. "Minor dysfunction" refers to milder impairments for which natural compensation occurs, or that are remediable to the extent that they allow a full and independent existence.

Several points regarding the spectrum of developmental dysfunction deserve emphasis. First, there is a great deal of overlap among the subdivisions. For example, children with cerebral palsy also often (but not always) have mental retardation. Second, different forms of minor dysfunction frequently occur together in a given child as a variety of syndromes referred to as minimal cerebral dysfunction, minimal brain dysfunction, attention deficit disorder, and hyperactivity. Third, the impact of any particular developmental dysfunction must be viewed within an understanding of the child's whole developmental profile.

Mild, or minor, developmental dysfunction is the most common developmental problem occurring in the premature infant. It can but need not necessarily include varying degrees of each of the following disorders:

- learning disability, which refers to subnormal learning achievement despite normal intelligence and adequate educational opportunity
- mild motor or perceptual dysfunctions, such as poor eye-hand coordination and gross motor clumsiness
- mild visual and hearing problems
- behavior disorders such as hyperactivity, attention deficit, aggressiveness, and tantrums
- mild developmental language disorders, which very frequently lead to a later learning disability.

It is important to note that the impact of combined forms of mild dysfunction may in some cases take on the magnitude of a major disability, with corresponding difficulties for the family of the affected child.

In regard to minor dysfunction, *seizures* and *hydrocephalus* should also be noted, as they are specific signs of dysfunction in the brain. Their functional impact is highly variable and probably relates directly to the degree of underlying brain injury. The vast majority of seizures are adequately controlled by medication and thus do not constitute a handicapping condition. Hydrocephalus, too, can be well controlled by medication or surgical intervention. At the same time it is important to bear in mind that these signs of brain dysfunction should alert professionals to look for associated deficits in perception, learning, and behavior.

The forms of *major developmental dysfunction* include cerebral palsy, mental retardation, severe language disorders, severe sensory impairment, and autism. *Cerebral palsy* (CP) refers to a chronic static disorder of posture and movement appearing before the age of 3 years. In moderate and severe forms, the child's motor development is very delayed for age,[10] and there are abnormalities of muscle tone and coordination that interfere with normal acquisition of motor skills. In premature infants, the most common type of CP is *spastic diplegia*, which involves hypertonicity and abnormal movement patterns, predominantly in the legs. Other types of CP can also occur in premature infants, including *spastic quadriplegia* (involvement of all four limbs) and *spastic hemiplegia* (involvement of arm and leg on one side).

Mental retardation refers to subnormal intelligence, as indicated by an IQ usually less than 70, associated with deficits in adaptive skills. In *mild* mental retardation (IQ of 55 to 70) there may be an extensive capacity for learning self-care and social skills and some potential for functional reading and arithmetic as the child grows. In *moderate* retardation (IQ of 40 to 55), however, basic self-care must be laboriously taught; and in *severe* mental retardation (IQ below 40) there often is a need for constant supervision and regular assistance with basic self-care activities.

Retardation is generally distinguished from *borderline intelligence,* in which the IQ is 70 to 80. These less severe deficits, however, frequently give rise to learning problems that mimic learning disabilities.

Severe *language disorders* are found in children with language intelligence and verbal skills in the retarded range, with preservation of visually mediated intelligence in the nonretarded range. *Autism* refers to a disorder involving pervasive and profound disturbance of social relatedness and is usually associated with severe mental retardation and language disorders.

ASSESSMENT STRATEGIES AND TERMINOLOGY

Developmental assessment and intervention for the premature infant with multiple and complex problems should begin well before discharge from the nursery. Initial evaluation can begin as soon as the infant's condition is sufficiently stable to allow a neurodevelopmental examination by someone skilled in the use of neonatal assessment tools (such as a development pediatrician, psychologist, occupational or physical therapist, neurologist, or neonatologist).

It is usually possible to categorize the infant's developmental findings as one of the following:

1. appropriate for gestational age OR
2. suspect abnormal OR
3. abnormal for gestational age.

When findings are abnormal, the specific pattern of problems should be identified, and suggested home management routines outlined by the appropriate therapist.

For example, problems with tone and movement may require specific positioning suggestions for the infant's prone, supine, sidelying, and sitting postures. Feeding problems involving suck-swallow dysfunction can be addressed by an occupational therapist, who will suggest positions and jaw or mouth manipulations to improve the feeding pattern. A psychologist can suggest visual, auditory, and social activities to encourage attachment and learning.

The ongoing evaluation of an infant's developmental progress continues with assessment of both the developmental rate and sequence in each major field of development: gross motor, fine motor, language, personal-social, and adaptive. In some disorders, motor skills are predominantly affected, whereas in others, language and adaptive skills are affected. This historical developmental information is supplemented and confirmed by findings of the neurodevelopmental examination in order to make a comprehensive set of diagnostic statements about a child's developmental status and any developmental disorders.

Terminology

With respect to understanding and interpreting information about an infant's development, the nurse should be familiar with three terms in particular: developmental delay, development quotient, and development sequence.

Delay refers to a slower-than-normal rate of development and is best measured by a *development quotient*, or DQ. For each stream of development (see Table 17–1), the rate of development—the DQ—is determined from the ratio of developmental age to chronologic age. For example, an 18-month-old child with certain developmental skills at a 9-month level would have a DQ of 50 for that area. It is important to note that a single DQ in a given stream is not equivalent to an IQ as measured by standardized intelligence tests in later childhood. Rather, the DQ is one index of neuromaturational integrity. In this regard, the DQ is an indicator of the severity of the child's developmental problem and can be translated into a specific developmental age for purposes of planning intervention.

Another feature of abnormal development is deviation from the normal *sequence* in acquisition of developmental milestones. For example, a baby usually crawls before walking and uses jargon before speaking in sentences. Deviance from these normal patterns of development can be viewed as a sign of dysfunction and should prompt a more careful search for associated problems. Specific patterns of deviation may also serve as a clue to the diagnosis of a specific disability. For example, a clear hand preference before 12 months of age is a sign of hemiplegia.

THE ROLE OF THE NURSE IN ASSESSMENT AND INTERVENTION

The role of the community health nurse in implementing home-based assessment and intervention varies depending on the individual's level of training. At the very least, the nurse should have a basic awareness of both the developmental problems faced by premature infants and the community resources available for further assessment and intervention.

A nurse with additional knowledge of normal developmental patterns and progressions will be able to observe the high risk infant's development, noting either any abnormalities in the rate or deviations in the normal sequence of attainment of developmental skills. In this way, the nurse can facilitate timely referral for problems.

Various developmental assessment tools exist to assist the nonspecialist. These tools have been concisely reviewed by A. Castiglia.[10] The tools chosen must fit the training limitations of the practitioner and must be suited to the infant's needs. For example, a screening tool such as the Denver Developmental Screening Test is useful for monitoring the progress of infants originally found to be developmentally normal. More sophisticated tools, such as the Revised Developmental Screening Inventory and the Minnesota Child Development Inventory, provide more specific and detailed information. In any case, parents are probably the most effective screening tools available; any parental concerns should be elicited and thoroughly explored.

Table 17–4 provides some practical guidelines for designing a developmental monitoring strategy at the time of hospital discharge. It is based on a combination of historical risk factors and the results of neurodevelopmental examination. The discharge plan should clarify who will be responsible for subsequent monitoring and what community resources will be available to supplement these efforts.

Table 17–4 Monitoring Strategies for High Risk Neonates

Discharge Status	Monitoring Strategy
1. High risk inventory (all high risk infants)	Hearing and vision tests at age 1 year (see Chapters 14 and 16)
2. High risk history, normal findings on neurodevelopmental examination	Developmental screening with well baby care; referral for definitive evaluation only as needed
3. High risk history, suspect findings on neurodevelopmental examination	Developmental screening with well baby care; definitive evaluation and school programming at age 2 or 3 years if abnormalities persist
4. High risk history, definitely abnormal findings or neurodevelopmental examination	Specialized developmental monitoring every 3 months including on-going therapy as appropriate
5. High risk inventory, abnormal findings on neurodevelopmental examination, active chronic disease	Same as for status 4 plus close linkage with medical care

One of the greatest frustrations faced by parents and health care professionals is the fragmentation of community services for children with disabilities. There are no simple rules of referral that will be applicable in every state for every child. However, it would be worthwhile for the community health nurse to become familiar with a few reliable entry points to the service network for infants in the local community. The following list suggests places to start:

1. public school system parent-infant programs
2. local health departments and child health clinics
3. university-affiliated child development centers
4. state Crippled Children's services
5. United Cerebral Palsy Association schools for the handicapped
6. National Easter Seal Society local chapter.

Whenever an infant is referred for services, the nurse can follow up by communicating observations and concerns to therapists or teachers and by stressing to parents the importance of carry-through of therapeutic techniques at home. (See also Chapter 20.)

Specific information about assessment and intervention related to hearing, speech, and vision is provided in this book in Chapters 14, 15, and 16, respectively. Additional suggestions regarding developmental intervention are described in L. Beckwith's *Intervention Strategies for High Risk Infants and Young Children.*[11]

CONCLUSION

As the studies cited in this chapter indicate, some developmental trends may be noted in the population of premature infants. However, extreme caution must be used in applying the study data to any particular infant. Rather, developmental assessment and intervention, and the determination of prognosis, must be very individualized.

In this regard, the community health nurse, along with other professionals, faces a challenge in meeting the developmental needs of the premature infant. The role of the nurse must be built on a knowledge of normal developmental patterns, an awareness of the spectrum of developmental problems associated with prematurity, and an understanding of assessment strategies and terminology. The nurse must be prepared to collaborate closely with other professionals with respect to both developmental screening and the counseling and education of parents. The nurse's knowledge of community resources providing developmental assessment and intervention is also key in ensuring timely and appropriate services for the infant in need.

NOTES

1. Knobloch H: *Gessell & Amatruda's Developmental Diagnosis,* ed 3, Hagerstown, Md, Harper & Row Publishers Inc, 1974.

2. Frankenburg WK, et al: *Denver Developmental Screening Test: Reference Manual,* rev ed, Denver, University of Colorado Medical Center, 1975.

3. Prechtl H: The neurological examination of the full-term newborn infant, ed 2, *Clin Dev Med,* no 63, 1977; Brazelton T: Neonatal behavior assessment scale, ed 2, *Clin Dev Med,* no 88, 1984.

4. Hack M: The sensorimotor development of the preterm infant, in Behrman RE, Driscoll JM, Seeds AE (eds): *Neonatal-Perinatal Medicine,* ed 2, St Louis, CV Mosby Co, 1977, pp 328–346.

5. Caputo D: The development of prematurely born children through middle childhood, in Field T (ed): *Infants Born at Risk,* New York, SP Medical Books, 1979, pp 219–248.

6. Further information may be found in the references already cited, and in a well-written concise book by Goldberg (Goldberg S: *Born Too Soon: Preterm Birth and Early Development,* San Francisco: WH Freeman and Co, 1983).

7. Bennett F: Growth and development of infants weighing less than 800 gm at birth, *Pediatrics* 71: 319–323, 1983; Drillien C: LBW children at early school-age: a longitudinal study, *Dev Med Child Neurol* 22: 26–47, 1980; Horwood S: Mortality and morbidity of 500 to 1479 gm birth weight infants live born to residents of a defined geographic region, *Pediatrics* 69: 613–620, 1982; and Kitchen W: Changing outcome over 13 years of VLBW infants, *Semin Perinatol* 6: 373–389, 1982.

8. Field T (ed): *Infants Born at Risk,* New York, SP Medical Books, 1979.

9. Developmental dysfunction is only one of a number of terms that have been used to discuss the spectrum of developmental disorders seen in premature infants. Other terms include handicapping conditions, long-term neurologic dysfunction, developmental disabilities, and developmentally at risk.

10. Castiglia P: Selecting a developmental screening tool, *Pediatr Nurs,* January/February 1985, pp 8–17.

11. Beckwith L: *Intervention Strategies for High Risk Infants and Young Children,* Baltimore, University Park Press, 1976.

REFERENCES

Accardo P: *The Pediatrician and the Developmentally Delayed Child.* Baltimore, University Park Press, 1979.

Accardo P: *A Neurodevelopmental Perspective on Specific Learning Disabilities.* Baltimore, University Park Press, 1980.

Beckwith L: *Intervention Strategies for High Risk Infants and Young Children.* Baltimore, University Park Press, 1976.

Bennett F: Growth and development of infants weighing less than 800 gm at birth. *Pediatrics* 71: 319–323, 1983.

Brazelton T: Neonatal behavior assessment scale. *Clin Dev Med,* ed 2, no 88, 1984.

Caputo D: The development of prematurely born children through middle childhood, in Field T (ed): *Infants Born at Risk,* New York, SP Medical Books, 1979, pp 219–248.

Castiglia P: Selecting a developmental screening tool. *Pediatr Nurs,* January/February 1985, pp 8–17.

Drillien C: LBW children at early school-age: a longitudinal study. *Dev Med Child Neurol* 22: 26–47, 1980.

Field T: *Infants Born at Risk*. New York, SP Medical Books, 1979.

Frankenburg WK, Dodds JB, Fandal AW, et al: *Denver Developmental Screening Test: Reference Manual*, rev ed. Denver, University of Colorado Medical Center, 1975.

Goldberg S: *Born Too Soon: Preterm Birth and Early Development*. San Francisco, WH Freeman and Co, 1983.

Hack M: The sensorimotor development of the preterm infant, in Behrman RE, Driscoll JM, Seeds AE (eds): *Neonatal-Perinatal Medicine*, St Louis, CV Mosby Co, 1978, pp 328–346.

Horwood S: Mortality and morbidity of 500 to 1479 gm birth weight infants live born to residents of a defined geographic region. *Pediatrics* 69: 613–620, 1982.

Johnson S: *High Risk Parenting: Nursing Assessment Strategies for the Family at Risk*. Philadelphia, JB Lippincott Co, 1979.

Kitchen W: Changing outcome over 13 years of VLBW infants. *Semin Perinatol* 6: 373–389, 1982.

Knobloch H: *Gessell & Amatruda's Developmental Diagnosis*, ed 3. Hagerstown, Md, Harper & Row Publishers Inc, 1974.

Prechtl H: The neurological examination of the full-term newborn infant. ed 2, *Clin Dev Med*, no 63, 1977.

Chapter 18

The Family of the High Risk Infant

Nancy Weinstock, MSW, ACSW

The transition of the high risk infant from hospital to home carries with it significant implications for the family. Discharge is often a sign to them that trouble is over and the crisis has passed. Although some medical procedures may need to be carried out at home, parents are still apt to expect life to proceed as they had fantasized it would with a new baby in the home. Unfortunately, hospital discharge marks the beginning of yet another crisis period for the infant and family members.

One role of the professionals working with the family during this transition is to offer both practical and emotional support that will foster effective crisis management and will effect positive long-term support for the infant. Many variables that accompany this challenging task are discussed in this chapter.

PSYCHOLOGIC ADJUSTMENT TO THE PREMATURE INFANT

A normal psychologic preparation occurring in both parents during pregnancy involves the wish for a perfect child and the fear of an imperfect one.[1] All parents, therefore, undergo a period of adjustment following the birth during which the discrepancy between fantasy ("I wanted a boy!") and reality ("At least she is healthy") is resolved. This adjustment may be experienced not only by the parents but by members of the extended family as well.

Many types of response to the birth of a handicapped infant have been identified. Drotar and coworkers have described seven specific stages in the grief reaction following the birth of such an infant: (1) shock; (2) denial; (3) sadness; (4) anger; (5) anxiety; (6) adaptation; and (7) reorganization.[2] Intertwined are

Note: One mother's view of home care of her high risk infant is presented in Appendix D at the end of this book.

times of ambivalence, numbness, disbelief, bereavement, a search for hope, intense reexperiencing of expectations for the idealized child, and, finally, a stage of acceptance of and commitment to the infant.

No two people pass through these stages of grief reactions at exactly the same rate; they may not even process emotions in the same order. In fact, the differences in individual coping styles of family members often intensify during times of crisis. This intensification can lead to family stress, marital difficulties, and sibling adjustment problems. No family member should be pushed through the grief process; however, it can be helpful to encourage family members to allow themselves time to devote to their own feelings, reactions, and supportive relationships. Professionals can also share observations to assist parents in identifying the issues with which they are struggling, to assure them of the normality of their feelings, and to facilitate discussion among family members to foster recognition and acceptance of each other's different coping strategies and grieving schedules.

As opposed to the grief reaction to the death of an infant, the reaction to the birth of a handicapped or seriously ill infant can be pervasive and chronic.[3] Professionals must accept ongoing and recurrent sorrow as a normal psychologic response. During the ongoing psychologic adjustment to a disabled infant, parents and family members will be dealing with a number of significant issues, listed in Exhibit 18–1.

THE FAMILY AS A SYSTEM

To provide the best help for the child, the professional working with the family of a handicapped or chronically ill infant must first understand the functioning of the family unit. Family members are interrelated in such a way that any behavior or change in one member affects the entire system. The family system is not limited to the nuclear family but also includes the extended family. As a system, a family operates by seeking to maintain a sense of order, balance, and continuity.[4] All change, whether positive or negative in outcome, is stressful because change challenges order.

In this regard, the arrival home of a premature infant with multiple problems causes sudden and dramatic changes in the normal order of the family system. Significant psychologic and role adjustments become necessary. Individual patterns of interaction that may have been minimally troublesome to family members during "normal days" may become more dramatic and difficult under the stresses of home care. The professional involved with the family during this time should help family members both to identify new and appropriate patterns of interactions and to develop new role responsibilities and problem-solving skills.

Exhibit 18–1 Responses to the Birth of a Handicapped or Chronically Ill Infant

Response	Description
Helplessness	Owing to long hospitalization and intensive medical attention, parents will often feel denied parental responsibility. They may experience resentment toward the medical team caring for their infant and a sense of loss of control over decisions involving their child.
Failure	Parents may feel that they have failed to produce a child acceptable to themselves, to their extended family, and to society.
Disappointment	Parents may experience painful disappointment that their infant requires medical support, attention, and, often, long-term follow-up.
Intense longing for idealized child	Parents may experience periods during which they long intensely for their fantasized "perfect" child.
Deprivation	Parents may feel deprived of the satisfaction of "normal" parent-infant interactions. This is especially true at feeding times when a premature infant is unable to breast feed.
Blame or guilt	Many parents experience guilt or try to assign blame for the infant's problems. They may ask: "Whose fault is this?" "From whose side of the family did this problem come?" "What did I do or think during pregnancy to cause this?"

STRESS FACTORS AFFECTING FAMILIES

Regardless of the strengths a family may bring to a crisis situation, psychosocial adjustment to the birth, hospitalization, and home care of the high risk infant is a highly stressful process, both for individual family members and for the family as a group. The degree and type of individual and group responses to stress are determined by the factors described in Exhibit 18–2.

The demands on time, energy, and finances, coupled with the psychologic adjustments to having an impaired child, place the family system in a position of vulnerability. It is therefore essential that parents learn effective stress management skills. Professionals who have a full awareness of the stresses faced by these families can best help families to master complex and highly technical home care. The rest of this section discusses some of the most common sources of stress and appropriate interventions that can be used by the home care professional to prevent or reduce such stress.

Family role changes are a frequently occurring source of stress. It is common for the medical staff to talk with only one parent, often the mother, about the infant's needs and prognosis and about parental involvement in the infant's care. The mother's involvement increases her expertise in caring for her infant. It may

Exhibit 18–2 Individual and Group Factors Influencing Family Responses to Stress

Factor	Effect	Assessment Intervention
Past experience	The past experiences of each individual family member and of the family as a group will influence coping styles.	Past experiences should be explored and coping styles related to illness, emotional trauma, financial difficulties, work-related problems, death, and other crises should be identified.
Attitudes	The individual attitudes that are brought to the family system by each of its members will affect the ability of the family as a whole to deal with the crisis.	Attitudes important to explore include family members' feelings toward medical authority, hospital personnel, illness, and seeking help.
Values	The values held by each family member—related to life style, need for order, tradition, religion, finances, and concept of family—will affect ability to adjust to the presence of an ill or disabled infant in the home.	Close observations of a family's day-to-day life patterns will give a clear picture of individual and family values. A non-judgmental attitude is critical for accurate assessment.
Interaction style	The way in which family members respond to one another will influence how well they can work together toward the common goal of caring for the premature infant.	Family interaction styles, as well as the expected role of the professional within the family interaction pattern, should be identified.
Expectations of self and others	Family members' expectations of themselves and others may be forced to change during a crisis period.	The family should be helped to identify prior expectations and to formulate more realistic expectations.
Goals	Having a premature infant in the home forces the family to rethink and reorganize individual and group goals.	Family members should be supported as they determine new directions and roles.
Resources	The degree to which a family will effectively manage the crisis of caring for a premature infant is related to how well parents and other family members make use of available resources (e.g., social, religious, cultural, economic, educational, and medical).	Appropriate resources should be identified, and family members supported in appropriate use of such services. (See also Chapter 20.)

also change her role within the family system, her self-perception, and how she is perceived by others. The exclusion of other family members from opportunities to gain similar expertise can lead to changes in the functioning of the family system. A feeling of helplessness or failure may arise in family members who have not been included in the day-to-day training related to the infant's care. In this regard, professionals working with the infant and family should attempt to ensure that all members of the family are included in the training to provide the infant's care, at least at some level. Additionally, fostering an atmosphere of psychologic "safety" is vital so that all family members begin to feel secure in sharing any questions or reactions related to the infant's care.

The *uncertain prognosis* of a high risk premature infant is another source of stress. Family members often experience an emotional "roller coaster" ride as they deal with repeated hospitalizations, renewed crisis, and uncertainty. When parents have questions, home care professionals should present realistic, simple, and honest answers. Asking the infant's physician to respond directly to questions can also be helpful.

Although planning and decision making may never before have been a problem for family members, the unpredictability of day-to-day events in caring for a high risk infant can make definite decisions regarding plans for typical family activities impossible. The resultant *feeling of loss of control* over one's life can be frightening for parents. Providing honest information, when requested, helps family members to gain some degree of control. This, in turn, will lead to more effective decision making regarding the infant's care.

Employment pressure is another source of stress to family members. Dual-income families, in which both parents had planned to maintain employment after the birth of their child, may be forced to consider alternatives. At the same time, insurance policies may need to be maintained, and the difficult choices parents face can be overwhelming. The parents of a high risk infant may find themselves making financial sacrifices and experiencing major changes in family life style. Single parents may find it impossible to arrange for home care for the infant owing to limited child care options. Professionals can help families to identify available financial resources and to secure child care support (see Chapter 20).

Exhaustion and isolation are common among parents of high risk premature infants. The amount of physical and emotional energy required for care of these infants is enormous. The lack of sleep resulting from 24-hour care requirements, as well as the emotional stress, can leave the parents exhausted. Professionals can help by identifying respite care programs, arranging for home nursing, or helping the family to identify friends who can offer support (see Chapters 2 and 20).

Although extended family members and friends can be supportive of and helpful to the parents of a high risk infant, this is not always the case. Grandparents in particular often experience denial and blame and are in need of much comfort. Such *extended family adjustment difficulties* can actually compound the problem for parents. The professional can help in this situation by a careful assessment of the role of extended family members and by identifying ways in which they can be helpful to the immediate family (such as transportation, assistance with routine household chores, care of the affected child's siblings, and babysitting for the infant).

Medical equipment can transform the home environment into a mini–hospital room. The *presence of medical equipment* forces changes in family life style. Siblings may have to change bedrooms to allow space for equipment; parents may lose privacy when monitors and suction machines surround them in their bedroom; and closets may be filled with medical supplies.

Transportation to and from the hospital or clinic for medical appointments also presents a difficult problem for the family and is discussed in Chapter 20.

Sibling adjustment difficulties are another common source of stress. Other children in the family often experience psychologic and even physical reactions to the parents' involvement in care of the high risk infant. Chapter 19 offers suggestions for how the home care professional can help parents to recognize and oversome sibling adjustment difficulties, thus decreasing potential long-term psychologic effects on these other children.

ADDITIONAL CONSIDERATIONS

Nurses and other health care providers in the home often develop a special attachment to the child and family. Providing care in the home affords the professional the unique opportunity of "knowing" the family as they really are and of promoting effective intervention. Care should be taken, however, that the professional does not totally assimilate into the family system but maintains a degree of professional distance.

In addition, since the professional is only a temporary support, the goal is to assist the family in becoming the infant's advocate. To accomplish this goal, it is important for professionals to recognize that they are not the most important care providers working with the infant. Home care professionals must realize that part of their responsibility is to "work themselves out of a job" as the family becomes more competent and confident.

Often the family will look to the professional as "the one bringing the care." Home care professionals should help the family realize that they do not, in fact, have all the answers. Rather, the professional's role is to listen, to respect the family members' reactions and needs, and to assist and support them in ways that will build *their* expertise and will strengthen and maintain the family system. The infant's parents and family are the lifelong care providers.

Another caution regards alliances. Too often the professional visiting the home relates to only one family member, and all information and training are transmitted to that person. Professionals must be aware that this will affect the family hierarchy and also the roles of each family member. For this reason, it may be wise to address interventions to as many family members as possible.

NONCOMPLIANCE

A final word on the responsibilities of the professional concerns parental noncompliance. Occasionally, negligence or forgetfulness may simply be due to exhaustion. However, in some cases parental failure to follow medical recommendations may be due to denial of the infant's needs to a degree that places the infant in jeopardy. Professionals who genuinely suspect that a parent is abusing or neglecting a child must report the case to the state child protective services agency. Indications of possible abuse and neglect are presented in Exhibit 18–3.[5]

Honest, direct discussions with family members are important if neglect or abuse is suspected. The reasons for concern should be explained, and the family informed of the professional's responsibility to report this suspicion to the appropriate state agency. In this circumstance, parents are likely to become defensive and angry. In such a situation it is best to continue to explain that the professional's role is to be as helpful as possible and that at times, families need additional support in order to provide optimal care for their children.

Exhibit 18–3 Signs of Child Abuse and Neglect

The Signs of Child Abuse

- Bruises, welts, burns, or broken bones that do not fit with the explanation of how they occurred
- Signs of excessively harsh punishment
- Signs of sexual abuse or exploitation
- Multiple injuries in various stages of healing
- A child's reluctance to discuss his or her injuries or apparent fear of parents

The Signs of Child Neglect

- Lack of proper nutrition, shelter, supervision, medical care, schooling
- Unsanitary or unsafe living conditions
- Lack of physical or emotional care
- Abandonment

Source: Reprinted from: "Helping the Abused or Neglected Child . . . While It Is Still a Matter of Conscience, It Is Now a Matter of Legal Obligation as Well," with permission of The Office of The Corporation Council, Washington, DC.

SUMMARY

The role of the professional working with the family of the high risk infant must include practical and emotional support. This support must be based on an understanding of common emotional reactions to the birth of a disabled child; factors frequently contributing to stress among families of chronically ill children; an awareness of the functioning of the family as a system; and an understanding of the professional's own role in relation to this system. The support of the home care professional can assist families, as needed, in achieving effective stress management, resulting in optimal long-term care for the high risk infant.

NOTES

1. Solnit A, Stark N: Mourning and the birth of a defective child, *Psychoanalytic Study of the Child* 16: 523–537, 1961.
2. Drotar D, et al: The adaptation of parents to the birth of an infant with a congenital malformation, *Pediatrics* 56: 710–716, 1975.
3. Olshansky S: Chronic sorrow: a response to having a mentally defective child, *Social Casework* 43: 190–193, 1962.
4. Berdie J, Selig AL: Family functioning in families with children who have handicapping conditions, *Family Therapy,* 8, no. 3 1981, pp 189–195.
5. Handicapped and health-impaired premature infants are at an increased risk of abuse and neglect owing to various factors, including low birth weight, long hospital stays, and a higher incidence of congenital defects. See Hunter RS, Kilstrom N, Kraybill EN, et al: Antecedents of child abuse and neglect in premature infants: a prospective study in a newborn intensive care unit, *Pediatrics* 61: 629–635, 1978, see also Elmer E, Gregg GS: Developmental characteristics of abused children, *Pediatrics* 40: 596–602, 1967; Klein M, Stern L, Low birth weight and the battered child syndrome, *Am J Dis Child* 122: 15–18, 1971; and Lynch MA, Roberts J: Predicting child abuse: signs of bonding failure in the maternity hospital, *Br Med J* 1: 624–626, 1977.

REFERENCES

Berdie J, Selig AL: Family functioning in families with children who have handicapping conditions. *Family Therapy,* 8, no. 3 1981, pp 189–195.

Caplan G: Patterns of parental response to the crisis of premature birth. *Psychiatry* 23: 365–374, 1960.

Elmer E, Gregg GS: Developmental characteristics of abused children. *Pediatrics* 40: 596–602, 1967.

Featherstone H: *A Difference in the Family.* New York, Penguin Books Inc, 1980.

Henig RM, with Fletcher AB: *Your Premature Baby.* New York, Ballantine Books, 1983.

Hunter RS, Kilstrom N, Kraybill EN, et al: Antecedents of child abuse and neglect in premature infants: a prospective study in a newborn intensive care unit. *Pediatrics* 61: 629–635, April 1978.

Klein M, Stern L: Low birth weight and the battered child syndrome. *Am J Dis Child* 122: 15–18, 1971.

Lynch MA, Roberts J: Predicting child abuse: signs of bonding failure in the maternity hospital. *Br Med J* 1: 624–626, 1977.

Madanes C: *Strategic Family Therapy.* San Francisco, Jossey-Bass Inc, 1982.

McCollum AT: *The Chronically Ill Child.* New Haven, Conn, Yale University Press, 1975.

Minuchin S: *Families and Family Therapy*. Cambridge, Harvard University Press, 1974.

Mitchell H: Crisis management for families living with chronic illness. *Wash St J Nurs,* Autumn 1983, pp 2–7.

Olsen E: The impact of serious illness on the family system. *Social Medicine,* February 1970, pp 169–174.

Schiff HS: *The Bereaved Parent*. New York, Penguin Books Inc, 1977.

Chapter 19

Siblings of Chronically Ill Children

Teri Peck, BSN, CPNP

The siblings of chronically ill or disabled children often become the forgotten members of the family. These other children tend to develop behavior changes that often go unnoticed by preoccupied parents. In some children, jealousy and anger can lead to aggressive behaviors against playmates, pets, the ill child, or themselves. Guilt, as well as the concern that "I may be next," leads other children to become withdrawn and uncommunicative; they attempt in this manner to avoid any behaviors that may draw punishment and therefore illness.

The concerns of some children with a chronically ill brother or sister may also generate excessive somatic complaints over minor illnesses and injuries. Separation anxiety often leads to regressive behavior such as bed wetting or thumb sucking. Sleep disturbances and fear of the dark can also occur, often as a result of misconceptions about the illness or disability. Although adjustment problems are inevitable in siblings of ill or disabled children, the knowledgeable and observant nurse can assist parents in noticing and understanding behavior changes and in planning purposeful interventions to mitigate problems that arise.

PREVENTING PROBLEMS

Parents should be encouraged to be honest with all the children in the family and to offer understandable and age-appropriate explanations without euphemisms. In this regard, the nurse may need to offer suggestions. For instance, to a sibling of a tracheostomized child, a parent can explain: "It was hard for your sister to breathe through her nose the way you and I breathe through ours. We took her to the doctors, and they helped her breathe this way instead." Similarly, oxygen can be simply described as "extra air," and a ventilator as a "special breathing machine." Children will need reassurance that the same problems will not happen to them: "You weren't born too early like your sister was; you won't need this special equipment."

303

The nurse should also encourage parents to help children discuss fears and other feelings. Parents should tell the other children in the family that they have no blame for the illness of their brother or sister. Likewise, they should assure and reassure children that they will not "catch" the disability (if this is true) and tell them that it is permissible to sometimes feel angry or frightened, just as the parents sometimes feel. In this connection, parents may need to be reminded that verbalizing these ideas will not put such thoughts into a child's mind. Rather, it will only acknowledge what the child already thinks, as well as correct any misconceptions.

Keeping the other children involved in the care of the disabled child is also important. Parents can be encouraged to ask a child to bring a diaper, for example, or to hold the feeding tube. The home care nurse can facilitate this involvement by dramatizing with the other children special procedures done for their brother or sister. For instance, the nurse might allow the well child to use a stethoscope on a doll, change a dressing on a doll, or weigh it. Other children's involvement with the disabled child must also include visitation during hospitalization.

It is also important for the well child to have a special place in the family, to be loved, and to have achievements acknowledged. Ideally, parents should spend time alone with each child, even if for only an hour or two a week. In addition, parents may wish to enroll the well child in sibling support groups, available through some hospitals.

THERAPEUTIC PLAY

Children often act out their daily concerns in their play; any parent who has eavesdropped on a "tea party" understands this behavior. Since children are very comfortable with play, they can be helped to utilize it as a medium for expression of anxieties related to their disabled brother or sister. In a therapeutically orchestrated play session, many of the well child's fears and misconceptions will become apparent and can be mitigated. A sound knowledge of development and an understanding of common fears and misconceptions are essential for facilitating this process. Pediatric mental health professionals are often experts at using play therapy. Nurses and parents can also develop some skills in the techniques. Two helpful resources are *Emotional Care of the Hospitalized Child,* by M. Petrillo, and *Therapeutic Uses of Children's Play*, by C. Shaefer (see References).

COMMON PROBLEMS

Although all siblings of a chronically ill child are affected by the related stresses imposed on the family, those between the ages of 3 and 7 years are especially vulnerable. The normal psychologic and cognitive processes in this age group, including magical thinking, separation anxiety, and concretizing, make these children susceptible to feelings of jealousy, anger, fear, and guilt. Such feelings can result in misconceptions and troublesome behavior changes upsetting to both the child and the family.

Between the ages of 3 and 7 years, the predominant psychologic characteristic is *magical thinking*. The natural egocentricity of this age group results in a sense of power; children believe that their thoughts and feelings can, and actually do, become reality. In addition, children want and expect all of their parents' attention. Even under normal circumstances, they want more attention than they can ever receive. In households with a chronically ill child, however, much of the parents' attention is diverted to the necessary medical care. As a consequence, the healthy child may feel a very natural jealousy and anger that can lead to spoken or unspoken wishes about the ill child. Such wishes typically envision a family environment without the ill child, where the healthy child would have complete and continual attention from the parents. Against the background of magical thinking, however, such wishes can lead to enormous feelings of guilt: the child may begin to believe that the illness was caused by destructive feelings toward the disabled child.

Another salient feature shared by children between the ages of 3 and 7 is a belief that illness is a punishment. Parental warnings of "Put on your raincoat or you'll catch cold!" reinforce this misconception. These children may have a fear that, if they misbehave, they too will become ill.

Separation anxiety is also a common occurrence. When the ill child was hospitalized, the parents may have frequently been absent from the home. This arrangement may have planted seeds of anxiety in another child in the family. After the ill child returns home, repeat hospital visits can recreate those anxious times for susceptible children. The child who once willingly stayed with a babysitter may no longer do so. Confidence in the continued presence of parents may have been undermined: "If Mommy and Daddy can leave Johnny alone at the hospital, then they can also leave me alone if they want to."

Because the cognitive thought processes in this age group involve significant *concretizing*, children tend to suffer from many misconceptions. For example, Susie, a 4-year-old, had been told that her 6-month-old baby brother, hospitalized since birth, was finally "home for good." When he was taken frequently to the hospital for follow-up examinations, Susie became convinced that their mother would leave him alone on the elevator! In fact, there was no apparent basis for this misconception, as is frequently the case. Susie apparently needed to label concretely or explain a phenomenon she otherwise could not understand: her brother's repeated hospital visits after he was supposed to be home for good.

SUMMARY

Behavior changes and adjustment problems are common among siblings of chronically ill or disabled children. An understanding both of the reasons for the behavior changes and of the roots of the problems is the first stage in planning purposeful interventions. The community health nurse, in the family's home, is in a position to observe sibling behavior and to assist parents in both noting behavior changes and planning interventions to alleviate problems that arise.

REFERENCES

Bank S, Kahn M: *The Sibling Bond*. New York, Basic Books Inc, 1982.

Craft M: Help for the family's neglected other child. *MCN: The American Journal of Maternal/Child Nursing* 4: 297–300, September/October 1979.

Dorn L: Children's concepts of illness: clinical applications. *Pediatr Nurs* 10: 325–327, September/October, 1984.

Lavigne J, Ryan M: Psychologic adjustment of siblings of children with chronic illnesses. *Pediatrics* 63: 616–627, 1979.

Nagora H: Children's reactions to hospitalization and illness. *Child Psychiatry and Human Development* 9: 3–19, 1978.

Perrin EC: There's a demon in your belly. *Pediatrics* 67: 841–849, 1981.

Petrillo M: *Emotional Care of Hospitalized Children*. Philadelphia, JB Lippincott Co, 1980.

Piaget J: Piaget's theory, in Mussen PH (ed): *Carmichael's Manual of Child Psychology*. New York, John Wiley & Sons, 1970.

Schaefer C: *Therapeutic Uses of Children's Play*. New York, Jason Aronson Inc, 1976.

Vernon D, Schulman J, Foley J: Changes in children's behavior after hospitalization. *Am J Dis Child* 3: 581–593, June 1966.

Chapter 20

Community Resources for the Family of the High Risk Infant

Janice George, MSW, ACSW
Elizabeth Ahmann, RN, MS, FNP

For the high risk infant or chronically ill child, the transition from the hospital to the home must be well planned to ensure continuity of care (see Chapter 2). An essential component of the planning process is the identification of community resources that are available to assist the family in providing care at home.

The availability and quality of resources in any given community is influenced by many factors, including economics, politics, and societal attitudes. As a result, available health care services, social services, and other community resources often vary greatly among different communities. Even federal programs, such as Medicaid, have eligibility requirements and home care coverage provisions that vary from state to state. The home care professional must become aware of the range of available community services and resources that can benefit families caring for the high risk infant at home. Financial, therapeutic, family support, and informational resources are identified and discussed in this chapter.

FINANCIAL RESOURCES

Seventy percent of families with a chronically ill child suffer a significant financial burden.[1] Indeed, financial concerns will often be a primary stressor for families providing home care for the high risk infant. These families not only have the basic living expenses faced by any family but have the following additional expenses:

- special supplies and equipment
- medications
- special formulas or foods
- transportation to frequent medical appointments

- increased utility bills related to use of medical equipment
- hospital and outpatient bills.

Even if a family has insurance coverage or Medicaid, all of these increased expenses will not be covered.[2] As Ratliff has noted,[3]

> The problem of total, continuous care for long-term patients remains a crucial one. . . . A person's ability to financially survive an illness often depends upon his own personal [financial and] insurance protection, government health care programs and the availability of both internal and external health care and financial resources.

The home care professional and the family may need to work together to develop a creative package of programs and funding sources in order to meet the multiple needs of the child while maintaining the family's financial viability. Sources of funding that may assist the family to provide home care include the following:

- private insurance
- health maintenance organizations
- Medicaid
- Supplemental Security Income (SSI)
- Women, Infants, and Children (WIC) programs
- food stamps
- state Crippled Children's services
- state and local social service agencies
- community organizations
- disease-specific organizations
- religious organizations
- state and local public health departments
- state and local departments of education
- private contributions.

The rest of this section discusses some considerations in identifying and choosing appropriate funding sources.

Insurance

If a family has insurance coverage, two points are important. First, it is essential to know whether the policy includes a lifetime limit for reimbursement. Families with infants who have been hospitalized for extended periods may have depleted a substantial portion of their available coverage. Second, to avoid sudden, unexpected costs, it is essential to query the company in detail about its home care coverage.[4] Some companies can be convinced to provide coverage for home care if their representatives are provided with figures that demonstrate the cost effectiveness of this approach.[5] (See also Chapter 2.)

Medicaid

If a family's insurance limit is reached, or if a family does not have insurance, the Medicaid program may provide coverage for medical and related expenses. Although specific criteria related to Medicaid eligibility vary from state to state, one of the following factors must apply:

1. family income is below the state-determined poverty level OR
2. child's medical expenses are high in relation to family income OR
3. child is blind or disabled, and family living on a limited income.

The local agency of the U.S. Department of Health and Human Services and the local Social Security office can supply eligibility criteria and application materials to interested families or professionals. The following materials are generally required in applying for Medicaid:

- birth certificate(s)
- identification
- verification of income
- medical bills or statements
- verification of residency.

Some states are also participating in the Medicaid Home and Community Based Waiver Program.[6] This program extends Medicaid coverage to some persons who, on the basis of diagnostic criteria, would otherwise not be eligible for Medicaid coverage. In some states, this program may include a variety of services generally not covered by Medicaid, such as case management, respite care, and even home repair.

The SSI Program

The SSI program is a federal income-maintenance program for the aged, blind, and disabled. Disabled children meeting eligibility criteria can receive monthly SSI payments, the amount of which is based on family income. In addition, if SSI eligibility criteria are met, the child automatically qualifies for Medicaid, regardless of the family's income. However, eligibility for other assistance programs, such as Aid to Families with Dependent Children (AFDC), may be adversely affected by receipt of SSI payments. The family applying for such assistance should therefore determine which programs offer the most advantages.

Further information about the SSI program and application materials can be obtained at any Social Security office. The following materials are generally required in applying for SSI:

- Social Security number
- proof of age
- verification of income
- medical records
- verification of residency.

The WIC Program

The WIC supplemental food program provides specific nutritious supplemental foods and nutrition education at no cost to eligible low-income persons. Pregnant women, those who have just given birth, and breast-feeding women, as well as infants and children up to their fifth birthday are eligible if they meet income standards and if they are determined to be at nutritional risk. Local health departments can provide further information and application materials.

Food Stamps

The food stamps program provides monthly benefits that help low-income persons buy food needed to maintain good health. Eligibility is based on the family's gross income. For the family with a disabled child, eligibility is based on meeting income guidelines after deductions. Further information and application materials can be obtained at the local Department of Human Services or Social Security office.

Other Financial Resources

Each state has a Crippled Children's program. In some states a portion of the funds for this program may be used to assist families in the purchase of equipment, supplies, or services needed by disabled children. Assistance in purchasing durable medical equipment or special supplies is also sometimes available from community organizations or disease-specific associations (such as the American Lung Association) if a special request is made. Church organizations and philanthropic contributions are yet another possible source of financial assistance. (See also Appendix 20–A.)

THERAPEUTIC RESOURCES

Home care of the high risk infant may involve any of a wide variety of therapeutic services:

- infant stimulation
- educational programs
- occupational therapy
- physical therapy
- speech therapy
- respiratory therapy
- audiologic evaluation and follow-up

- pharmacy services
- home nursing
- equipment and supply services
- transportation
- emergency services
- primary and specialty medical care.

When any service is needed, payment mechanisms should also be explored. Some agencies may provide a service only to self-pay families; others may accept reimbursement from third party payers or Medicaid; still other agencies may provide services on a sliding scale or even free of charge if a family's resources are limited. (Obviously, this will be true for only certain types of services.) Payment options will influence the family's choice of service provider.

Infant stimulation and education programs can be located through the local school system, state Crippled Children's program, or state or local Easter Seal Society office. (See also Chapter 17.) Programs may be home-based or center-based. The latter programs may or may not be prepared to provide services to children with a tracheostomy or those on oxygen. However, some program personnel may be willing to provide services to such children if special training can be arranged through the hospital or home health agency.

If occupational, physical, or speech *therapy* services are indicated, a physician's referral is generally necessary. A hospital rehabilitation department or the school system may be able to provide referrals to therapists with a pediatric background, an important criterion in the choice of provider.

Some infants with respiratory compromise may need *medications* that are not readily available in local pharmacies. If a family has difficulty obtaining specific medications, a hospital pharmacy is a possible resource. Alternatively, if a willing community pharmacist can be identified, special orders may be arranged, or the hospital pharmacist can instruct the community pharmacist in any unusual medication "recipes."

Several *transportation issues* may affect the family of a high risk infant: cost, convenience, and special needs. If a family has Medicaid coverage, some states may provide transportation assistance to medical appointments. Handicapped tags or stickers for privately owned vehicles may assist the family in parking convenience. If an ambulance or van is needed to transport a ventilator-dependent child to medical appointments, the Medicaid program, Red Cross, or the local ambulance or rescue squad may be of assistance.

Other therapeutic services are discussed in Chapters 2, 4, and 7.

FAMILY SUPPORT RESOURCES

When the high risk infant first comes home from the hospital, the family is most likely to need concrete support. For example, assistance in arranging transportation to and from the clinic, in finding a pharmacy that can supply the needed medications, and in arranging daily schedules to accommodate the child's care may be most welcome initially.

Most families caring for a disabled child will, with time, identify a need for respite care. Because of the complexity of care and the relative instability of some high risk infants, an appropriate source of back-up or respite care may be nursing services (see Chapter 2). Unless insurance or Medicaid covers the cost of home nursing, this arrangement may not be financially feasible for a family. As an alternative, a family may try to locate a babysitter willing to be trained to care for the infant. (Such training, however, must be as complete as that for the primary caregiver.)

Some communities have respite care programs that may serve as a source of relief for parents. In most cases, however, these programs are targeted to care for the mentally retarded and developmentally disabled populations, and the respite providers do not have the training to care for a child with medical impairments. Nevertheless, it may be possible to make special arrangements for training of program personnel if no other source of relief is available to a family.

In addition to some source of respite care, an important resource for parents of the high risk infant can be sharing both information and support with other parents. Support groups, arranged by hospitals, social service agencies, or by parents themselves, provide a useful forum for problem solving and for exchange of experiences, challenges, and ideas. If no such appropriate support groups are available, or if a parent is unable to attend meetings, telephone contacts with one or two other parents may be a helpful alternative. However, a family's desire for privacy should always be respected.

Psychosocial intervention is a needed service for many families. Although the cost of this service often is not reimbursable by third party payers, the importance of social work, psychotherapeutic, and psychologic support services should not be overlooked.

When the infant has been at home for some time, the family's needs may change; the home care professional must be sensitive to cues signaling such changes. Chapters 18 and 19 discuss sibling and family issues in detail, with suggestions for assessment, intervention, and referral. A variety of community resources are available to provide needed support to families caring for the high risk infant at home:

- back-up caregivers
- babysitting services
- respite caregivers
- parent groups
- sibling groups
- neighborhood organizations
- church groups
- psychosocial support services.

INFORMATIONAL RESOURCES

Family members and other caregivers may be interested in obtaining information about the infant's condition, prognosis, available treatments or services, and other topics. The physician, community health nurse, and other professionals involved in the infant's care may be helpful in this regard. Parent groups may also be an important information resource. In addition, books, articles, pamphlets, and newsletters are available to augment discussions with both professionals and other parents. (See Appendix 20–B for suggested newsletters and pamphlets; Appendix C at the end of this text lists recommended books. National organizations that provide information, publications including newsletters, and contacts with local affiliates are listed in Appendix 20–A.)

NOTES

1. Ireys HT: Health care for chronically disabled children and their families, in *Better Health for Our Children: A National Strategy* (Report of the Select Panel for the Promotion of Child Health, vol IV), DHHS publication 79–55071, US Department of Health and Human Services, Public Health Service, 1981, p 333.
2. Medicaid coverage of the pediatric population, *Caring,* May 1985, p 52.
3. Ratliffe B: *Leaving the Hospital, Discharge Planning for Total Patient Care,* Springfield, Ill, Charles C Thomas, 1981, p 164.
4. Private health care coverage for children, *Caring,* May 1985, p 53.
5. Cabin B: Cost effectiveness of pediatric home care, *Caring,* May 1985, pp 48–51.
6. Medicaid coverage, p 52.

REFERENCES

Cabin B: Cost effectiveness of pediatric home care. *Caring*, May 1985, pp 48–51.

Ireys HT: Health care for chronically disabled children and their families, in *Better Health for Our Children: A National Strategy* (Report of the Select Panel for the Promotion of Child Health, vol IV), DHHS publication 79–55071, US Department of Health and Human Services, Public Health Service, pp 321–332.

McCollum A: *The Chronically Ill Child, A Guide for Parents and Professionals*. New Haven, Yale University Press, 1975.

Medicaid Coverage of the Pediatric Population. *Caring*, May 1985, p 52.

Moore G, Morton KG, Southard A: *A Reader's Guide for Parents of Children with Mental, Physical, or Emotional Disabilities*. Maryland State Planning Council on Developmental Disabilities, 1983.

A National List of Voluntary Organizations in Medical Genetics and Maternal and Child Health. Washington, DC, National Center for Education in Maternal and Child Health, 1983.

Private health care coverage for children. *Caring*, May 1985, p 53.

Ratliff B: *Leaving the Hospital: Discharge Planning for Total Patient Care*. Springfield, Ill, Charles C Thomas, 1981.

Starting Early, A Guide to Federal Resources in Maternal and Child Health. Washington, DC, National Center for Education in Maternal and Child Health, 1984.

Travis G: *Chronic Illness in Children: Its Impact on Child and Family*. Stanford, Stanford University Press, 1976.

Appendix 20-A

Resource Organizations for Families of the High Risk Infant

American Cancer Society
777 Third Avenue
New York, New York 10017
(212) 371–2900

American Heart Association
7320 Greenville Avenue
Dallas, Texas 75231
(214) 750–5300

American Lung Association
1740 Broadway
New York, New York 10019
(212) 315–8700

Association for the Care of Children's Health
3615 Wisconsin Avenue, N.W.
Washington, D.C. 20016
(202) 244–1801

Association for Retarded Citizens
National Headquarters
P.O. Box 6109
2501 Avenue J
Arlington, Texas 76011
(817) 640–0204

Clearinghouse on the Handicapped
Office of Special Education and Rehabilitation Services
Department of Education
Switzer Building, Room 3119-S
Washington, D.C. 20202
(202) 732–1245

Developmental Disabilities Office
U.S. Department of Health and Human Services
200 Independence Avenue, S.W., Room 338E
Washington, D.C. 20201
(202) 245–2910

Federation for Children with Special Needs
312 Stuart Street, 2d Floor
Boston, Massachusetts 02116
(617) 482–2915

Cystic Fibrosis Foundation
6000 Executive Boulevard
Rockville, Maryland 20852
(301) 881–9130

Make Today Count, Inc.
Box 303
Burlington, Iowa 52601
(314) 348–1619
[for parents of seriously ill children]

March of Dimes Birth Defects Foundation
1275 Mamaroneck Avenue
White Plains, New York 10605
(914) 428–7100

Muscular Dystrophy Association
810 Seventh Avenue
New York, New York 10019
(212) 586–0808

National Association for Sickle Cell Disease, Inc.
3460 Wilshire Boulevard, Suite 1012
Los Angeles, California 90010
(213) 731–1166

National Association for the Visually Handicapped
305 East 24th Street, Room 17-C
New York, New York 10010
(212) 889–3141

National Center for Clinical Infant Programs
733 15th Street, N.W.
Washington, D.C. 20005
(202) 347–0308

National Center for Education in Maternal and Child Health
3520 Prospect Street, N.W.
Washington, D.C. 20057
(202) 625–8400

National Easter Seal Society
2023 West Ogden Avenue
Chicago, Illinois 60612
(312) 243–8400

National Genetics Foundation
555 West 57th Street
New York, New York 10019
(212) 586–5800

National Information Center for Handicapped Children and Youth
P.O. Box 1492
Washington, D.C. 20013
(703) 522–0870

National Information Center on Deafness
Gallaudet College
7th & Florida Ave., N.E.
Washington, D.C. 20002
(202) 651–5109

Parentele
1301 E. 38th Street
Indianapolis, Indiana 46205
(317) 926–4142
[for parents of children with handicaps]

Parents Helping Parents
47 Maro Drive
San Jose, California 95127
(408) 272–4774

Parents of Premature and High Risk Infants, International, Inc.
33 West 42nd Street
New York, New York 10036
(606) 277–0008

Premature Incorporated
10200 Old Katy Road, Suite 100
Houston, Texas 77048

SKIP [Sick Kids need Involved People]
216 Newport Drive
Severna Park, Maryland 21146
(301) 647–0164

Spina Bifida Association of America
343 South Dearborn, Room 317
Chicago, Illinois 60604
(312) 663–1562

United Cerebral Palsy Association, Inc.
330 West 34th Street
New York, New York 10001
(212) 481–6300

Appendix 20–B

Newsletters and Pamphlets for Families of the High Risk or Handicapped Infant

Newsletters

Compassionate Friends, Inc.
P.O. Box 1347
Oak Brook, Illinois 60521
(312) 323–5010
[for bereaved parents]

"Sibling Information Network Newsletter"
Department of Educational Psychology
Box U-64
University of Connecticut
Storrs, Connecticut 06268

"The Independent"
Center for Independent Living
2539 Telegraph Avenue
Berkeley, California 90704
[published quarterly]

Pamphlets

Social Security Handbook
U.S. Department of Health and Human Services
Social Security Administration
6401 Security Boulevard
Baltimore, Maryland 21235

A Guide to Supplemental Security Income
U.S. Department of Health and Human Services
Social Security Administration
6401 Security Boulevard
Baltimore, Maryland 21235

Medicaid and Medicare: Which Is Which?
U.S. Department of Health and Human Services
Health Care Financing Administration
Publications Management, D-3
Gwynn Oak Building
Baltimore, Maryland 21235

Many of the organizations listed in Appendix 20–A also publish newsletters and pamphlets that may be of interest.

Sample Forms for Emergency Notification

Exhibit A–1 Rescue Squad Notification

TO: Rescue Squad or EMT Unit   DATE:_____

                    _____
                          Address

FROM: _____   PHONE:_____
                    Address
       _____   DOB:_____

RE: _____
                     Child
       _____
                    Parents
       _____
                    Address
       _____

This child is at home in your catchment area.
The child named above has the following medical problem(s):

Medications:

Treatments:

Please verify above information with parents to determine if it is up to date.

Exhibit A–1 continued

The child's heatlh care providers are:

_____   Phone:_____
_____   Phone:_____
_____   Phone:_____

In the event of an emergency, please transport the child to _____
_____ Hospital. If this is not possible, please share the above information with the receiving hospital.

Thank you.

Source: Reprinted with permission of Home Care Program, Children's Hospital National Medical Center, Washington, DC.

Exhibit A–2 Telephone Company Notification

TO: Telephone Company, Customer Services
           _____

FROM: _____   Telephone_____
           _____
           _____

RE: _____   Billing Party_____
Address   _____
           _____
Telephone _____

The child named above has a severe medical problem requiring continuous telephone service in the home.

This child should be placed on your priority list. In the event of anticipated interruptions of service, the parents should be notified beforehand. In the event of unexpected interruption of service, this family should have their service reinstituted on a priority basis.

Thank you.

Source: Reprinted with permission of Home Care Program, Children's Hospital National Medical Center, Washington, D.C.

Exhibit A–3 Electric Company Notification

TO: Electric Company, Customer Services

FROM: ——————————————   Telephone————————

RE: ——————————————   Billing Party————————
Address   ——————————————

Telephone ——————————————

The child named above has a severe medical problem requiring continuous electrical service for the following equipment:

This child should be placed on a priority service list. In the event of anticipated interruptions of service, the parents should be notified beforehand. In the event of unexpected interruption of service, this family should have their service reinstituted on a priority basis.

Thank you.

Source: Reprinted with permission of Home Care Program, Children's Hospital National Medical Center, Washington, D.C.

Cleaning Respiratory Equipment

Maintaining clean respiratory equipment is essential in preventing respiratory infections. A routine schedule of cleaning and disinfection is important, and the guidelines presented here are recommended for most respiratory equipment used in the home.

A cardinal principle is, of course, to clean equipment in a clean area. Cleaning should not be done under an open window or after vacuuming because of the risk of contaminating equipment with dust in the air. Hands should be washed before cleaning equipment. The screen-trap filter on the sink can be a breeding ground for *Pseudomonas* and should be removed. All apparatus, after it is disinfected, should be stored in jars or plastic bags to prevent contamination between uses. Any vinegar solution used for disinfecting supplies and equipment can be reused if stored in a covered jar for no more than four days.

Ambu Bag and Nebulizer

Wash every 1 to 3 days depending on frequency of use. Disassemble all parts, wash in warm soapy water, rinse thoroughly, air dry, and reassemble. Every 3 days soak parts for 20 minutes in half-strength white vinegar solution, rinse thoroughly, and air dry.

Suction Apparatus

If catheters are to be reused, aspirate saline through after each use, store in a clean dry towel or bag, and use for no longer than 2 to 6 hours. Then, soak used catheters in warm soapy water and rinse well. A large syringe can be used to force water through the catheter. Every 2 days, soak the catheters in half-strength white vinegar solution for 20 minutes, rinse thoroughly and air dry.

The collection bottle contents should be emptied daily, and the bottle cleaned. To clean, warm soapy water from a jar should be aspirated through the connecting tube, followed by warm clear water. The collection bottle should then be washed in warm soapy water, rinsed, and air dried.

Every 2 days, the connecting tubes, bottles, and rubber stopper should be washed in warm soapy water, rinsed, and disinfected. To disinfect, fill the bottle with half-strength white vinegar, insert connecting tubing and used catheters, and soak the apparatus for 20 minutes, followed by a thorough rinse and air drying.

Tracheostomy Tubes

If *metal* tracheostomy tubes are used, the inner cannula should be removed and cleaned daily with hydrogen peroxide and a small brush or pipe cleaner. Each week, the tracheostomy tube, inner cannula, and obturator should be cleaned with hydrogen peroxide and a small brush or pipe cleaner. Following this, sterilize by boiling the tube, jars, and lids for 10 minutes in a porcelain, Pyrex, or stainless steel pot. Remove apparatus from the pot, taking care to touch only the flange of the tracheostomy tube and the outside of the jars and lids. Allow to air dry. When it is dry, store the tracheostomy tube in a sterilized jar. Sterilize the tube again just before using.

If *plastic* tracheostomy tubes are used, the tube and obturator should be washed first with soap and water prior to sterilization. Hydrogen peroxide can be used to remove crusted mucus. If a pipe cleaner is used, care should be taken not to scratch the tube. After rinsing, soak the tube in half-strength white vinegar solution for 10 minutes, rinse well in sterile water, and allow to air dry. When it is dry, store the tube in a sterilized jar. Sterilize the tube again just before using.

Ventilator Apparatus

The humidifier jar, ventilator tubing, water traps, exhalation valve, and tracheostomy swivel from the ventilator must be replaced with clean equipment every 2 to 3 days. To clean, completely disassemble the apparatus, wash in warm soapy water, and rinse thoroughly. Then, soak overnight in half-strength white vinegar solution and rinse thoroughly. Allow to air dry.

Alternatively, after a first washing with warm soapy water, ventilator apparatus can be disinfected in the dishwasher. Set tubes in the upper rack with their ends facing down; secure small parts to prevent floating during the wash and rinse cycles; and place the humidifier jar in the lower rack facing down. Regular dishwashing detergent and a normal wash cycle can be used. Thoroughly dry tubing by attaching to the aspirator or compressor for several minutes, followed by air drying.

REFERENCES

Bell CW, Blodgett D, Goike CA, et al: *Home Care and Rehabilitation in Respiratory Medicine.* Philadelphia, JB Lippincott Co, 1984.

Guidelines to home ventilator (LP-4) (patient information sheet). Philadelphia, Children's Hospital of Philadelphia, Department of Respiratory Therapy, undated.

Hennessy P (ed): *Home Care of Your Child with a Tracheostomy: A Parent Handbook.* Washington, DC, Children's Hospital National Medical Center, 1983.

National Medical Home Care: Cleaning the equipment, in *Catalog of Equipment and Services.* Orange, Calif, National Medical Home Care, undated.

Books for Parents (and Professionals)

Many of the suggestions in this bibliography are drawn from the Health Resource Collection of the Family Library at Children's Hospital National Medical Center, Washington, D.C., the largest such library collection in the United States. Interested readers may wish to purchase the library's more complete bibliography of books for both parents and children, available for $20.00:

Willard C: *Family Library Health Resource Collection Subject Bibliography of the Children's Hospital National Medical Center* (95 pp).

Two bibliographies of books for children are also available:

Azarnoff P: *Health, Illness and Disability: A Guide to Books for Children and Young Adults*. New York, RR Bowker Co, 1983.

Books That Help Children Deal with a Hospital Experience, DHEW publication (HSA) 78-5224. US Department of Health, Education and Welfare, Public Health Service, rev. 1978.

Coping with Illness

Association for the Care of Children's Health: *The Chronically Ill Child and Family in the Community* (pamphlet). Washington, DC, Association for the Care of Children's Health, 1982.

A Reader's Guide: For Parents of Children with Mental, Physical, and Emotional Disabilities, DHEW publication (HSA) 77-5290. US Department of Health, Education and Welfare, Public Health Service, 1977.

The author thanks Carolyn Willard, MLS, for her assistance in the development of this appendix.

Dickens M: *Miracles of Courage: How Families Meet the Challenge of a Child and Critical Illness*. New York, Dodd, Mead & Co, 1985.

Featherstone H: *A Difference in the Family*. New York, Penguin Books Inc, 1981.

Hosford B: *Making Your Medical Decisions: Your Rights and Hard Choices Today*. New York, Frederick Ungar Publishing Co, Inc, 1982.

Jones M: *Home Care for the Chronically Ill or Disabled Child*. New York, Harper & Row Publishers Inc, 1985.

Kupfer F: *Before and After Zachariah*. New York, Delacorte Press, 1982.

McCollum AT: *The Chronically Ill Child*. New Haven, Yale University Press, 1981.

Schulman J: *Coping with Tragedy: Successfully Facing the Problem of a Seriously Ill Child*. Chicago, Follett Publishing Co, 1976.

Travis G: *Chronic Illness in Children: Its Impact on Child and Family*. Stanford, Stanford University Press, 1976.

Cerebral Palsy and Handicaps

Finnie N: *Handling Your Cerebral Palsied Child at Home*. New York, EP Dutton, 1975. (Selected chapters available in Spanish from local offices of the United Cerebral Palsy Association.)

Hale G: *The Source Book for the Disabled*. New York, Paddington Press, 1979.

Development

Bailey R: *The Dynanic Self: Activities to Enhance Infant Development*. New York, Delacorte Press, 1972.

Brutten M: *Something's Wrong with My Child*. San Diego, Harcourt Brace Jovanovich Inc, 1973.

Brazelton TB: *The First 12 Months of Life*. New York, Bantam Books, Inc, 1971.

Brazelton TB: *The Second 12 Months of Life*. New York, Bantam Books, Inc, 1977.

Fraiberg S: *The Magic Years*. New York, Charles Scribner's Sons, 1959.

Kaban B: *Choosing Toys for Children*. New York; Schocken Books, Inc, 1979.

Leach P: *Your Baby and Child from Birth to Age Five*. New York, Alfred A Knopf, Inc, 1978.

Hearing and Speech Impairment

Barach C: *Help Me Say It: A Parent's Guide to Speech Problems*. New York: Harper & Row Publishers Inc, 1983.

Miller A: *Your Child's Hearing and Speech.* Springfield, Ill, Charles C Thomas, Publisher, 1974.

Ogden P: *The Silent Garden: Understanding the Hearing Impaired Child.* Chicago, Contemporary Books Inc, 1983.

Infant Death, SIDS

Bergman A: *Why Did My Baby Die?* New York, Third Press, 1975.

Derain J: *Coping with Sudden Infant Death.* Lexington, Mass, Lexington Books, 1982.

Donnelly K: *Recovering from a Loss of a Child.* New York, Macmillan Publishing Co Inc, 1982.

Parenting and Child Care

Brazelton TB: *Infants and Mothers.* New York, Dell Publishing Co Inc, 1983.

Brazelton TB: *Toddlers and Parents.* New York, Dell Publishing Co Inc, 1976.

Brewster D: *You Can Breastfeed Your Baby Even in Special Situations.* Emmaus, Pa, Rodale Press, 1979.

McBride A: *The Growth and Development of Mothers.* New York, Harper & Row Publishers Inc, 1973.

Parke R: *Fathers.* Cambridge, Harvard University Press, 1981.

Spock B: *Baby and Child Care.* New York, Simon & Schuster, Inc, 1976.

White B: *A Parent's Guide to the First Three Years.* Englewood Cliffs, NJ, Prentice-Hall Inc, 1980.

Premature Infants

Brazelton TB: *On Becoming a Family.* New York, Delacorte Press, 1981.

Harrison H: *The Premature Baby Book: The Parent's Guide to Coping and Caring in the First Years.* New York, Saint Martin's Press, Inc, 1973.

Henig R: *Your Premature Baby.* New York, Charles Scribner's Sons, 1983.

Lieberman A: *The Premie Parents' Handbook.* New York, EP Dutton, 1984.

Nance S: *Premature Babies: A Handbook for Parents.* New York, Arbor House Publishing Co, 1982.

Shosenberg N: *The Premature Infant, A Handbook for Parents.* Toronto, Ontario Ministry of Health, 1979.

Safety

Arena J: *Child Safety Is No Accident*. Durham, NC, Duke University Press, 1978.

Green M: *A Sigh of Relief: First Aid Handbook for Childhood Emergencies*. New York, Bantam Books, Inc, 1977.

Tracheostomy Care

Adamo P: *A Guide to Pediatric Tracheostomy Care*, Springfield, Ill, Charles C Thomas, 1981.

Hennessy P: *Home Care of Your Child with a Tracheostomy: A Parent Handbook*. Washington, DC, Children's Hospital National Medical Center, 1983.

Visual Impairment

Lowenfeld B: *Our Blind Children, Growing and Learning With Them*. New York, Charles C Thomas, Publisher, 1971.

Scott C: *Can't Your Child See?* Baltimore, University Park Press, 1977.

Home Care: A Mother's Perspective

Karen D. Dixon

Our son, David, was born August 4, 1983. He was premature, born at 28 weeks. He weighed 2 lb 7½ oz. It is frightening when your baby is born so early because you don't know why . . . or what the chances are he'll survive . . . or what his problems will be if he does survive.

David was born with immature lungs and required a tracheostomy, ventilation, and oxygen. He also had Pierre Robin syndrome (small chin and a complete cleft palate). He ended up staying 5 months and 9 days in the hospital.

When he came home, everybody came to see him, but they all shied away when I had to do his care. Before he came home, people would look at pictures of him and say, "He's so cute," but when he came home they didn't want to get near him. Friends and relatives gave me a lot of verbal support, but when I brought David to them they got glassy-eyed and would say, "No, I don't want to hold him—he's too small." Yet if any other baby came into the room, everybody would fight to be first to hold it. This was very frustrating to me. I cried over it many times. It is better now, though. Many of my friends have learned his care.

When David came home, I felt ready for him. I had been at the hospital every day or two and had gone through so much training in the nursery. (My husband, though, felt he shouldn't come home until he was more stable.) David came with the tracheostomy, a gastrostomy tube, lots of medicines, and all the equipment. I wasn't too concerned, though, because I knew the monitor would tell me if this or that went wrong . . . and I had learned all the care.

What was different, though, was having all the equipment and supplies in our apartment. At first we had the monitor, a suction machine, an air compressor, an aerosol machine, medicines, and catheters, tubing, and other supplies. Later, we also got oxygen. You see, a baby's dresser is usually decorated with baby items. My baby's is decorated with medical machines. I'd rather have lotions and powders instead of distilled water—but I had to have my own nursing station.

The other important thing about the equipment has been to keep it clean and have it always working. This is very time-consuming. Even the littlest things can make it work improperly. For example, the filter on the back of the air compressor needs to be cleaned every week. One time the compressor stopped working. I had the mechanic out here with a new machine before I realized I had forgotten to wash that filter. It was so embarrassing!

Well, David had been home for three weeks. He had been to see the doctor, and the nurse had been to visit once or twice each week. But in that third week he became seriously ill, so we rushed him to the hospital. This kind of thing happened many times. It often gave me feelings of guilt. I thought I knew what I was doing, and he'd still get sick. I would think maybe there is something I did or didn't do that caused it . . . or I should have noticed it earlier. It helped a lot when the doctors or nurses would tell me that I didn't cause it. Sometimes, I would think he was getting sick and I'd take him to the hospital, but the doctors couldn't find anything . . . then, two days later he'd be sick, and they'd admit him. These babies with BPD can get sick very easily, and mothers really know when something is wrong.

David's care has been a 24-hour job. At the beginning, it was helpful to have someone around just to watch David while I got organized to do all the little details of his care. It's also a good idea to have two or three people trained in the care so you can get a break now and then. Even when I finally get a break, get time to rest, I still feel uncomfortable, as if there were something I am supposed to be doing. For example, from 6 AM to 12 midnight David is getting medications or feedings or aerosol treatments at least every hour. He often needs suctioning in between. So all day I am very busy. Then when midnight comes, it is hard to fall asleep. Maybe by 3 AM I fall asleep. Then, I'm up again at 6 to start over. Even though he's been home for a year and a half, I still have this schedule.

His care is also demanding because I feel if I make a mistake, I risk his getting sick. For example, he was getting potassium. The dose was 3 cc twice a day. I read the bottle. It said 6 mEq.* For some reason, trying to be exact, I gave him 6 cc twice a day. When I found out, I was really upset. I was lucky he didn't OD on it.

I have had some nurses to take care of him, and that is very helpful. Still, it takes a lot of time to train them to do things the way you want them done for your baby. And if a nurse is sick and another one comes as a replacement, you have to start the training all over again. Some nurses have been really good with him, though.

Caring for a child like David can be a strain. It is very time-consuming, and both parents can get very tired and end up annoyed at each other because of the care they have to do for the baby. It also puts a limitation on your social life. You have to arrange anything you do for yourself between what the baby needs done (like

---

*6 mEq of potassium chloride is equivalent to 3 cc.

feedings and medications). You have to be careful of the conditions you expose him to, so you can't take him everywhere you might want to go.

Another strain is the uncertainty. Once when David was in the hospital with a serious respiratory infection (from respiratory syncytial virus), the doctors and nurses held an important meeting with us. They told us he was doing very poorly and might not live. After that meeting, I went up to David's room and cried. Then I yelled at him to get himself together . . . and I prayed to God, saying we wanted to have David with us longer. The next morning, the doctor called me on the phone and said, "I don't know what you did to that boy, but he's looking much better today."

Another big uncertainty is his development. I have a goddaughter a year younger than David. When she was 6 months, she was sitting up. At that time, David was 1½ years old and was still lying there. It really hurt to see that. All parents look forward to the time when their babies walk. I knew that sitting up was a goal for David. Finally, when he was 16 months old he sat up. Then he saw more, imitated more, played more, and developed much more quickly. He has found his own way of doing things. At 2 years, he is just starting to walk around, holding onto things . . . just beginning to express himself verbally (with his finger over the tracheostomy hole) . . . and although he still has the gastrostomy tube for feeding, he is starting to sample flavors. He is really fun now. At 14 months, his developmental scores ranged from 2 to 8 months. Now he is 2 and they are much higher. He'll be in school (a special program) in the fall, and I think he'll progress rapidly. The doctors are talking about maybe taking his "trach" out soon, too.

Working with David for the past 2 years has been very time-consuming, and I haven't had much time to myself. But it can't be all bad because I am due to have another baby any day now!

Index